"I am very happy to recommend this book, which contains detaile
to carry out research projects on anti-social behaviour. It should appear
psychology and criminology students, but everyone who is interested in anti-social behaviour will
derive useful information from it."

David Farrington, Cambridge University, UK

"David Canter reveals his experience as a seasoned, practicing social scientist by embracing 'the value of doing science, rather than just reading about it'. The ten invaluable studies in this book encapsulate the lifeblood of crime psychology."

Benjamin Baughman, Mercyhurst University, USA

"David Canter's expertise shines through this book and a good deal of the material – notably the discussion of forgery, fraud, and geographical profiling – will, I'm sure, interest crime writers and all those interested in true crime, and perhaps surprise them."

Martin Edwards, former chair of the Crime Writers Association, UK

"The book is great. It poses some interesting and complex ideas while still being easy to understand."

Rosie Jacobs, sixth form (high school) student, UK

"This book is easy to read and provides a lot of useful and easy to understand details of how to carry out studies and make sense of the results. These are things that I had to learn over a period of time from here and there that would mostly use maths jargon. Seeing it all in one place makes it significantly easier."

Miraslava Yaneva, MSc student, UK

Experiments in Anti-Social Behaviour

For a practical, hands-on approach to studying criminal psychology, *Experiments in Anti-Social Behaviour: Ten Studies for Students* presents a collection of unique projects for students that illustrate the many ways research into anti-social behaviour can be conducted while also highlighting social psychological aspects of criminality.

Drawing on over half a century of supervising many hundreds of projects at high school, undergraduate, master's, and doctoral levels, David Canter provides well-grounded and detailed guidance for students on how to execute a range of different research studies through several psychological approaches, including quantitative cognitive studies, qualitative discourse analysis, and social identity theory. After introducing the ethical and practical challenges of studying crime and criminality, *Experiments in Anti-Social Behaviour* outlines broad approaches to research. This is followed by ten practical studies for students to carry out in order to engage directly with experimental research. These studies cover experiments, surveys, and case studies, and include a controlled examination of how easy it is to forge a signature, descriptions of experiments trying to detect deception, and an exploration of what is involved in linking actions in a serial killer's crimes to his characteristics.

Both engaging and interactive, *Experiments in Anti-Social Behaviour* is an invaluable resource for instructors and students from colleges and universities around the world in many different fields, such as psychology, criminology, and socio-legal studies. It will also be of interest to all those who want to know more about the psychology of crime and criminality.

David Canter is internationally known for his many publications in environmental psychology and for creating the field of investigative psychology. He has supervised research projects for over half a century, at every level from schools to PhDs, as well as large-scale studies for government departments, industry, and research councils.

Experiments in Anti-Social Behaviour

Ten Studies for Students

David Canter

Routledge
Taylor & Francis Group

LONDON AND NEW YORK

First published 2021
by Routledge
2 Park Square, Milton Park, Abingdon, Oxon OX14 4RN

and by Routledge
52 Vanderbilt Avenue, New York, NY 10017

Routledge is an imprint of the Taylor & Francis Group, an informa business

British Library Cataloguing-in-Publication Data
A catalogue record for this book is available from the British Library

Library of Congress Cataloging-in-Publication Data
A catalog record has been requested for this book

ISBN: 9781138354104 (hbk)
ISBN: 9781138354128 (pbk)
ISBN: 9780429425011 (ebk)

Typeset in JoannaMT
by Newgen Publishing UK

A range of PowerPoint presentations, published papers, and other material of
relevance to this book can be found at www.davidcanter.com.

For
Rosie, Robin, Felix, Byron, and Ivor.

Brief contents

Contents

Figures

Tables

Preface

One inspiration for the present volume was a book I had in my early teens. It was called *Chemistry Experiments at Home for Boys and Girls*. It was written by my chemistry master H.L. Hayes, published in 1959. I remember the excitement of acquiring the chemicals and equipment (no package sets in those days – not much concern about health and safety). Then the delight of trying out the experiments. It gave me a flavour not only of what chemistry was all about, but the exhilaration of doing science. Mr Hayes expressed disappointment when I told him I was going to study psychology at university. But his inspiration in showing me the value of doing science, rather than just reading about it or preparing for exams in it, has stayed with me. Hence this book about doing psychological research in perhaps the most difficult, although some would claim one of the most important of areas – criminality, and related anti-social activity.

Collecting data and analysing them in order to test ideas, or develop them, is what scientists do. No matter what results your studies achieve (although the unexpected results are often the most interesting), by actually carrying out a project you get inside the scientific process. You learn about the challenges and how to overcome them. This gives you a much better insight into the studies you read about. The experience enables you to evaluate other people's work in a much more informed way.

The ten studies proposed here are all versions of projects I've carried out with a variety of students in different contexts. I've selected them to be feasible for students to do without the need to access especially sensitive or difficult to obtain data. The move to 'evidence-based' policing (Sherman, 2013) and 'predictive' policing (e.g. Mohler et al., 2015) has opened up a whole new era of criminological research. But that tends to be carried out by police officers or others who have exclusive access to police databases and procedures. It also often provides little insight into the psychology of crime, tending to be a branch of statistics and operational research. Other important studies are built around large-scale databases, such as those carried out by the prolific researcher Professor David Farrington.[1] These studies require considerable experience and research skills. The studies described in the present volume are to get students started on the adventure of research. Taking the first steps on a fascinating journey.

It therefore is important to emphasise that the studies proposed here are a very small proportion of all the possible studies of criminals and their offending. A recent review of experiments in criminology by Farrington and his colleagues (2019) provides a broad canvas that goes beyond the issues and examples tackled in the present volume.

ANTI-SOCIAL ACTIVITY

Crime and offending cover a vast array of activities. If put along an alphabet you could run from arson to the consequences of xenophobia. Major components of modern society are set up to manage and attempt to control criminals and what they perpetrate. The police, of course, and the creation of laws and their operation are a massive part of any economy. The prison system and other forms of punishment, or attempting to rehabilitate offenders, take up major resources. Then there is the large-scale commercial enterprise of insurance and protection against crime. On top of this, it is impossible to turn on the television, enter a bookshop, or search the Internet without coming across crime fact and fiction. As I've discussed recently (Canter & Youngs, 2016), what/where would society be without crime?

It is therefore rather surprising that the systematic study of crime and criminals has only recently become a significant area of psychology. Until the 1980s most consideration of criminality was left to sociological and socio-legal explorations. Psychologists dealt with mentally disturbed offenders that came to them through their criminal practice and aped psychiatric diagnoses with notions of personality disorder and psychopathy. But if you wanted to find out how a burglar decided which house to break into, or how rapists differed from each other you would find very few studies.

In the twenty-first century this has all changed. The field of forensic psychology and the overlapping area known as crime psychology has developed extremely rapidly over the last quarter of a century. Textbooks on the topic abound as do many academic journals. Almost every undergraduate psychology course will have at least one module on the topic.

Yet, this area is not divorced from mainstream psychology. Those studying memory, for example, have contributed significantly to the understanding of the distortions in remembering that are crucial for evaluating eyewitness testimony, or carrying out effective interviews of victims or suspects. Taking these links to mainstream psychology further, it can be seen that just about any topic that has a chapter in an introductory psychology textbook can be explored through the lens of crime, criminals, and criminality.

However, the psychological study of crime has tended to be somewhat limited. In general, the focus has been on criminals and their characteristics. This is understandable because offenders typically come into contact with psychologists in a clinical, legal, or prison setting, where they are being assessed and/ or helped. But crime is fundamentally social. It is an interaction between an individual and others. It may be contact with other criminals that encourages, facilitates, or requires criminal acts. There will also be victims with whom the offender interacts either directly, as in some forms of abuse, deception, or violence, or implicitly, as in burglary and various types of fraud. Therefore, it is productive to consider crime as an aspect of anti-social behaviour.

This means that an important development in understanding the psychology of crime is the growing awareness that criminality is embedded in social interactions. It cannot be understood as merely a product of dysfunctional or mentally disturbed individuals. As a consequence, studying anti-social behaviour also provides a fascinating gateway into many aspects of social interaction.

Furthermore, the range of topics that are revealed by these considerations provide the opportunity for many different types of study. The study of anti-social behaviour excitingly opens up many different ways of doing research. This enriches an understanding of the different sorts of research questions that can be asked. It demonstrates that the way research questions are phrased carries implications for the research methods that are appropriate for answering them. I have therefore chosen a variety of different forms of anti-social behaviour as the focus of the ten[2] studies in this book. They each raise their own theoretical questions and require their own research design and type of analysis.

NOTE TO STUDENTS READING THIS BOOK

Except for Parts one and two of the volume, I've deliberately written each of the ten studies as independent chapters. This has entailed some repetition of background material so that you can benefit from any chapter without reading the others. There is a sequence though, from the most constrained and clearly defined experimental study through to a much more open-ended exploratory case study and simulation.

A Note to Lecturers, Tutors, and Others Using this Book as Part of a Course

The example studies described are only the start of a very wide range of possibilities. Many details to turn them into publishable accounts are inevitably omitted from such a short volume. There are also many topics that can be opened up for more detailed consideration to enrich any pedagogical activity. Crime and related aspects of anti-social behaviour is always fascinating, but the light it throws on many topics in psychology and related disciplines, beyond offending, is even more interesting.

Hopefully, you will see how to use this book to achieve three different areas of contribution to education:

1. Enrich the understanding of how to carry out many different types of psychological research.

2. Develop knowledge and appreciation of many fascinating issues in crime, forensic psychology, and related disciplines.

3. Broaden an understanding of central theories in applied psychology as varied as pattern recognition, the study of attitudes, and social identity theory.

The statistical analysis in the examples given have deliberately been kept as simple as possible. However, you will be aware of many more sophisticated possibilities. A range of inferential statistics such as t-tests, analysis of variance (ANOVA), correlations, and multiple regressions can all be utilised in one or more studies. I have not given the details of these because there are plenty of other sources that can assist and explain these possibilities.

Plagiarism is an inevitable risk of providing the sorts of guidance offered in this book. Being aware of that I have tried to ensure that there is plenty of room for development in each study. A slavish following and cut and paste from the chapters would be readily spotted. I've also kept the style relatively conversational, which would not be appropriate for a formal dissertation submission.

Acknowledgements

I'm deeply grateful for the largesse of my colleagues in commenting in various chapters. The book was written when the world was in lockdown due to the Coronavirus (COVID-19), but despite the anxiety this caused, many people were ready to scrutinise whatever I sent them. I would like to specially acknowledge the help of Aldert Vrij, Chris Street, Louise Porter, Laura Hammond, John Drury, Miroslava Yaneva, Rosie Jacobs, Jonathan Ogan, Michael Bamberg, and Donna Youngs.

Mikko provided the delightful drawings to lighten the mood of what could otherwise be a very intense book.

Although all of the material in this book has grown out of student projects, which I've supervised over the last half century, the opportunity to try aspects of them out with a regular meeting of Ruthin University of the Third Age was extremely helpful. Their enthusiasm and intelligent involvement, drawing on their personal and professional experiences, was encouraging and rewarding.

I would also like to record my gratitude to Christina Chronister and Danielle Dyal at Taylor & Francis for guiding me so well through the editing, production, and publishing process.

Not least to my wife, Sandra, for her loving support as ever, and tolerance of the inevitable distraction of my working on a book.

Notes

1 He lists over a thousand publications at www.crim.cam.ac.uk/global/docs/cv/david_farrington_ publications, many of which were conducted over a number of years.
2 Actually Study 2 contains two related studies. So if you are being pedantic there are at least 11 studies described.

References

Canter, D., & Youngs, D. (2016). Crime and society. *Contemporary Social Science, 11*(4), 283–288. doi: 10.1080/ 21582041.2016.1259495.

Farrington, D.P., Lösel, F., Braga, A.A., Mazerolle, L., Raine, A., Sherman, L.W., & Weisburd, D. (2019). Experimental criminology: Looking back and forward on the 20th anniversary of the Academy of Experimental Criminology. Journal of Experimental Criminology. https://doi.org/10.1007/ s11292-019-09384-z.

Mohler, G.O., Short, M.B., Malinowski, S., Johnson, M., Tita, G.E., Bertozzi A.L., & Brantingham, P.J. (2015). Randomized controlled field trials of predictive policing. *Journal of the American Statistical Association, 110*(512), 1399–1411. doi: 10.1080/01621459.2015.1077710.

Sherman, L. (2013). The rise of evidence-based policing: Targeting, testing, and tracking. *Crime and Justice, 42*(1), 377–451.

PART ONE

Challenges and concerns when studying anti-social activity

SYNOPSIS

Ethical and practical challenges dominate the study of anti-social behaviour. These include the demands of ethical committees, the requirements of professional organisations, and legal requirements. These are discussed with examples from my own research. However, the burgeoning number and variety of studies in this area demonstrate that there are many possibilities for obtaining interesting and important data. These range from material that is available in the public domain to private information that can be acquired through direct contact with individuals. Some of this is generated without any connection with any research process, other data is collected as an integrated aspect of a study. All of these sources of information have their strengths and weaknesses.

SOME KEY CONCEPTS

- ethics committees
- proportionality
- informed consent
- professional competence
- plagiarism
- pathways to data
- data sources.

ETHICAL, PROFESSIONAL, AND LEGAL CONCERNS

Unlike testing students' reaction times in a university laboratory or getting school children to complete an attitude questionnaire, although these activities do have ethical implications, every project that deals with something that is not socially acceptable, and may even be illegal, has much greater alarm bells ringing. The very first aspect of any such study to consider is what are the ethical, professional, and legal constraints that need to be taken into account. You should also be aware that in any major institution, whether it be a university, high school, hospital, or other organisation there will doubtless be some bureaucratic hoops to jump through, usually known as an 'ethical committee'. They will require detailed information of what you are planning to do and will not allow you to carry on with your study until they are satisfied it is acceptable.

What follows is coverage of the major ethical, professional, and legal matters that you need to be aware of when planning and carrying out your studies. These will probably be more significant for studies of anti-social behaviour that go beyond those detailed in the present volume. I've selected studies here that you should be able to carry out with minimum difficulty, but they each illustrate issues that could be developed further, opening up more onerous challenges.

To be clear, although they overlap, ethics, professionalism, and legal requirements are distinct and you need to take account of all of them; for clarity, they are dealt with in what follows under each heading. But you need to be aware that each country, jurisdiction, and organisation will have its own take on the details of what is required. The comments that follow are only the basics; the general principles are indicated here. You can find much more detailed documents on the Internet, some of the key websites being listed in what follows. There are even freely available online tests that will guide you through ethical considerations, which some **ethics committees** insist you complete successfully before you even submit your research proposal. Descriptions of the sort of information required by ethical committees are given in Appendix A at the end of this book.

Ethical issues

Do no harm

Ethical aspects of the study of anti-social activity take on many different forms. Probably the most fundamental is the same as Asimov's 'first law of robotics'. In this case it is the researcher rather than the robot who "may not injure a human being or, through inaction, allow a human being to come to harm".

It is important to be clear that the 'human beings' in this principle includes both the participants in the research as well as the researcher herself. Harm and injury also include psychological damage. This can require consideration of indirect consequences.

A controversial example

Consider, for example, the notorious Milgram experiments into 'obedience' in which the researcher required participants to apparently punish subjects taking part in the experiment. Of course, it would be unethical to actually punish a person. But the participants are likely to have had some traumatic response if they really thought they were hurting someone. Even if afterwards they were told they were not really giving the subjects electric shocks, they may still suffer from the experiences. What about the researcher who had to cheat the participants? Was this white-coated individual free from the consequences of having to lie to others?

Researchers may convince themselves that the quest for knowledge made all of Milgram's subterfuge acceptable. But I have to say I would be surprised if any ethics committee approved of such a study today. Indeed, any study that uses subterfuge runs into real ethical problems. I would also say that it runs into methodological problems too. If the researcher is cheating the participants what guarantee is there that they are not cheating him? In the detailed examination of Milgram's own notes, Perry (2013) reveals that many of the subjects in that experiment did not believe they were really hurting someone.[1] What light does that throw on Milgram's claim of individuals' readiness to obey?

Proportionality

If there is some risk of distressing those involved but the researcher wishes to argue that this is for the greater good, as may be the case for example in some medical research, then there are concerns about whether the level of distress is proportional to the possible benefits. There would need to be considerable evidence already amassed, of course, to demonstrate that there are really likely to be benefits from the research.

Worthwhile

In psychological research there is always some effort required from participants. Even when existing records are used, such as police reports of crimes, someone needs to prepare the material or make it available in some way. It could therefore be regarded as a moral obligation, as well as ethical, that the study is worthwhile. It should be carefully planned and not some casual 'suck it and see' project.

Adding to the value of the research is the way its results will be disseminated. Those who fund research usually require an indication in a research proposal of what the output of the research will be. These days the intended benefits, or 'impact', may also need to be specified. I discuss the issue of reporting on research and getting published later, but I do consider it an ethical and moral obligation to make findings from research open to being utilised. Many people usually support and contribute to the possibility of the research, often without payment or benefit. Certainly, the public at large supports research and are often "happy to help you get your degree, dear".[2] Therefore, at the very least a decent report of the study is an ethical requirement. This is often given to the organisation that supported the research. Wherever possible more formal publication adds to the value of the study.

Privacy and confidentiality

Information about people is sacrosanct. Even if you are dealing with police records or some other source of information, rather than what people have told you directly, you have an obligation to ensure that no one else can learn about what you have found out, or been told. You may be able to share it with others in your research team, such as a supervisor or colleague, if you agree that with those who provide the information. Normally, participants are informed that no accounts of the research in a report, thesis, or publication will identify individuals. Or if you are writing about case studies you will take care to anonymise reference to individual cases. This applies just as much to the age and gender of respondents as to some very serious aspect such as a crime they have committed. It is usual even to change some details of no importance to the research so that the individual cannot be recognised. For example, as well of course as changing their name, you might change an indication of where they live and their occupation.

In rare cases people may want their identity recognised. For example, there is one professor I know who later in life published an account of how he had murdered someone who bullied him at school, having spent time in prison for doing so. But you have to be very cautious about breaking such confidentiality because the person may not fully understand the consequences of doing so.

Informed consent

A process that is generally considered fundamental in all research involving human beings, is **informed consent**. This is the antithesis of misleading research participants. It is the requirement of ensuring that the participants in the study know why you have approached them, what you want of them, what you will do with the information, who will have access to it, and how long it will be kept for. This includes making clear that any records or other information you have been given has been made available with a clear understanding that it will be used for your research project. They will also be told that they can withdraw from the study at any time without any recriminations.

Most organisations require that participants in a study actually sign a form to indicate that they understand what the study is about and what will happen to any responses they give. A typical informed consent form is given in Appendix A at the end of this book.

There is an important consequence of the idea that consent to participate in a study is based on being properly informed about that study and understanding that information and its implications. There are many groups of possible participants that may not be regarded as able to give informed consent. Children, for example, may not be able to understand the process and the freedom they have to participate or not. Therefore, their parents or guardians would be required to give permission as well as the children.

Rare access

A notable example of access to a hard-to-reach, but important respondent group was the PhD study carried out by Sudhanshu Sarangi in India. He mange to interview 49 convicted terrorists, most of whom were in prison. But to get permission to do this he had to choose prisons that were regularly visited by the Red Cross and not only did he require agreement from the police and prison governors, he also had to get permission from the senior 'officers' in the terrorist organisation. These interviews did produce some fascinating results (Canter, Sarangi, & Youngs, 2012; Sarangi, Canter, & Youngs, 2013).

Another group, especially relevant to forensic psychology, are those people in various forms of custody. It may be regarded that any request for them to participate in research either has an implicit coercion associated with it, or they may think it will benefit their case, or decisions about their parole. As a result, many ethics committees do not regard prisoners as able to give informed consent, reducing the possibility of studies with them. If permission is granted by authorities to involve prisoners in a study it is therefore incumbent on the researcher to make clear that such involvement will have no consequences for their life in prison or other aspects of their case.

These concerns can spread over into considerations such as whether to give participants any recompense (e.g. payment, sweets, or cigarettes, etc.) for their involvement. Does this reduce their freedom to participate in an informed, non-coercive way?

Extreme instances

As with all these requirements they can be taken to annoyingly extreme lengths. In one study I wanted to research anonymous threatening letters sent to large organisations such as supermarkets or banks. These are typically extortion notes that threat to commit some dastardly deed, such as putting broken glass in baby food, unless the company pays a substantial sum of money. However, I was told by the supermarket I'd approached that the letters were actually the copyright of the anonymous villain so I could not study them without his permission!

I suspect this was partly a concern that the company had about the possibility of it becoming public knowledge that they received so many threats. The lesson here is that whatever you do, in relation to the information you are working with, can have consequences for other researchers in the future as well as having implications beyond those you may have thought of. This can become very contentious when research has political and related implications. Another illustration of this from my own research into arson, was the discovery that some fires are set by firemen who want to see some action. Of course, this type of arsonist is extremely rare, but no fire brigade will allow a study of that being the slightest possibility, because of its public relations implications.

Professional issues

Professional concerns are best understood by reference to the demands on research provided by professional bodies such as the British Psychological Society and the American Psychological Association. These 'codes of conduct' as they are known technically, apply to members of those professional bodies. They also cover professional practice as well as all other aspects of working as a psychologist, including research activity. They provide helpful indicators for anyone involved in psychological research. Their codes of conduct are widely available online (indicated in Appendix A at the end of the book). The basic principles from which the codes are derived were articulated by Katz (1972) in his review of issues relating to studies of people. He called them the 'Nuremberg Rules' (summarised in Table 0.1) as a reference to the trials of war criminals at the end of World War II. They are particularly relevant to invasive experiments, as may be common in medical research, but they are a salutary set of guidelines for any study of people.

One significant aspect of these codes of conduct in relation to research is the nature of the research design. Psychologists are very fond of experimental studies in which control and experimental groups are randomly assigned different experiences. This aping of the natural sciences is claimed to indicate the causal influences on the topic being studied. The weaknesses of this approach to scientific research are discussed in detail later, but from a professional point of view the controlled experiment does raise many challenges. Central to these is the problem of deception already mentioned. How can a person give informed consent if they are either actively deceived by the experimenter, for example by a misrepresentation of the purpose of the study, or passively by concealed observation?

The reason for deceptive instructions to research participants relates directly to a central challenge in psychological research; the great sensitivity to being observed that people have. A fundamental implication of this is that all psychological research is a form of social interaction. That interaction carries consequences for how the relationship between the researcher and participants is managed. Even if it is

Table 0.1 The 'Nuremberg Code' for any study involving human subjects

1. Voluntary participation, aware of any risks
2. Purpose of the research is for human benefit not otherwise available
3. Unnecessary physical or psychological harm to be avoided
4. Based on valid background knowledge from earlier research
5. Death or disablement not expected
6. Any risks proportional to the potential benefits
7. Precautions against any possible harm
8. The researcher (or their supervisor) is highly qualified in the area of study
9. Participants free to discontinue at any point
10. Procedure in place to discontinue if unforeseen negative consequences emerge

Table 0.2 Five ethics principles for social science research as summarised by the Academy of Social Sciences

1. Social science is fundamental to a democratic society and should be inclusive of different interests, values, funders, methods, and perspectives
2. All social science should respect privacy, autonomy, diversity, values, and dignity of individuals, groups, and communities
3. All social science should be conducted with integrity throughout, employing the most appropriate methods for research purposes
4. All social scientists should act with regard to their social responsibilities in conducting and disseminating their research
5. All social science should aim to maximise benefit and minimise harm

Note: For further information on ethics in social science, see, for example, www.acss.org.uk/developing-generic-ethics-principles-social-science.

just the records of previous activity, such as in police records of crimes, that are the basis of the research, there are still implicit relationships with the people recorded and their activities. Due care about privacy and confidentiality is essential. The people who supplied access to the records are also part of the research process and need to be effectively informed about the research (see Table 0.2).

If deception is deemed appropriate because of the potential benefit of the research, then some form of debriefing after participation is essential. This is the need to restore the relationship of trust and openness between researcher and participant that is essential for effective psychological research. This is crucial not just for that particular project, but for the message it sends out to others about participation in psychological studies. If psychologists get a reputation for deceiving those who are subjects in their studies, as can easily happen, then this clouds all participation in psychological studies, especially if the deception is unnecessary or disproportionate to the potential benefits of the study.

One requirement is that people should never act beyond their level of **professional competence**. This may not seem relevant to research projects. However, many of the studies in forensic psychology involve working with other agencies, such as the police, lawyers, prison authorities. It would not be unusual for people in these organisations, on learning of the project, to ask for some guidance on an ongoing investigation or other study in which they are involved. The researcher could be very tempted to 'do something useful' and respond positively to such a request. Yet such a response is potentially fraught with difficulties. One of these is that the involvement with ongoing work in the organisation may distort any results of the project (see my comments on 'consultancy' later in this section). Another difficulty is that the researcher may just not be competent to give this advice. Certainly, any such advice if carried out in a professional way, would require careful consideration of the facts and great caution in not stepping into a hornets' nest of internal debate within the organisation around the guidance being requested. There is also the possibility of the researcher being drawn into some legal process that the request is part of.

Is it professionally acceptable for psychologists to guide torturers?

The issue of proportionality can raise some profound ethical challenges. One example of direct relevance to studying anti-social behaviour is the American Psychological Association's concern about whether professional psychologists should provide guidance on how to torture people. Discovering that some members of the professional body had helped the

American military in Guantanamo Bay, there was a great outcry that this broke the key ethical principle of doing no harm. Those involved, who made a great deal of money out of the consultancy they provided to generate torture, claimed it was proportionate because it was for the general good.

Legal issues

Beyond the ethical need for privacy and confidentiality, in the United Kingdom and across Europe stringent new laws have been introduced to ensure any information held about an individual is kept private and confidential. This is often known as 'data protection'. The Data Protection Act of 2018 that has generated General Data Protection Regulations (GDPR) carries stringent punishments for any organisation that does not make sure information about people is used fairly, lawfully, and transparently. Note that it is the organisation that would attract serious fines if it does not follow GDPR properly. So be sure that even if you think you've got it all sorted the people responsible in your organisation are going to want to make sure you definitely have.

Illustrative example

There are other direct legal concerns that are particularly important when studying criminals. A crucial one is that in many countries it is illegal to reveal the identity of a rape victim unless the person has deliberately revealed it themselves. The identity of juveniles is also legally kept confidential. This may seem obvious and be part of the concern with privacy and confidentiality, but in one contribution to a police investigation I carried out an analysis as part of the investigation that considered a number of rape victims. Because it was part of the actual police investigation, the report I gave the investigators had the victims' names on. Many years later I wanted to present these results at a scientific meeting. Fortunately, I realised in time that the names would be visible to the audience and laboriously blanked them all out.

Copying the work of others

Plagiarism is often regarded as illegal. To be clear about it though, most academic and professional institutions have specific rules describing what it is and how to avoid it. They make clear that it is an offence to substantially copy the work of another person without appropriate acknowledgement. The law on copyright is relevant too. Anything that a person writes, even a message on Twitter, is the property of that person. It is against the law to use that material for your benefit without the copyright holder's agreement.

However, there are many people who consider the use of other people's work, with acknowledgement, is a good thing. They have created what is known as *Creative Commons*. To facilitate this there are special forms of copyright licences under which people can publish their material.[1]

It is worth noting, also that there are laws against defamation, libel, and slander. The privacy and confidentiality aspects of research should protect against drifting into this unwittingly. But it is worth being aware that mentioning a person who is publicly acknowledged as being criminal has to be done

[1] See www.creativecommons.org.

with some caution. The person may have subsequently been exonerated or you may have confused identities.

There is one further legal issue that is very important when interviewing people who may have committed crimes. These could be people who are not in prison and have never been convicted of a crime (as with Study 6 in this book). If they were to tell you about a crime they have committed for which they have not been charged, or even a crime they plan to commit, then in most jurisdictions you would be legally obliged to inform the authorities about this. If you don't you could be regarded as an 'accessory' to that crime, with legal consequences. This can make the exploration of a person's criminality very problematic.

Your account of what you have been told in an interview would be regarded in a court as 'hearsay', which would not usually be admissible as evidence. You would need more details for law enforcement agencies to follow up. As a consequence, minor misdemeanours, such as stealing sweets when a child, would not normally cause much problem, but more serious crimes could. It is therefore common practice, especially when talking to people in prison, to tell them that you do not want to know about any crimes they have committed for which they have not been convicted. You could even go further and say that if they do tell you about any serious crimes, or those they plan to commit, then you would be legally required to inform the authorities.

A particularly challenging aspect of this form of disclosure is when a victim tells you about crimes they have suffered and may possibly inform you of who the culprit is. This can happen, for example, when interviewing victims of abuse, possibly in a therapeutic encounter. The confidentiality of the interaction is usually regarded as sacrosanct, but the legal demands of not hiding a crime pull in the other direction. The victim may not wish their experience to be told to anyone else because of fears of reprisals and other consequences. The interviewer/therapist may encourage the victim to report the crime and leave it at that. But this does show that researchers need to go into such encounters armed with information about victim support and related organisations that can help manage claims by victims. Ethics committees would usually require that you have plans in place for giving such guidance to any participant in your research who may benefit from it.

An ethical conundrum

In academic life, and increasingly in other areas of professional activity, publishing accounts of research is crucial for career development. The scholarly tradition of recognising the person who contributed most to the work covered in the publication, by putting her/his name first in the authorship (known as the 'senior' or 'first' author) of the work, therefore takes on serious significance. The issue of authorship and especially who is 'first' author can consequently be very fraught. The challenge is determining who has made the major contribution. Indeed, who has a right to be recognised as one of the authors at all? The person who first thought of the project and ensured it was carried out effectively, possibly even turning the draft of a publication into something acceptable to a journal may consider himself the rightful senior author. This may often be the supervisor. But the student who got access to the data, assiduously collected it, and did all the statistical analysis may think she did the real legwork and therefore may believe she ought to be the first author. She may even think her supervisor should merely be acknowledged in a 'thank you' in the paper and not be an author at all. The resolution of this and similar disagreements may be resolved by reference to declarations by the university or the professional body as to what is appropriate, or be dealt with by some agreement prior to the research being undertaken.

Such plans should cover any aspect of the potential distress or concern that the research may generate. This could even be, for instance, having available information about help for drug abusers who become more aware of their problems during the research. Or even more general requests for help that may arise because you have been listening to a person's account of their current situation.

Ethical committees

Being effective in handling the ethical and related matters does ease the way to getting access to appropriate data of quality. In addition, there is usually one other important hurdle to jump – the ethical committee. An ethical committee is a group of people appointed by the organisation to overview all research proposals in order to ensure that they are ethically acceptable. These people have their own ideas of what is ethically acceptable and, in my experience, rarely have a detailed set of guidelines or criteria that overtly specify what makes a proposal satisfactory. They will be aware of all the matters discussed here and may also (to steal a line from Larkin's poem about families, 'This Be the Verse') "add some just for you".

They will want a detailed account of exactly what you plan to do: the procedures you will use to obtain data, the permissions you have or will get to allow you to use that information, what you intend to do with it, and anything else they can think of to satisfy themselves that you are not putting the institution at risk. You can even get into an infinite loop as I have on occasion when seeking to carry out a study in the health service. The university ethics committee required evidence the health service would give access, but the health services would not give access until the university had approved it. The project, some five years later, has still not taken place.

Insuring researchers

Sometimes an ethics committee may require some sort of insurance cover for the project. This happened when I wanted to study actions in fires in buildings that would require researchers travelling out with fire engines to fires. The fire brigade insisted the university insured the researchers, but the university insisted the fire brigade insurance should cover it. That project never happened.

ACCESSING DATA

In forensic psychology, perhaps more than any other area of psychological research, determining the source of data and how/if it will be accessed is crucial. Indeed, when students propose a research project my first question is always, "What data will you use?" Until you've been actively involved in studies in this area you may have an unhelpful mixture of naivete and optimism about what data will be available. I've already mentioned the ethical problem of gaining access to even the literally captive audience of prisoners, but many other seemingly accessible sources of data may be equally out of reach. However, that has not stopped the explosion of research in this area over the last two decades, but for you to be able to contribute to it you have to learn from the masters who have gone before.

I should note that the studies proposed in this volume have all been selected because there is a very strong possibility that, if approached in the right way, the data for carrying them out will be available. But never finalise your plans for research until you actually have the data in your hands (at least electronically). Police officers who I have supervised have been certain of access to not particularly sensitive source material only to discover at the last minute that access has been denied. As you develop your research career and go beyond what is listed here, as I hope you will, the demands become even more challenging.

Pathways to data

The idea that there is a process or pathway to gaining information on which to develop a project is taken from Habenstein (1970). The subtitle of his book is *Field Methods for Studying Ongoing Social Organisations*, but many of the experiences described by researchers in that book are directly relevant to studying anti-social behaviour. They draw attention to the following issues, which need to be considered from the earliest stages of planning a research project.

Access

Who do you need to contact in order to get the material needed for your project? What authority do they have? Who may they need to contact? Do not forget that anything you pass on to your initial contact, which describes what you want and why, is likely to be passed on to someone else for approval. This other person(s) may well be someone you've had no contact with before. Therefore, the document must be self-explanatory and clear enough to overcome any confusions your initial contact may have garnered.

Consider the people you are asking for help with access. To be brutal, what's in it for them? This may seem cynical but when I approached the director of a national police institution, sitting on vast amounts of interesting information about offences and offenders, collected of course using taxpayers' money, he blatantly asked me if he would get a university degree out of providing me with this material. This illustrates the fact that many of the institutions you may be dealing with, most notably law enforcement agencies, have no tradition or culture of research. They are set up to deal with the here and now of crime and criminals. I was even asked early in my contact with the police why I published my research: "Do you just want to see your name in print?" I was challenged. There was no notion of the career development and indeed moral demands of making research findings available to others.

As a friend of mine who had a career as a management consultant pointed out, the person you are in contact with, the liaison, for any organisation, is both your key associate and potential source of disruption. This individual is likely to have a personal agenda for why she or he is involved in the project. That may not be related to your objectives at all. An illustration of this are the many police officers who have supported my studies, who it later turned out were close to retirement and were looking for an academic career thereafter.

The benefits of the research have already been mentioned as an aspect of the ethical, and professional, aspects of any studies. In addition, besides any personal reasons for helping you, those who give access to data are likely to have to defend the benefit of the proposed research to their organisation. The British Home Office, for example, who fund a lot of crime-related studies, are very reluctant to fund any project, or give necessary approval for access to the relevant sources of data, that does not accord with the current political requirements. The government's science budget may happily spend millions trying to measure gravitational waves or determine if there is life on Mars, which only has the very slightest relevance to daily life, if at all, but try to get funding for the psychology of criminality without a direct benefit clearly specified and you'll be whistling into the wind.

It is also of value to emphasise that the skills required for gaining access to data go far beyond technical knowledge, say of how to run a factor analysis, or the relevant scholarly literature. Skills in communication and social interaction are probably more important. Those who give access will want to trust you and believe you have the appropriate expertise and authority to carry out the research appropriately. For sure, they'll want to be confident you will not get them or anyone else associated with the work into any sort of difficulty. For example, will the questions you ask upset anyone? Will you require their organisation to devote a lot of time and effort to helping you? Will you be at risk from anyone/thing that they are not willing to protect you from?

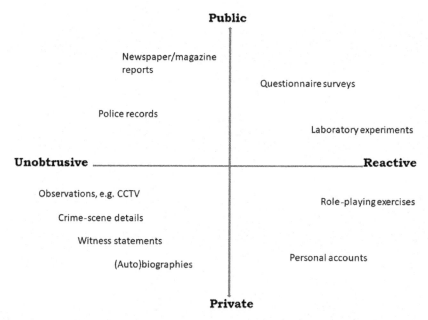

Figure 0.1 The range of sources of data on anti-social and criminal behaviour

Sources of data

Despite the challenges of access, the burgeoning literature covering the very wide range of studies of many different aspects of anti-social and criminal activity demonstrates that many different sources are available. These can be helpfully considered along two axes. One ranges from how directly involved with the participants the researcher is – how *intrusive*, at one end, to *unobtrusive* at the other end, with the participant not being aware at all of the research. The other axis is from how public the source of information is to how private. These two axes with proposed examples indicated are given in Figure 0.1.

This intrusive–unobtrusive continuum reflects the degree to which the researcher needs to consider the impact of the study on what is being studied. Webb, Campbell, Schwartz, and Sechrest ([1966] 2000) revisited by Lee (2005) proposed that 'unobtrusive', or as they also suggested 'non-reactive' measures, could enhance the objectivity of psychology because they reduced the possibility of the participant responding to the experience of the study as well as what was being studied. There are many such **data sources** available in criminal research, from newspaper reports and police records through to details of crime scenes and even gangsters' autobiographies. None of these is influenced by the acts of carrying out the research. I did explore this some years ago (Canter & Alison, 2003) as a way of considering the claims of Webb, Lee, and their colleagues about the objectivity of such data sources.

The irony is that although the non-reactive sources of information are not influenced by the researcher, precisely because they are not collected for research purposes, they have many flaws and biases. The people who do make this material available have their own purposes and agendas. Journalists want an interesting and exciting story, preferably with some 'human interest'. What they choose to report will therefore be biased towards those events and people that are particularly dramatic. Even the more formal police records are often distorted and inaccurate. As Farrington and Lambert (1997) showed in their study of the accuracy of police data even the gender and the age of culprits are not always correctly recorded. I have found much the same in more recent studies. The biographies and autobiographies of criminals are invariably justifications for their actions rather than completely honest accounts of what they were trying to do and why. Crime-scene photographs and related reports from experts require interpretation. They are raw information that must be converted into data for analysis.

At the other end of this continuum are those research interventions for which the participants, respondents (or as they are called in experimental studies – the subjects) are required to act on instructions given by the researcher. This may be responses to questions on a pro forma or in an interview, participation in an experiment, or even acting out a role (as in Study 9, planning a bank robbery).

The other dimension that is worthy of note runs from material that is publicly available, through to that which is essentially private. At the public end are reports in newspapers and other published accounts. True-crime magazines and websites are a remarkable resource for researchers. Often the articles are written by professional historians who pride themselves on getting their facts right. Although the covers of these magazines and the gory photographs on the websites are often sensationalist to draw in readers, the details there may be a useful basis for research provided they are cross-checked with other sources.

At the private end of the continuum are personal accounts. This could be victim or witness statements that increasingly are available to bona fide researchers. Typically, they are collected by police officers looking for evidence, unaware that a more extended account of what they are dealing with could be used as research data. In some cases, the researcher herself is able to interview people. This, of course, can be a very reactive process. The witness or offender may wish to present themselves in a good light and try to hide anything they think would be embarrassing, or that they would not want others to know about. For this reason, questionnaires that can be completed anonymously, without direct interaction with the researcher, may be preferable. In a number of studies in prisons I have given out questionnaires for prisoners, and also prison officers, to complete. But in doing so I have taken special care to ensure that each questionnaire is given out with an envelope that the respondent can seal. The collection of responses has also been carefully organised so that no one can tamper with these envelopes, thereby maintaining strict confidentiality for the answers being given.

Recording an interview

It may be regarded as non-threatening to record an interview with a victim or witness. But most people are aware of the evidential value of such a recording. In one study I interviewed a witness who seemed happy to let me record what he said. But once the recorder was clearly turned off, he then told me things that he was aware had legal consequences. This despite my original assertion that the recording would stay confidential to me. I of course made careful notes immediately after the interview. But since then I've used the turning off of the recording device as a clear action to encourage other, possibly more significant, comments to be forthcoming.

CONCLUSIONS

Despite the difficulties of studying crimes and criminals there is a plethora of material available on which to base significant and important research. Police records and other accounts that are in the public domain of offences and offenders are increasingly available. Personal descriptions from victims and those convicted of many different sorts of crime are readily available in books and online. In addition, there are many possibilities for getting offenders, victims, and those involved in law enforcement to participate in research. Yet all of these opportunities carry with them ethical, professional, and legal requirements that are more stringent and onerous than in many other areas of social science research. Managing these requirements effectively ensures that your research will be possible and worthwhile.

TOPICS FOR DISCUSSION

1. Is it appropriate to conduct research on the positive benefits or negative effects of torture? How would you carry out such research ethically?

2. What are the challenges in interviewing prisoners? How would you overcome them?

3. Under what circumstances is it appropriate to misinform participants about the purpose of a research project?

4. What professional and ethical issues are raised by using criminals' (auto)biographies for research?

5. What considerations are crucial if using videos of robberies for research?

NOTES

1   Although the detailed criticisms of Perry's critique available as comments in response to her YouTube interview at www.youtube.com/watch?v=UFxOnaa1BQg show just how problematic and contentious social psychology experiments can be.
2   As I remember kindly people said to me when I collected data for my PhD.

FURTHER READING

There are many journals that publish studies in crime psychology, forensic psychology, and criminology. An overview of an experimental approach to crime and criminality is given in:

Horne, C., & Lovaglia, M.J. (2008). *Experiments in criminology and law: A research revolution.* Plymouth, UK: Rowman & Littlefield.

REFERENCES

Canter, D., & Alison, L.J. (2003). Converting evidence into data: The use of law enforcement archives as unobtrusive measurement. *Qualitative Report*, 8(2), 151–176. Retrieved from https://nsuworks.nova.edu/tqr/vol8/iss2/1.

Canter, D., Sarangi, S., & Youngs, D. (2012). Terrorists' personal constructs and their roles: A comparison of the three Islamic terrorists. *Legal and Criminological Psychology*, 19(1), 160–178. https://doi.org/10.1111/j.2044-8333.2012.02067.x.

Farrington, D.P., & Lambert, S. (1997). Predicting offender profiles from victims and witness descriptions. In J.L. Jackson & D.L. Bekerian (Eds.), *Offender profiling, theory, research and practice* (pp. 133–158). Chichester, UK: Wiley.

Habenstein, R.W. (Ed.) (1970). *Pathways to data: Field methods for studying ongoing social organisations.* Chicago, IL: Aldine.

Katz, J. (1972). *Experimentation with human beings.* New York, NY: Russell Sage Foundation.

Lee, R.M. (2005). *Unobtrusive methods.* London: Elsevier.

Perry, G. (2013). Behind the shock machine: The untold story of the notorious Milgram psychology experiments. New York, NY: New Press.

Sarangi, S., Canter, D., & Youngs, D.E. (2013). Themes of radicalisation revealed though the personal constructs of Jihadi terrorists. *Personal Construct Theory and Practice*, 10, 40–60. Retrieved from www.pcp-net.org/journal/pctp13/sarangi13.ht.

Webb, E.J., Campbell, D.T., Schwartz, R.D., & Sechrest, L. [1966] (2000). *Unobtrusive measures* (rev. ed.) Thousand Oaks, CA: Sage.

PART TWO
Approaches to research

SYNOPSIS

Over many years of teaching research methods, I have found it fruitful to distinguish the overall design of the research – its strategy – from the way in which the data is collected – its tactics. While there is a natural relationship between the chosen strategy and the tactics used, they are still distinct aspects of research planning. They also imply types of research question, with their related theoretical perspective about ways of thinking about human nature. This framework has implications for the mode of analysis. Putting all these components together provides a rich set of guidelines for considering what a project is about and for developing a research proposal. Designing projects that consider aspects of anti-social behaviour is particularly demanding, therefore this framework can be of considerable assistance in formulating the details of the study. This approach to research design is of course also of value for all other areas of research.

SOME KEY CONCEPTS

- theoretical perspectives
- research strategies
- research tactics
- modes of analysis
- report writing.

THEORETICAL PERSPECTIVES

Louis Pasteur, who helped to develop the microbial theory of disease, so relevant to fighting COVID-19, emphasised the importance of theory for any scientific activity. As he put it, "Without theory, practice is but routine born of habit. Theory alone can bring forth and develop the spirit of inventions." This is somewhat at variance with the view that all you need to be a scientist is some data and statistics. There is a fundamental weakness in analysis without any theory or explanation of what the results mean, or the underlying processes that generated them. This is that the results are only relevant to the particular data set from which they were derived. Pasteur put this succinctly when he said that theory in science helps you to "go beyond the data". General principles, sometimes known as 'laws' in science, can be applied to new circumstances and data sets that are related to, but different from, those used in the original research.

The proposed studies in this volume are therefore all introduced with some brief background to the concepts and theories that are relevant to the projects. These generate questions to be answered or hypotheses to be tested. As a consequence, these studies provide an introduction to a wide range of **theoretical perspectives** that exist across psychology and related social sciences. The main types of theory are summarised here.

Cognitive models

Theories about how people think and the mechanisms of different mental activities are common across many considerations of anti-social activity. These include the pattern recognition processes used to determine if a signature is genuine or not (Study 1), as well as the mental maps that influence where criminals choose to commit their crimes (Study 4). The challenges of being deceptive are also better understood in terms of the cognitive demands that lying entails (Study 2). All judgements about offending, whether it is how serious a crime is (Study 5), or the distorted views gangsters have that justify their crimes (Study 8), require some sort of modelling of the cognitive processes.

Geo-spatial activity

All crimes happen at a time and in a place (even if that is in cyberspace). Consequently, the social and psychological mechanisms that influence where and when crimes occur help to reveal what generates criminals' spatial activity (Study 4). This illustrates that different theoretical perspectives are not usually in competition with each other. The cognitive models of criminals' selection of where to commit a crime are complemented by an understanding of the geo-spatial possibilities that influence people's lives.

Narrative perspectives

An emerging area of research across studies of criminality, as well as other areas of the social sciences, are theories about the underlying narratives that shape and explain human actions. The way criminals see their lives unfolding, their personal storylines, is a fruitful way of understanding the links between their characteristics and their actions (Study 3), as well as how they understand their criminality (Study 8). These personal narratives support the continuation of criminality by providing roles that keep the offences significant for the criminal (Study 6). It also is an intriguing aspect of the methods fraudsters use to persuade (Study 7).

Social processes

Criminality is inherently a social activity. There is always an explicit or implicit victim. Criminals often act in relation to each other, either as part of a gang or a network. Explanations of how social interactions operate are therefore relevant to group behaviour in bank robberies (Study 9), as well as the social interactions that help fraudsters to persuade (Study 7).

Organisational theory

Those criminal activities that require larger networks for their operation take on the characteristics of organisations. These are paralleled by the organisations that large-scale police investigations require (Study

10). This introduces the rich area of organisational theory and the more recent aspects of this, which explore how people form their personal identities as part of social groups. The nature of group cohesion, leadership roles, and the fundamental significance of communications between individuals all have relevance to understanding illegal and legal networks.

An Alternative Vocabulary

The many weaknesses in the experimental laboratory model of psychological research, discussed later, including the hijacking of its vocabulary for the study of real-world events, has led me and others who discuss 'real-world' research, such as Robson and McCartan (2017), to utilise a different vocabulary for research methods and design. The purpose of this different vocabulary is to recognise that there are many rigorous scientific procedures available to psychologists and other social scientists, but that their effectiveness relies on understanding their particular strengths and weaknesses, rather than regarding them as watered-down versions of randomised controlled laboratory experiments.

The vocabulary I have chosen draws loosely on military theories. If you wish you can consider research as a series of battles against ignorance. The overall approaches to these battles are *strategies*. The detailed ways in which they are carried out are the *tactics* of the research. There is a certain compatibility between certain tactics and specific strategies, but to understand them it is clearer to deal with each set of them separately.

In order to understand their implications, I present the strategies and tactics in order from the most structured – the 'lab 'experiment' – to the most 'open-ended' – case studies and simulations. It is important to emphasise that each of these is a valid basis for scientific research. Each type of strategy and each kind of tactic has its own rules. They can be used successfully producing good science, or they can be misunderstood and generate incoherent and invalid results of little utility.

Each combination of strategy and tactic has an appropriate mode of analysis, as described in the following section.

Research Strategies

'Lab' experiments

In their desire to make psychology as much like the natural sciences as possible, those engaged in the study of human activities and experiences have tended to regard the randomised, controlled-trial experiment as the epitome of scientific endeavour. This is typified by bringing people (usually referred to as subjects) into a sequestered room (what for simplicity I'm calling a 'lab') in which they are requested to react to different stimuli presented to them. Further, in what is regarded as the ideal study, these subjects are randomly assigned to different experimental conditions. In some conditions they will experience the manipulation the researcher is interested in (called the 'experimental' conditions) and in another they will not experience that condition (the 'control' condition). For example, the ability to solve mathematical puzzles would be studied in the experimental conditions of different types of noise in comparison with no noise.

The argument runs that because the researcher has control over the conditions the subjects experience, then any differences in their performance between experimental and control conditions can be confidently assigned to being caused by the experimental manipulations. This gold standard for research is therefore heralded as the only truly scientific way to do psychology and reveal underlying causes. Consequently, a whole vocabulary and associated set of analytical techniques have grown up around this form of laboratory experiment. The manipulation introduced by the experimenter is known as the 'independent variable'. The outcome activity generated by the subjects is called the 'dependent variable'. Statistical procedures are carried out that explore the amount of variability in the results that relate to the different conditions (or 'treatments' as they are often called), most notably 'analysis of variance'. Even the much-vaunted inferential statistics with its 'level of significance' and test of the 'null hypothesis', is really based on the assumption that the study is at least some diluted version of the controlled laboratory experiment.

There are situations, in the context of legal processes, for which there is no alternative but to set up some sort of representation of reality that may take the form of an experiment. A clear example is the jury decision-making process. In most jurisdictions members of a jury are not allowed to mention what happened in their actual deliberations. Therefore, in order to understand those processes, 'mock' juries have to be set up. This also has the advantage of allowing the evidence to be presented to them in different ways as experimental manipulations.

What is an experiment?

Ex.per'i'ment (ik-sper'e-mant): [Middle English from Old French from Latin experimentum, from experiri, to try]; 1. (a) A test under controlled conditions that is made to demonstrate a known truth, examine the validity of a hypothesis, or determine the efficacy of something previously untried. (b) The process of conducting such a test; experimentation. 2. An innovative act or procedure: "Democracy is only an experiment in government."

The term 'experiment' is frequently used promiscuously to refer to any study at all. Rooms full of completed questionnaires, which have no control or experimental conditions associated with them, may be referred to as laboratories. Even just a group of people doing research may call themselves a 'laboratory'. This broadening of the use of this label is unhelpful because it reduces the possibility of identifying the particular experimental design strategy. Therefore, from now on, I will keep the term 'experiment' for these rarefied explorations that have the paraphernalia of controlled conditions with dependent and independent variables. Sometimes, to be absolutely explicit about the sort of study I am referring to I will make clear I am writing about laboratory experiments. This implies studies that are carried out under reasonably controlled conditions within physical confines. Study 1 in this book illustrates this research strategy by presenting people with genuine and forged signatures (the independent variable) and asking them to say which are genuine and which are not (the dependent variable). Aspects of the signature provide variations in the independent variable.

At this point I should apologise about the title of this book. In popular parlance the term 'experiment' is often used to describe any systematic study. It has a certain connotation that implies something interesting, exciting, and even a little exotic. The publishers therefore wanted the word 'experiments' in the title rather than the more mundane 'studies' or 'projects'. However, now that we've got to consider exactly what strategies and tactics are available for studies of anti-social behaviour, I hope you will forgive the slight confusion when I now declare that most of the projects I describe in the book are not 'experiments' in my stricter usage of the term.

The limits of the laboratory experiment

Even though, or possibly because, the laboratory experiment is so highly regarded it is fraught with problems. In a recent publication, dealing directly with the idea of experimental criminology, Farrington and his colleagues (2019) discuss the fact that the purist form of experiment – the randomised controlled trial – is not necessarily the best research design for studies of criminality. The weaknesses of variations in controlled experimental designs, for example by using naturally occurring differences in conditions (sometimes called 'quasi-experimental designs'), also raise questions about the utility of using the laboratory experiment vocabulary to describe all applied research.

Example of experimenter effect in a witness identification

When investigators examined the bomb that blew up the aeroplane over Lockerbie on 21 December 1988 they found clothing in the suitcase near it. They thought they traced this clothing to a shop in Malta. Convinced that Antony Gauci had put the bomb on the plane, a year later, they showed the shopkeeper 12 photographs, including that of Gauci. The shopkeeper was asked if he could recognise the person who had bought the clothing the previous Christmas. He selected the picture of Gauci, much to the delight of the police. Gauci denied his involvement and for a subsequent appeal I was asked to examine the evidence. I therefore set up a study to see if there might be an experimenter effect influencing the selection of the target photograph. This was subsequently published (Hollinshead, 2014), as was the full report examining all the evidence from the Malta 'eyewitness' (Canter, Youngs, & Hammond, 2012).

   This study showed that if the experimenter asking respondents to identify a suspect knew who the suspect was in the set of photographs, then the experimenter was far more likely to get the suspect selected than an experimenter who did not know. This topic is discussed in more detail in Study 1.

The problems with laboratory experiments (especially when studying anti-social behaviour)

1. There are ethical and practical constraints on what is allowable, or possible.

2. Only a limited set of conditions/treatments can be used. Any effects within or outside of those conditions cannot be known.

3. It is assumed that the process being studied is a relatively simple input–output one, essentially that human beings are mechanical mechanisms.

4. The paradox that attempts are made to control variables that may influence the results, even though it is important to understand what variables will influence the results outside of the laboratory.

5. The meaning of interventions for participants are difficult to explore, as are the effects of naturally occurring contexts.

6. Participants try to make sense of what they are asked to do and will often try to give the results they think the experimenter wants. These are known as the implicit demands the experimental situation makes or 'demand characteristics' (as explored in great detail by Orne, 1962 and Rosnow, 2002).

7. The experimenter can unwittingly influence how people respond within the experimental situation. This is known as 'experimenter effects' (as studied extensively by Rosenthal and Rosnow, 2009). The fascinating book by Perry (2013) examining the detailed records kept by Milgram from his notorious 'obedience' experiments, as well as interviews with participants, reveals how much of the reported results were a result of artefacts, demand characteristics, and experimenter effects, not obedience to authority as Milgram claimed.

8. The experimental situation is one of asymmetrical power. The researcher dominates and participants volunteer to be manipulated. This means open, honest interaction is extremely difficult (as Schuler, 1982, discusses at length).

9. A history of misleading subjects who participate in experiments by psychologists makes subjects suspicious and sceptical of what they are asked to do. Only a few days ago, a member of the audience for a lecture I gave came up to me afterwards and implied I'd not been honest with the audience, that the whole lecture was an 'experiment', even though nothing could have been further from the truth.

10. The ritualistic vocabulary of experimental and control groups, testing the null hypothesis, dependent and independent variables, distract researchers from actually understanding the processes they are studying, unravelling the complex patterns of relationships that characterise human actions and experiences.

11. The modes of analysis, such as analysis of variance and related inferential statistics do not provide a clear indication of the processes being studied, as Guttman (1977) made clear in a seminal paper titled 'What Is Not What in Statistics' for the Royal Statistical Society. Perhaps his most telling point is that measures of statistical significance do not measure significance.

Field experiments

The inherent artificiality of the lab experiment, but its ability to indicate a clear direction of causality, has led to the development of a research strategy that attempts to use naturally occurring circumstances while still having some of the benefits of the experimental process. These have been called 'field experiments'. These approaches were given great impetus by the slim book titled *Experimental and Quasi-Experimental Designs for Research*, written by Campbell and Stanley (1963).

Campbell and Stanley's book proposed ways of enabling the causal interpretations that laboratory experiments are supposed to be so good at, but applied in a wider range of contexts. They called these 'quasi-experiments' because they were not carried out in the controlled conditions of a laboratory. They adapted this format in naturally occurring settings. Some of their research designs were even called 'field experiments'. This way of thinking about research still has a huge following, with Campbell involved in an update of his perspective in a more recent book (Shadish, Cook, & Campbell, 2002) and in a more recent account by Levy and Ellis (2011).

The idea is that instead of the controlled conditions of a university room, something similar would be done in a natural setting, such as a classroom. For instance, students could be randomly assigned to one of two different ways of teaching maths and the outcome compared, or even what they called 'natural experiments' would be used. In this research two comparable situations, which came about without the intervention of a psychologist, would be examined. For example, patients with similar symptoms who had different treatments would be compared with each other. Study 2, here, examining the detection of deception, proposes two projects: one using experimental and the other quasi-experimental strategies. Study 4 takes the naturally occurring differences between rural and metropolitan areas to compare the distances offenders move from home to commit a series of crimes. This can be regarded as a rather crude field experiment.

I had the privilege of meeting Dr Campbell at a conference once and put it to him that his research designs should really be called 'quasi-naturalistic' because they distorted actual occurrences to make them fit the experimental paradigm. He agreed. He also accepted my point that he would not have sold so many copies of his book if had not had the reference in the title to the implicit magic of the 'experiment'.

It is worth noting that the motivation for the development of these not quite experimental approaches to research was Campbell's own interest in educational research. He was aware that the pure experiment was not producing results that could readily be applied to what happens in a classroom. Getting children to do things under laboratory conditions is not very predictive of how they will behave in the classroom.

Similar comments have been made about studies of psychological therapies. The more 'controlled' the experiment is the more artificial and consequently the less applicable to actual practice.

Studies of criminal activity are similarly difficult to squeeze into the laboratory experiment box. Could you randomly assign people convicted of crimes to different forms of punishment and some to no punishment at all in order to determine the 'effects' of punishment? Even if you were able to carry out such an outrageous study, wouldn't there be a public outcry because of the perceived unfairness of the process?

The problem of any study done in a natural, existing context is that it has a range of associations and expectations already tied into it. The meanings of the interventions the researcher introduces derive from their context. They can never have the purity of influence that is assumed in the laboratory. There is also the issue of the impact any observations may have on those being observed, which may be more obtrusive in a naturalistic setting, but always has to be assumed in a laboratory.

There are also many situations where controlled experiments are just not possible. One example that many of us live with are hospital operations. Each surgeon develops a particular way of carrying out a specific operation. The complex mix of the interpretation of the problem and how to deal with it, combined with the particular skills and experience of the surgeon, mean that it would not be expected that any two operations would be carried out in exactly the same way. Nor would we want them to be. Of course, the success of each surgeon can be assessed. If that reveals a weakness, such as killing more than an acceptable number of patients, the individual's procedures can be examined and appropriate remedies and training authorised. But this is not anything like the formal process of an experiment.

In effect, any sort of field study (i.e. one carried out in a natural setting), is never appropriately considered as an 'experiment'. It is really a comparison of different situations. One in which the details of each situation need to be understood in order to make sense of the differences in outcomes. These field studies may be more appropriately called 'comparative case studies'.

Surveys

In contrast to the detailed account of one, or a few, conditions for which the outcomes/consequences are compared, surveys cover more cases with fewer features. The great advantage of this research strategy is that it covers a range of values for the topics being examined rather than selecting a very limited number of particular levels, as required for experimental designs. The examples in this book, for instance, cover issues like the degree and kind of emotions people feel when committing crimes and attitudes towards various forms of deviance. They illustrate that surveys can also deal with a range of related issues rather than just one or two 'dependent' variables as is typical of experiments.

There are also many studies for which a range of values on one variable may be usefully related to a range of values on another variable. One intriguing example would be to explore the relationship between how serious a crime was thought to be and the severity of the punishment it received, as proposed for Study 5. Hamilton and Rytina (1980) did examine this by getting people to rate the seriousness of a wide range of crimes and then to consider the severity of the punishments they considered appropriate. This enabled them to test sophisticated, statistical models of the relationship between seriousness and severity as well as showing that this relationship was different depending on the subgroup's experience of crime and punishment.

An important distinction needs to be made between the exploration of the relationships between sets of variables mentioned here and the widely used 'public opinion' questionnaire, which is often called an 'opinion survey'. This is more relevant to sociology than psychology. Typically, a few direct questions are asked to a carefully chosen sample of individuals, representative of the population of interest. A powerful example would be a survey of the population to determine if homosexuality should be illegal. The crucial aspect is that the frequency of people expressing a particular opinion is the outcome. The value of this result depends on how clearly the question is posed and, crucially, on how representative the sample is.

Such surveys are the basis of a referendum, such as the silly one that asked whether the United Kingdom should leave the European Union (EU).

The form of survey I am considering here is not so critically dependent on the representativeness of the sample or respondents. This is because it is the relationships between the range of questions being asked that is at the heart of any such study, such as the proposed Study 5 looking at the relationship between the rated seriousness of a crime and the legal punishment for it. A very distinct, or biased, sample will provide different relationships between questions. For example, relating religiosity to how often a person lies would probably get quite different results for a sample of Christians when compared with people diagnosed with psychopathy.

The weakness of surveys is that, although they can give important descriptions of a sample's reactions and the relationships within a variety of such reactions, it is a complex and challenging process to unravel any causal mechanism within that material. This can be illustrated by the previous example of the relationship between lying, religiosity, and psychopathy. Would any results be due to religious beliefs, psychological processes, or some interaction between the two? A lot of additional questions would need to be asked and probably some quite sophisticated statistical analysis applied to sort this out.

When there are a variety of questions in a survey the issue emerges of what the underlying 'structure' of the questionnaire is. In other words, the task is to identify the components that make up the issue that is being explored. Although not a survey in the usual sense, a clear illustration of the idea of 'structure' is the finding that items in intelligence tests are made up of either spatial, verbal, or numerical components, as well as a general component (Guttman & Levy, 1991). In Study 6 it is proposed that there are a set of roles that underlie the experience of committing crimes.

Across the social sciences in general, and in many areas of psychology, questionnaire surveys are the dominant form of research strategy. It is therefore somewhat amusing to note that William James, one of the founders of modern psychology, stated well over a century ago that, "because of its ease of use the questionnaire survey is the bane of modern society". The ease of setting up such surveys on the Internet has taken this a leap further in frequency, although the challenges in using online surveys are not small, as illustrated in Study 6.

Inevitably, the lockdown caused by COVID-19 is making the online survey the strategy of choice for many areas of research. You cannot purchase anything – from a 5-amp fuse, to an expensive car, or a holiday in Italy – without being asked soon afterwards your view of the object or service and the process of buying it. It is therefore perhaps not surprising that very few people respond to these requests, often as few as 10% of those approached. If the topic is of serious, personal interest a higher proportion are likely to respond. Or if the respondent has some relationship with the people conducting the survey a good number may participate. The warning here is that you should not jump to the survey as the strategy of choice without careful consideration of the possibilities and other options.

Case studies

In psychology individual case studies are often dismissed as 'merely descriptive' but when dealing with anti-social activity a crucial starting point is to get a detailed, clear account of what it is, what happens. The value of this can be seen when considering serious crimes such as rape or murder. Although we may think we know what actually happens in these crimes, close consideration reveals that they can take many forms. The differences between them are vital for understanding their origins and motivations.

Describing what happens in a crime requires a variety of skills and processes. Access to the information is itself a challenge. But even if the information is available there is the demanding task of determining how to organise that information in a way that is of scientific value. There are a number of approaches to this depending on whether one complex system is being explored or a number of cases are being compared. There are a variety of ways of carrying out case studies, which Robson and McCartan (2017) elaborate on. Baxter and Jack (2008) also consider the various possibilities in their review. Early authorities, notably Bromley (1986), emphasised the use of case study material to develop a reasoned argument. He proposed an analogy to presenting evidence for a case in court. In general, though, case studies always draw on the need to identify the salient components of the case(s) being examined, and how they relate to each other. This is illustrated in Studies 7, 8, and 9.

Study 8 proposes a consideration of the autobiographical accounts given by gangsters and other violent criminals about their life and times. Straus and Corbin (1998) and other followers of what is called 'grounded theory' propose that the researcher can enter the mire of naturally occurring events and derive from that some hypotheses and frameworks without any prior conceptions. I do not believe that is possible. A researcher always has some background that makes her interested in the topic and the reason for the case study. The more clearly that can be articulated the more effective the analysis can be. For example, in studying criminals' autobiographical books about their actions it is very likely they have a reason for publishing such accounts. They can therefore be read with a view to why they are writing. I would propose that justification for their actions is one such purpose. This then leads to the search for the forms of these justifications.

Simulations

A process that lies on the border between training and research is what I call a 'simulation'. This can take many forms: from simulating the impacts of climate change using complex computer models to setting up a mock jury to simulate what happens in a jury room. Sometimes, as with computer games, they mirror activities to create competitions. The aspect of this strategy that I emphasise in Study 10 is that people participate in a task in which they take different roles. The way this task is set up allows the detailed recording of how they interact with each other. It also allows different communication networks to be created so that the effect of being at any node in this network can be examined.

There is a sense in which the sort of simulation I am describing may be regarded as a controlled set of case studies. Besides recording how they participate in the 'game' they can also be asked about their involvement. The intense nature of actually playing a role, under controlled conditions, turns the research aspect of the activity into a personal experience. This has educational and training features not so powerful in other research strategies. It can therefore be a useful vehicle for enabling people within organisations to develop the way they deal with each other – a form of consultancy.

A note on consultancy

As has been mentioned a few times, a central challenge of psychology, especially in the area of crime and criminality, is that the actual process of research may, indeed is likely to, change what is being studied. Various procedures therefore have to be harnessed to make allowances for this and to mitigate these effects as much as possible. But there is one form of research in which the primary objective is to change what is being studied. I call this 'consultancy', but what I am referring to often goes under the umbrella title of 'action research' (Stringer, 2014). An example in which I have been engaged is in trying to improve police detection rates.

This is a research project because it is necessary to understand the distribution of crimes, say for instance burglaries, and the current police practice (as illustrated in Study 4). Furthermore, any guidance given needs to take account of what is possible and legal for the police to do. This can be illustrated by my discovery that police clear-up rates for burglary are disturbingly low: usually less than 10% of crimes are solved. The resources available to law enforcement are also minimal. One consequence of this is that they cannot readily follow up individual cases, but if a set of burglaries can be linked to a common offender then it is more cost effective for these to be investigated. This means that research needs not only to consider individual burglaries, which may have been the initial requirement, but to build into the advice to the police proposals on the linking of crimes.

The input of proposals to the organisation requires skills in addition to those that may be relevant for effective research. One point that I discovered early on is that decision makers who have little scientific background are greatly influenced by 'successful' cases. They like to think there are big numbers and research behind the example case, but it is the example that influences their decision. No amount of general findings that indicate the value and potential of an approach or idea will usually encourage them to change what they do or how they do it. On the other hand, a one-off case that successfully drew on that research and principles will sometimes create a swirl of activity.

One implication of this is that being able to communicate effectively with the organisation you are consulting with, being able to understand their expectations, needs, and limitations, is a significant part of working with them. The arcane language of research, the delight in advanced statistics and the other paraphernalia that makes many academics believe they have real skills, are no substitute for being able to get your message across in a way the people who must use your findings can understand and are able to act on.

All of the strategies and tactics that are relevant to the research process can also be used as part of a consultancy or action research project. The crucial aspect, though, is how the methods, and especially the results, can be communicated to the organisation. I mention aspects of **report writing** later, explaining how a consultancy report differs in important ways from an academic account of what you have done.

Advising the police in a major investigation

The simple fact is that I would not be writing this book if over 30 years ago I had not used straightforward psychological ideas to act as a consultant to a major investigation into a series of rapes and murders around London. The value of my contribution to that one case opened the doors to work with the police that would otherwise never have happened, no matter how much background research I could quote (Canter, 1994).

RESEARCH TACTICS

In contrast to the broad design of a study, what I have called the 'strategy', there are the details of the data that is to be collected and how it will be prepared for analysis. These 'tactics' also carry implications for underlying assumptions about the nature of people, 'models' of humankind. I think of these models as being along a continuum from those that give the person and their understanding of what is going on a central role through to those that deal with people as objects for study.

At the former end are processes that treat the person as what the Australian philosopher Harré (1984) called "experts on their own experiences". There is a long tradition in psychology of seeking to work with people on their own terms. Trying to understand how they see the world and what they consider the most appropriate way to express that. They are participants in the research, or even in some projects co-researchers. The tactic most used in this context is the interview and case study. People also generate accounts outside of the demands of research, as when they write autobiographies. These can be a rich source of unstructured data, as in Study 8.

At the other end of the continuum people are treated as organisms that the researcher has the authority to study and whose actions the researcher has the right to interpret. Here they are treated as objects of study, although, as mentioned, they are usually referred to as 'subjects'.

Of course, neither extreme is total. Even when observing people, some sense needs to be made of what they are doing and subjectively undergoing. Personal accounts have to be treated with as much objectivity as possible, distancing the researcher from the emotions they may be expressing.

Interviews can be structured or open-ended with various degrees of focus in between. There is relatively little point in using a very structured, multiple-choice interview. That questions might as well be written down in the form of a questionnaire, unless the participants in the research may have difficulty reading or understanding what is required of them, such as children.

A further step beyond understanding the opinions, experiences, or attitudes of the participants as they express them, is to give people tasks to perform, to record what they do. This is really what an intelligence test is and many forms of occupational assessments. In most studies in this volume people are required to make some choices and related decisions. How they do this are the key measurements of the study. However, to make sense of their actions it is necessary to explore with them why they did what they did.

When participants in research are observed in a research set-up or in more naturally occurring situations, the researcher tends to impose her views on what is going on and why, unless the observations are accompanied by some form of interview. Nonetheless, there are areas of research for which this is an appropriate tactic. The project in Study 2, which uses television appeals by people whose loved ones have disappeared, is an observational examination of those appeals. However, to turn these observations into data, observers are asked to complete questionnaires to describe what they see or hear. This illustrates how, as with strategies, a variety of tactics may be employed in any one study.

MODES OF ANALYSIS

This book would be far too long and complex if it included the details of the statistical procedures that many books about research methods cover. The *Statistical Package for the Social Sciences* (SPSS) manual is also very helpful. In addition, it is surprising how much can be achieved with Excel and other spreadsheet software. Therefore, I just want to draw attention to broad types of research question. Each type of question implies its appropriate form of analysis and statistics.

Comparing groups

The standard experimental procedure is to compare the results generated by two or more sets of participants. The key example is comparing the experimental group (that have received the experimenter's manipulation) with the control group (who did not get any manipulation). Perhaps the clearest example in this volume is the comparison of truth and lies in Study 2. The comparison of the distances burglars travel from home in rural and metropolitan areas would be another example.

The most commonly used statistics for this are the t-test, or analysis of variance. Although when there are only frequencies available the chi-square test may be appropriate.

Examining relationships

Where there are two variables being compared, as in Study 5, where ratings of seriousness are compared with legal sentencing, then measures of correlation will indicate how closely related the two variables are. It is often very useful to draw the relationship in a scatter plot, as illustrated for Study 5. This enables you to see if the relationship is not a simple straight line. It also allows you to look at individual cases that have rather different results from the others, so that you can look more closely at these and determine what is making them different.

Describing cases

When you are examining one or a few cases closely you build up an account of those cases. This may seem like a purely descriptive activity, but it requires the identification of the main aspects to specify. To be of real value, it is also useful to relate what you describe to underlying theory. For example, in Study 4 the different roles that are indicated in the accounts offenders give can help to make the description of their backgrounds and actions of more general relevance.

RESEARCH STYLES

One of the myths of research is that there is one best way to do any project. This ignores the fact, obvious if you study the work of any active researcher, that people develop a style of doing research. I had a colleague who was an excellent laboratory researcher. He was called on to do some field-based research, but soon gave it up because he could not cope with the lack of control that was part of the project.

As you read through the studies in this book you will doubtless gain a flavour of the sort of research I feel most comfortable with. You will quickly realise, for example, that the strict randomised controlled trials, or large-scale studies with thousands of participants and heavy number-crunching, are not part of my portfolio. Nor will you find that I have carried out intense, extremely detailed qualitative explorations, although I have given examples of this important approach in Study 8. Nonetheless, I have tried to be as eclectic as possible in the examples I've selected, but we all have our styles of doing research. You need to find yours.

REPORT WRITING

Students often mistakenly believe that the products of research are findings or results. If they are a bit more sophisticated, they may think the outcome is the testing of an hypothesis or the support of a theory. All of these beliefs miss the point that if there is no account of the research, in a publication or at least a presentation at a conference, then those results will never be known. They can certainly not be evaluated without the appropriate details being available to view. Consequently, it is important to recognise that a crucial stage in any research activity is the production of a report of that research. There are many books and journal articles that give guidance on report writing, including my own (Canter & Fairbairn, 2006). Or the salutary article by Pinker, Munger, Sword, Toor, and MacPhail (2014). I would also make the point that there is a moral obligation to produce reports of your work. There will be many people who have helped either as participants or in other ways. The least they can expect is that you make the results of your work available to others.

There are few basic points about writing a report, which I summarise here:

- *Knowing your audience.* Different recipients of your report will have different expectations and understanding of what you are writing. It is always good to find a document written for the audience you have in mind, whether it is your lecturer, a general audience, a newspaper, etc., and see how that is written. You should consider both how it is organised and the vocabulary and content of the material presented. There will be standard ways of organising the material for each outlet.

- *One page at a time.* Often it is very daunting to start writing an account of your research if you've not had any experience of doing that. This is especially true if you are writing about an extensive piece of research, say for a master's or PhD dissertation. My guidance is to work with the material by first outlining the overall structure on one sheet of paper. Then take a section and develop that as a page of headings. Then take one of those headings and develop it further. Keep on doing this, but always only thinking of the current page you are working on. You can go back and change things, move sections and pages around. This way you will not be frightened by the overall scale of the task and you will be aware where every paragraph and section fits in the overall framework.

- *A general framework.* When planning the framework and contents of your report do not be confused into thinking it is a logbook or journal that describes what you've done. It is an argument. It may very well present a case that is rather different from what you intended to write when you first started thinking about collecting data. That does not matter. The report must do the following:

(a) Put the work in context and show how and why it answers questions raised by other research.
(b) It needs to make clear what questions you are seeking to answer, or hypotheses you are testing.
(c) It needs to describe clearly how you collected the data to answer those questions/test those hypotheses. This description should be clear enough for another experienced researcher to be able to repeat it, in principle at least.
(d) The way in which the data was analysed has to be specified.
(e) The results should be reported in as objective a way as possible.
(f) The implications of those results should be described.
(g) The overall conclusions you reach about what you have done and how it might be developed in the future should be described.

It is interesting to note that this gives seven sections to a report. If you are involved in a major study, such as for a PhD, then you may be expected to have five projects that make up your dissertation. In simple terms the five projects and seven sections would give 12 chapters. You will see that many PhDs (in the United Kingdom at least) have around 12 chapters.

• *Getting published.* If your aspiration is to have your work published in an academic journal then you have to jump through some significant hoops. The crucial aspect of this is to determine the journal you want to submit your work to, then to look closely at what content it covers and exactly how the material is to be organised for that specific journal. Almost invariably you will have to submit your paper online and the journal will have specific guidelines to follow. If you do not follow them your paper will be rejected before anyone looks at it.

Also remember that a journal article usually makes one direct point with supporting information. You might helpfully prepare a journal article by first deciding on its title, then on the conclusions you want to draw. After that you could identify the main tables or illustrations that support your argument. You are then ready to write the introduction to the paper.

• *Consultancy reports.* A report to an organisation, or a court of law, or an individual, has a rather different set of requirements to those required for academic publications. Consultancy documents are read by busy people whose main interest is what they should do about your results. They need to know what your conclusions are very directly and clearly, as well as any recommendations you are willing to make. There is therefore usually a 'management' or 'executive' summary at the start of the report. Then what you did to come to those conclusions. Details of analyses and the data collected could then be in an appendix. As mentioned earlier, graphic case examples that illustrate the results help to bring the study to life for those who are interested in acting on your conclusions.

General headings for most reports or publications

Remember, though, that each outlet or audience has its own preferred format.

• *Title.* The title should be a simple, clear statement of the main purpose of the document. Avoid clever titles, e.g. 'Bridging the Gap: Links Between Psychology and Law', as search engines may pick that up in searches by civil engineers, who will get very annoyed!
• *Abstract.* The abstract describes what question you are addressing, what data or other material you collected to address it, how you analysed it, the results, and conclusions – usually in that order.
• *Introduction.* The introduction sets the context for the report. This can be the challenges that are being faced, or the issues that emerge from previous research. It is useful to think

of this starting with 'Although'. That forces you to present the report as dealing with a problem rather than just recounting of what others have done that vaguely relates to it.
- *Research questions*. What hypotheses are you testing, or what questions are you seeking to answer? The origins of these in previous studies or other material should be made clear.
- *Analysis*. The analysis should be clear enough for others to be able to repeat, but does not usually require detailed working out unless you've been specifically asked for that.
- *Results*. Tables and figures should be appropriate for the audience and as succinct and limited as possible, but well labelled. People often look at the tables and figures first, so if possible, they should tell the story of your report.
- *Conclusions and implications*. Where do these results take you? What consequences do they have for:
  - theory development;
  - policy and practice;
  - the methods and procedures you've employed.

QUESTIONS FOR DISCUSSION

1. What areas of criminality would benefit from randomised controlled trials? How would you set about creating such experiments?

2. What relationships can you see between the different forms of theory and the different research strategies?

3. What relationships can you see between the different forms of theory and the different research tactics?

4. Which tactics are most compatible with which strategies? Can you create a table that shows the relationships?

5. Describe two studies of drug dealing with each study utilising a different mix of strategies and tactics.

FURTHER READING

A comprehensive textbook that follows the general approach described here is:

Robson, C., & McCartan (2017). *Real world research* (4th ed.) Chichester, UK: Wiley.

REFERENCES

Baxter, P., & Jack, S. (2008). Qualitative case study methodology: Study design and implementation for novice researchers. *Qualitative Report*, 13(4), 544–559. Retrieved from www.nova.edu/ssss/QR/QR13-4/baxter.pdf.
Bromley, D.B. (1986). *The case-study method in psychology and related disciplines*. Chichester, UK: Wiley.
Canter, D. (1994). Criminal shadows: Inside the mind of the serial killer. London: HarperCollins.
Canter, D., & Fairbairn, G. (2006). Becoming an author: Advice for academics and other professionals). Maidenhead, UK: Open University Press.

Canter, D., Youngs, D., & Hammond, L. (2012). Cognitive bias in line-up identifications: The impact of administrator knowledge. *Science and Justice*, 53(2), 83–88. http://dx.doi.org/10.1016/j.scijus.2012.12.001.

Campbell, D.T., & Stanley, J.C. (1963). *Experimental and quasi-experimental designs for research*. Boston, MA: Houghton Mifflin.

Farrington, D.P., Lösel, F., Braga, A.A., Mazerolle, L., Raine, A., Sherman, L.W., & Weisburd, D. (2019). Experimental criminology: Looking back and forward on the 20th anniversary of the Academy of Experimental Criminology. *Journal of Experimental Criminology*. https://doi.org/10.1007/s11292-019-09384-z.

Guttman, L. (1977). What is not what in statistics. *Journal of the Royal Statistical Society. Series D (The Statistician)*, 26(2), 81–107. doi: 10.2307/2987957.

Guttman, L., & Levy, S. (1991). Two structural laws for intelligence tests. *Intelligence*, 15(1), 79–103.

Harré, R. (1984). Personal being: A theory for individual psychology. *Ethics*, 95(4), 947–949. doi: 10.1086/292700.

Hamilton, L.V., & Steve Rytina, R. (1980). Social consensus on norms of justice: Should the punishment fit the crime? *American Journal of Sociology*, 85(5), 1117–1144.

Hollinshead, J. (2014). *Administrator effects on respondent choice* (PhD thesis, University of Huddersfield, UK). Retrieved from http://eprints.hud.ac.uk/id/eprint/24473/1/Master_Revised_Final_Jemma_Hollinshead_July_2014.pdf.

Levy, Y., & Ellis, T.J. (2011). A guide for novice researchers on experimental and quasi-experimental studies in information systems research. *Interdisciplinary Journal of Information, Knowledge, and Management*, 6, 151–160. Retrieved from https://core.ac.uk/download/pdf/51072279.pdf.

Orne, M.T. (1962). On the social psychology of the psychological experiment: With particular reference to demand characteristics and their implications. *American Psychologist*, 17, 776–783.

Perry, G. (2013). *Behind the shock machine: The untold story of the notorious Milgram psychology experiments*. London and New York, NY: New Press.

Pinker, S., Munger, M.C., Sword, H., Toor, R., & MacPhail, T. (2014). *Why academic writing stinks and how to fix it*. New York, NY: Chronicle of Higher Education. Retrieved from www.chronicle.com/article/why-academics-stink-at-writing-and-how-to-fix-it.

Robson, C., & McCartan, K. (2017). *Real world research* (4th ed.). Chichester, UK: Wiley

Rosenthal, R., & Rosnow, R.L. (2009). *Artifacts in behavioral research*. New York, NY: Oxford University Press.

Rosnow, R.L. (2002). The nature and role of demand characteristics in scientific inquiry. *Prevention & Treatment*, 5(1), 37.

Shedish, W.R., Cook, T.D., & Campbell, D.T. (2002). *Experimental and quasi-experimental designs for generalized causal inference*. Boston, MA: Houghton Mifflin.

Schuler. H. (1982). *Ethical problems in psychological research* (M.S. Woodruff & R.A. Wicklund, Trans.). New York, NY: Academic Press.

Straus, A., & Corbin, J. (1998). *Basics of qualitative research: Techniques and procedures for developing grounded theory* (2nd ed.). Los Angeles, CA: Sage.

Stringer, E.T. (2014). *Action research* (4th ed.). Los Angeles, CA: Sage.

PART THREE
Ten studies

Experiments

FORGERY

STUDY 1

How to forge a signature

SYNOPSIS

As an illustration of a formal 'laboratory' experiment, a study is described that considers how easy
it is to create and detect forged signatures. The nature of signatures in relation to how easy people
think a signature is to forge is also considered. Consequently, although this is an intriguing aspect of
criminal behaviour it also illustrates aspects of pattern recognition as well the basis of judgements of
verisimilitude. How do people identify a genuine signature? Do they focus on small details or form an
overall opinion?

This is a controlled experiment. Although it uses actual stimuli generated by people in a context that
is close to what would happen in the 'real world', it is systematic and carefully managed. It therefore
demonstrates the kinds of details that are necessary in any psychological experiment. Many of the features
that have to be considered in the constrained context of such a controlled study must be kept in mind.
The basis for other studies of the unintentional biases in experiments that can be introduced into many
psychological studies are also provided by the example in this chapter.

SOME KEY CONCEPTS

- forensic linguistics
- graphology
- index of accuracy
- pattern recognition
- experimental procedure.

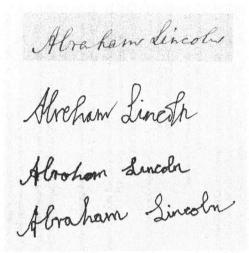

Figure 1.1 Genuine and forged Abraham Lincoln signatures

How Easy is it to Forge a Signature?

Figure 1.1 provides four signatures reputed to be written by President Abraham Lincoln. But at least one of them is suspected as being forged. Can you tell which one it might be? Why do you make that judgement?

To be more precise, a forgery is an alteration of a bona fide document/item, such as attaching another person's picture to a real passport or ID card. It is useful to distinguish this from a counterfeit item, which is a spurious document/item that has been created from scratch. So technically in this experiment the study is to see what is involved in counterfeiting or recognising a counterfeit signature.

Background

Despite the growing use of electronic indicators, personal signatures are still widely used on legal documents to signify that the person signing approves, accepts, and/or acknowledges the contents of the document. Websites illustrating legal examples of this are given in the references. As Dey (2019) claims, "check fraud costs banks about $900M per year with 22% of all fraudulent checks attributed to signature fraud". This use is based on the assumption that the way people sign their names is unique to each person. Moreover, for centuries it has been assumed that copying – forging – another person's signature is difficult to do. Indeed, people who can forge signatures effectively have been at the heart of many criminal activities. This may be to fraudulently sign cheques to obtain money from another person's account, or to produce a contract or a will that indicates the beneficiary is someone other than the actual person the document was intended to benefit.

When signatures are treated as 'autographs', especially of famous people, forgeries of them can sell for a great deal of money. There are many notorious examples of this criminal activity. Forgeries of the signatures of Elvis Presley, the Beatles, and Neil Armstrong, to select just a few, have sold for many thousands of dollars. It is interesting that the signature is regarded as something special, unique to the person. People pay a lot of money for this because they feel that owning it brings them closer to their hero.

The sanctity of the signature is therefore an interesting social psychological, even cultural, phenomena. This therefore raises the interesting question of how easy it is to determine if a signature is genuine. That determination is part of the more general issue of identifying whether handwriting has been generated by the person who is assumed to have written a document. This was very important in the days before typewriters and electronic printing. When all legal documents were handwritten, forged wills or other statements that had financial implications could be a basis for significant criminality. Many other forms of written communications could also be the foundation of criminal activity, such as extortion letters, blackmail or ransom notes, threatening material, false confessions, and much more. An especially notorious example was the claim that diaries written by Adolf Hitler had been found (described in delightful detail by Hamilton, 1991; see Knight and Long 2004 for a general review of such fakes). For all of these, being able to link the writing to that of the perpetrator could be crucial for establishing who the author was and obtaining a conviction in court.

Document examination

The comparison of questioned documents with those of known writers is a branch of forensic science, not unlike the identification of fingerprints, discussed by Harrison (1981). An objective study of the distinguishing characteristics of the writing are determined and used to link various sources of handwritten material. Forensic document examination is often carried out by people with a background in physics who are trained in the careful measurement of objects.

Forensic linguistics

Forensic linguistics is very different from document examination. It is carried out by linguists. They comment on the meaning and use of language in a criminal context. Sometimes they attempt to link different texts to a common author using aspects of the style of the writing – an aspect of 'stylistics' (not to be confused with the US soul group of the same name!). These aspects of 'style' may include the vocabulary used, the syntax, or a particular way of organising textual material. John Olsson (2018) has made a career out of this type of linguistic analysis in legal cases. Although linguistic issues are a common basis for discussions about the authorship of literary texts.

Not graphology

The objective examination of the physics of handwriting for legal purposes is very different from what is generally known as **'graphology'**. Although confusingly, some studies of objective examination of handwriting use the term to describe a very different process (e.g. Oliveira, Justino, Freitas, & Sabourin, 2005).

Broadly speaking, graphologists claim that a person's character or personality, as well as such issues as mental or physical health, can be determined from their handwriting. In relation to signatures, graphologists assume that the uniqueness of a signature enables them to determine a person's character from the way they sign their name.[1] The claims of graphologists do lend themselves to empirical test. The many studies that have been conducted (e.g. Beyerstein & Beyerstein, 1992) provide no support for these claims. The interesting question therefore is why it is still accepted as of value by many professionals. Some companies even still use handwriting analysis as a part of their process of selecting staff. See, for example, Negi's (2018) recent claims for its value.

The study described in this chapter could be developed to test assumptions about graphology, although, as I found when I tried this, the problem is getting any agreement among graphologists about what any particular aspect of a person's writing reveals about them. Unlike in a scientific discipline, there is no definitive agreement between graphologists as to what aspects of the writing should be considered. It is not even clear if any given practitioner would use the same aspects of the writing on different occasions. This does make this a rich area for study, which is considered at the end of this chapter.

PROPOSED STUDY: DETECTING FORGED SIGNATURES

The present study has much simpler aims than testing the claims of graphology. It seeks to determine the following:

(a) The proportion of people who can correctly identify the genuine signature among a set of forged signatures.

(b) Which forged signatures are more readily confused with genuine signatures.

(c) The characteristics of those forged signatures that are mistaken as genuine.

(d) The characteristics of those individuals who are most able to determine whether a signature is genuine or not.

This exact number of participants and signatures studied depends, of course, on the number of people available. These numbers can be readily adjusted to suit your opportunities. For the present study I'm assuming that you will use five signatures and there are 25 people participating.

If you are so minded, I'm sure the study could be set up to collect data online. If you set this up as a study online then what follows could all be online. Issues in the use of online studies are discussed in Study 6.

Equipment

The signatures

Genuine signatures

TARGET SIGNATURES

Obtain 35 index cards. (When I've done this, I've used A7 sized cards – about 3 inches by 5 inches). Say, 10 white and 25 yellow.

For each person giving their signature you require one white card and one yellow card. Let us call these five people Alan, Bronwyn, Charles, David, and Eric.

They are each to sign one white card once. Making these cards white so that you know they are the original signatures will make it less confusing. These are the five *target signatures*.

Carefully mark on the back of each card (in a way that does not shine through) what they are. So, you will have AT on Alan's *target signature*, BT on the back of Bronwyn's, and so on.

Now number each of the *target signature* cards on the side with the signature with the following random number sequence:

Alan = 5

Bronwyn = 1

Charles = 2

David = 4

Eric = 3

Keep the original writing implement used to write the signature with each of the signatures.

Carefully put all five *target signatures* to one side.

COMPARISON SIGNATURES

Using the same writing implement that they used to sign the *target signature*, the original person should now sign a second card. They are each to sign one yellow card once. This is the *comparison signature*. Carefully mark on the back of each card (in a way that does not shine through) what they are. So, you will have AC on Alan's *comparison signature* card, BC on the back of Bronwyn's, and so on.

You will thus have five white *target signature* cards and five yellow *comparison signature* cards.

If you do not want your participants to produce signatures, there are many example signatures (autographs) of famous people available online. You could get two of these for each famous person to use as your *target* and *comparison signatures*.

Forged signatures

You could use as many forged signatures for comparison as you wished, but to keep the arithmetic simple at the moment, I use just four *comparison signatures* for each *target signature*.

Now for each *comparison signature* get four people each to copy the signature on to a new yellow card. This should be done out of sight of the other participants, using the same writing implement that the genuine signature was written with.

You now have five *experimental signatures*, that is the four forged signatures and the one *comparison signature*, for each of the original five signatures, on yellow cards. You should shuffle these so that you can randomly assign letters to all five of these *experimental signatures*, A, B, C, D, E, for each of the five sets of experimental signatures.

Write the name (or indicative letter) of the signatory on the front of each of the five *experimental signature* cards. (Unless of course you want to do an even more complex experiment in which people have to work

Figure 1.2 Example set of signatures for the experiment

out which is the *target signature* they should be making the comparison with!) This will give you AA, AB, AC, etc. BA, BC, etc. for *experimental signatures* for Alan, etc. BA, BB, BC, etc. for Bronwyn, and so on.

Keep a separate, secret, list of which of these five signatures on the yellow cars is the is the real signature, e.g. AB is the genuine one, DC is the genuine one, etc.

You should also keep a careful note of which person has forged each signature.

Ensure all cards are signature side up and instruct all participants that they are not to turn the cards over until the end of the experiment.

Pro forma to record judgements

Table 1.1 is the form for each participant to record their judgements. They can be kept with each of the five *experimental signatures*. Each participant completes the form for the five signatures and also the assessment and other information noted later in the chapter. You should consider whether you want to include the people who forged the signatures in making judgements about the signatures they forged. If you have used different people to forge each sets of signatures then they could be asked not to make a judgement on the signature they forged.

For each of the five target signatures judges are presented with the six cards as illustrated in Figure 1.2.[2] The white card is the *target signature*. Four of the yellow cards are *experimental* (forged) signatures and one is the *comparison* (genuine) *signature*.

Questionnaires

There are many possible issues you can explore with this material beyond the direct assessment of how accurate people are. These issues could be to do with:

(a) *The task and aspects of the signatures.* This can be explored by asking people to indicate on a scale from 1 to 10 how difficult they think each signature would be to forge, with 1 being very easy indeed, 10 being extremely difficult. Recording this against each of their judgements gives data for further analysis.

You can also ask for comments on signatures, which can be analysed later to see what respondents notice about each signature in relation to the ease or difficulty there may be in forging it.

(b) *Individual differences between the participants in their ability to correctly identify the signature.* Age and gender are always useful to record. Background, such as their experience with visual judgements or being an artist or graphic designer would be interesting. Using law enforcement personnel or forensic scientists would be another interesting group. Then there is the range of personality differences and measures such as intelligence, especially spatial intelligence, if you want to explore that. For this illustration I will keep it simply age, gender, and occupation.

Process for carrying out the study

Please note that the general instructions and informed consent need to be prepared for this study as for all the others, as discussed in Part two. Example documents are given in Appendix A at the end of this book. Although this may seem like an amusing exercise (and when I've run it people do enjoy it), it nonetheless has ethical implications and some people may find it is something they do not wish to participate in.

Each person is given a set of the five experimental cards and the one target card at a time, as illustrated in Table 1.1. They are asked to decide which of the five cards has been signed by the same person as the *target card*. They indicate their decision by putting a tick in the appropriate box using the form in Table 1.1. There is one form for each participant. The sets of five cards can be passed round the group so that everyone can make a decision for each of the five signatures. The people who forged any given signature should not make a decision about that signature. The form also allows them to indicate how difficult they think the signature is to forge. There is also space for any other thoughts they have about the signature.

Table 1.1 To be completed by each participant in signature identification study

Participant number ( ) Name[a]:		
Card ID	Tick the signature that you believe is the genuine one. Put a cross in the box if you forged that signature.	On a scale from 1 to 10 how difficult do you think each signature would be to forge? (1 being very easy indeed, 10 being extremely difficult)
AA		Signature 5
AB		Do you have any comments about this signature?
AC		
AD		
AE		
BA		Signature 1
BB		Do you have any comments about this signature?
BC		
BD		
BE		
CA		Signature 2
CB		Do you have any comments about this signature?
CC		
CD		
CE		
DA		Signature 4
DB		Do you have any comments about this signature?
DC		
DD		
DE		
EA		Signature 3
EB		Do you have any comments about this signature?
EC		
ED		
EE		
Please now provide some information about yourself. As already mentioned all this information will be confidential to the research team.		
Are you: Female/Male/Other What is your age?		
What is your occupation (if a student your area of study)?		
Do you have any further comments?		

[a] This study could be carried out anonymously if you wish. In which case of course you would not ask for a name. The advantage of having a name is you could follow up issues that may arrive subsequently.

At the bottom of the form are questions about the respondent.

Recording the results

Once all respondents have completed the task for all signatures you can then prepare a table that lists the respondents in rows and the five signatures in columns, as in Table 1.2

Table 1.2 The basic matrix that summarises everyone's decisions, with illustrative results

Signatures	AA	AB	AC	AD	AE	BA	BB	BC	BD	BE	CA	CB	CC	CD	CE	DA	DB	DC	DD	DE	EA	EB	EC	ED	EE	Proportion correct for each person
Correct match				✓				✓					✓					✓							✓	
Participants' choice																										
1		✓							✓				✓					✓								1/5
2		✓					✓					✓						✓						✓		2/5
3			✓				✓					✓						✓					✓			2/5
4				✓			✓				✓					✓					✓					1/5
5								✓						✓				✓							✓	3/4
6				✓							✓						✓				✓					1/4
7			✓								✓						✓							✓		2/5
8			✓				✓					✓						✓								2/5
Etc.																										
Proportion correct for each signature			2/7	2/7			2/7	2/7			3/8		3/8					5/8					2/8			14/38 = 37%

Note: Person 5 only offered decisions on four signatures, presumably because that person forged signature A, similarly for person 6.

Analyses

Accuracy of identifying the correct signature

In the results indicated in Table 1.2 approximately one in three (37%) of genuine signatures were selected from among those forged. In the present experimental design, choosing one signature from five, there is a one in five chance (20%) of getting a correct guess by chance alone. Conventional inferential statistics, such as chi-square can therefore be applied to this result to determine if it is above chance level.

Index of accuracy

Each signature can be given a score to indicate how readily people can tell if it is genuine or not. This is the proportion in the bottom row of Table 1.2. For example, signature A can be given a value of $2/7 = 0.29$, which means only two out of the seven judgements were correct, whereas signature D is $5/8 = 0.63$. D is more readily identified correctly, showing signature A is easier to forge.

Overall, in the example data in Table 1.2 there is 37% accuracy. That is above the 20% that would be achieved by chance, indicating that these respondents are slightly better at identifying the genuine signature than tossing a coin to decide. Although the appropriate inferential statistics would test this assertion more effectively.

Assumed ease of forging

Table 1.3 shows how to record the values each person assigns to each signature in terms of 'how difficult it is to forge', as recorded in the form given in Table 1.1.

The average ratings of difficulty to forge from Table 1.3 can then be correlated with the accuracy values derived from Table 1.2. A simple scatter plot (or more technically a correlation coefficient) of one against the other, as shown in Figure 1.3, can be used to examine whether people's assumptions about the ease of forging a signature do relate to how difficult these participants find it to tell genuine signatures from forged ones.

Are people's assumptions about what make a signature easy to forge correct?

Figure 1.3 is an invented illustration, not from actual data, using the signatures of famous people. Careful consideration of this does indicate that, if this were real data, broadly speaking, as the average assessed difficulty of forging increases so does the proportion of errors in correctly identifying the genuine

Table 1.3 Data recording form for 'difficulty of forging a signature'

Judge / Signature	1	2	3	4	5	6	Etc.
A	3	6	2	Etc.			
B	Etc.						
C							
D							
E							
Average							

Note: The numbers in the cells of the table are the values from 1 to 10 recorded on the form given in Table 1.1.

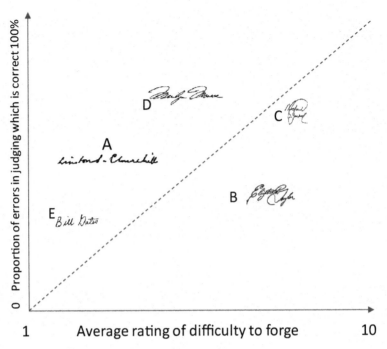

Figure 1.3 Illustrative scatter plot of five signatures showing the relationship between ease of forging and how difficult to forge people thought they were

matched signature. Figure 1.3 can also be used to explore where the mismatch is between assessment and difficulty. In the illustrative example, for instance, those signatures below the dashed line ('Elizabeth Taylor' and 'Michael Jackson') appear to be more difficult to forge than is actually the case. Whereas those above the dashed line are easier to forge than is typically assumed. By looking closely at the signatures above and below the dashed line it is possible to generate hypotheses about what it is about a signature that makes it easy or difficult to forge. Also, what people assume to be the factors that make a signature easy or difficult to forge can be hypothesised from looking at the results for each signature.

The sorts of hypotheses that could emerge from the results represented in Figure 1.3, might be that simple signatures without elaboration, such as 'Bill Gates' and 'Winston Churchill' are actually more difficult to forge than people realise. Perhaps small details are easily spotted. If people are using this micro-level form of **pattern recognition**, they are more likely to notice those details. By contrast, Elizabeth Taylor's highly embellished signature is much easier to forge than people realise. Perhaps that is because it stimulates a more global consideration of its overall pattern? These findings could have practical implications, especially for people whose signatures are, for one reason or another, significant.

A systematic approach to the task of what can be used objectively to identify genuine signatures is provided by Oliveira et al. (2005), using the rather unhelpful label 'graphology'. They give a detailed set of descriptors of signatures that they claim are of value in distinguishing the genuine from the false. These provide a set of measures that can be applied in the present study. Their claim is that these measures could be automated to allow computer pattern recognition analysis to be applied to the forensic document examination task. It would also be of interest to see if specific distinctions between forged and genuine signatures could be identified from the current study. They could then be used in future studies to determine if they made identifying fake signatures any more accurate.

Differences between people

Are some people better at identifying the correct signature?

The right-hand column of Table 1.2 indicates how successful each person was at correctly identifying the genuine signature. It can be turned into a simple measure by calculating the proportion of genuine signatures correctly identified. For example, person 1 was the least successful with a score of $1/5 = 0.20$ and person 5 was the most successful with a score of $3/4 = 0.75$ (note this person had provided one of the signatures, so did not make a judgement on that one).

These scores can be used to explore the characteristics of good and bad judges. People of different gender, age, or background could be compared with each other. Or if you had also asked respondents to complete a personality inventory you could correlate their scores on that with their scores of identifying the correct signatures.

Are some people better at forging signatures than others?

To answer this question, you need to prepare a table of the people who had forged the signatures and how many respondents thought their forgery was the genuine one. You could then explore the characteristics of the 'good' forgers with those of the less successful ones. If a particular skill or set of skills can be identified, it may be possible to train people to use them so as to improve forensic document examination techniques. In this way the application of the study could have real-world utility. What are the aspects of signatures that are most effective for comparing the genuine and false?

Psychological processes

There are other more psychological issues beyond consideration of the objective features of a signature. In essence this is what is often thought of as a 'pattern recognition' problem. On what basis do people compare two phenomena? How do they determine that two sets of stimuli are the same? These questions take us back to fundamental questions in the psychology of perception (discussed, for example, by Neisser & Weene, 1967; Sekular & Abrams 1968). The debate is whether sets of stimuli are compared detail by detail, or as some overall form, a *gestalt*, or what is sometimes referred to as a *schema* (Reed, 1973).

The forensic analyst is likely to operate at the detailed level, examining specific aspects of the signature, such as a loop over an L or the apparent sequence in which the strokes of the letters are carried out. Do the curves on a K, for instance, indicate the < component is drawn distinctly from the vertical line or as part of the same stroke? Non-specialists, by comparison may be expected to take the whole signature in a composite view and estimate what proportion of the target pattern is similar to the comparison. These issues are explored in some interesting detail by Dey (2019)

It may help to disentangle what is going on by assigning signatures to different categories, such as 'florid', 'tidy and print-like', 'leaning – italic'. These are global aspects of the signatures. Is there any difference in the rate of successfully distinguishing genuine from fake signatures for these different groups? Or do the sorts of objective criteria of details of each signature give a better explanation? Distinguishing these approaches may be achieved in the current study by asking people how they decided. Future studies could identify signatures that have a specific form to them in order to test these hypotheses.

OTHER STUDIES THAT COULD USE THIS RESEARCH DESIGN

Signatures have been the focus of this study both because they are a readily available and quite straightforward set of stimuli to use for such a study, and because they are still widely used as indicators of significance in legal documents. But there are many other things that involve judgements of veracity that could use a similar format. Those that come to mind include:

- Various messages that could be genuine or not, say from famous people, or from agencies requesting information or help. In these cases, there would not be a target 'genuine' message. The central assessment would be to decide whether the communication is honest or not. Further aspects of such a study are considered with the perspective of case studies in Study 7, which examines how fraudsters persuade.

- Images can also be used. What about genuine and fake paintings attributed to particular artists? Or just drawings? How easy is it to copy someone else's drawing of a face? (There are drawing claiming to be the work of Adolf Hitler in his youth. People realised they were fraudulent when experts pointed out that they were much better than any Hitler had drawn.)

- The debates about music that has been plagiarised or copied and other attempts to fraudulently offer works as by particular composers, offers a more rarefied, but equally fascinating area of research. In this area also, though, overall judgements about the 'feel' of the music could be contrasted with detailed assessment, such as the harmonies used and their sequence.

The crucial aspect of all these possibilities is that they allow consideration of the basis on which people judge authenticity and what it is that is most useful in these judgements. This also allows studies to be set up that test specific hypotheses about what informs these judgements. As noted, specifically selected signatures, or messages or images, could be chosen to reflect a model of what influences the judgements. The procedure outlined above can then be used to test these hypotheses. Similarly, by carefully selecting participants in the studies it is possible to test whether those hypothesised to be more effective at detecting fakes do indeed show that capability.

A broadening of approach relates to the large number of studies exploring the detection of deception. These use a similar overall framework, but tend to focus on judgements of whether or not a particular communication is deceptive. In more complex studies a comparison of effectiveness of discerning deception compared with establishing genuineness is carried out. Although it is still rare to explore what it is that leads people to judge an account to be plausible. I did study an aspect of the qualities of an account that were more likely to lead people to think it was plausible (Canter, Grieve, Nicol, & Benneworth, 2003). Detailed consideration and proposed studies of the detection of deception is given in Study 2.

BIAS IN EXPERIMENTS

Experimenter effects

In any experiment, there is always the possibility of the influence of the **experimental procedure** on the outcome, rather than the objective aspects of the study. In other words, the way the experiment is carried out may bias the results. This is not the case just for psychological experiments. The history of science is fraught with examples of people getting the results they wanted or expected rather than the untrammelled consequences of the experimental manipulations. Even the significant and universally quoted studies of genetics carried out by Mendel have been shown to have generated results that were much more in accord with his theories of inheritance than the actual facts of the studies revealed (Piegorsch, 1986). The very widely cited results of the experiments on 'obedience' by Milgram have been shown by Perry (2013) to be rather different from the real results Milgram obtained.

There are many aspects of scientific research that can contribute to distorted results, but those studies requiring respondents (usually called 'subjects') to make a judgement are particularly prone to unwanted influences from the many different aspects of the experimental procedure. Although similar impacts have been found on, for instance, albino rats (Rosenthal and Fode, 1963). The study of these influences has been carried out for well over half a century under the general heading of 'experimenter effects'. In summary, two particular influences are worth emphasising.

One is the influence of experimenters, usually without them being aware that they are doing it. This can be implicit gestures, ways of asking the respondents to check their decision, and a range of other actions that encourage the respondents to give the answers the experimenter wants. A forensic example of this is the study I carried out with some colleagues (Canter, Youngs, & Hammond, 2012). We examined whether the identification of the person who had placed the bomb on the plane that exploded over Lockerbie was influenced by the desire of the police carrying out the investigation to establish Abdelbaset al-Megrahi as the culprit. The police had given a possible witness a set of 12 photographs and asked him which photograph was the person he remembers buying clothes, a year earlier, that were found round the bomb.

We presented the same set of photographs to people unaware of the investigation under two conditions. In one the interviewer knew which the target picture was. In the other condition the interviewer did not know. Of course, in both cases the interviewer was told not to indicate to respondents who the target was. Yet, in significantly more cases the target was selected when the interviewer knew which it was. In a larger-scale study, in which the people briefing the interviewers knew or did not know who the target was, similar results were found (Hollinshead, 2014). It would be relatively straightforward to repeat these sorts of studies with signatures.

Demand characteristics and confirmation bias

A second major influence that can arise in experiments are the expectations that the whole set-up indicates the likely results to those participating. Orne (1962) called these the 'demands' the experimental procedure makes on the respondents. Perry (2013) shows the power of these in the Milgram experiments. By talking to those who took part she discovered that many did not believe the whole procedure and behaved as they thought they were expected to. The irony of this is that Milgram claimed this was an illustration of obedience to authority, when in fact the respondents were more sophisticated than that. They understood what the experimenter wanted without necessarily trusting his account of what was happening.

Orne, Dinges, and Orne (1984) provided an interesting forensic example of these demand characteristics in practice. He interviewed Kenneth Bianchi (the 'Hillside Strangler'), who claimed he had multiple personalities and that it was one of these other personalities that had carried out the murders. Orne showed that suggesting likely personalities to Bianchi led him to generate those. Orne took this to indicate that Bianchi had never been hypnotised but was aware of the demands hypnosis offered and was thus a clever malingerer. It is important to note, however, that other experts, notably Watkin (1984) drawing on other procedures, challenged Orne's conclusions, claiming that Bianchi did indeed have multiple-personality disorder. This debate therefore illustrates the subtlety of the concept of experimental demand characteristics and the difficulty of disentangling their presence in naturally occurring settings. Nonetheless, there is little doubt that many psychological experiments suffer from these biases. They are therefore something that should be borne in mind when carrying out any of the studies indicated in this book.

Another interesting example of this, which draws on the idea that people perceive what they expect, known as 'confirmation bias', are the studies by Kukucka and Kassin (2013). They found that when participants read a summary report indicating a defendant had previously confessed, they were more likely to erroneously conclude that handwriting samples from the defendant and a different perpetrator were written by the same person.

TESTING THE CLAIMS OF GRAPHOLOGY

One other interesting area of research that can follow the research design described in this chapter is the testing of the claims of graphology. I did once set in motion a test of graphology, but the research assistant lost all the material (he was not kept on in such a role thereafter), so it was never completed. But here is what I did. I obtained some documents in which criminals talked about their crimes. I then got five research students to copy out one different account each in their own handwriting. I did this so that the topic of the material was distinct from the handwriting because I wanted to see if the graphologists would actually read the material rather than look closely at the handwriting, thus basing their claims on what the person had written, not how they had shaped the letters (as the study by Kukucka and Kassin, 2013 suggests can happen).

The students who wrote the documents also completed a standard psychological personality inventory. I then managed to get five graphologists to examine each of the five documents and produce a report about the personality of the author of the document.

For analysis purposes the following things were noted:

- The details of the form of the writing that each graphologist commented on. This could be anything from how the writing sat on the page to the angle or shape of the letters, spacing between words and so on. Graphologists do each have their own idiosyncratic aspects of the writing that they draw on.

- The aspects of the writer's personality that each graphologist inferred from the written material.

- The personality profiles of the five research students.

All of these indicators could then be compared both between graphologists and relating their inferences about personality to the scores on the personality inventory.

If you could get the graphologists to complete a personality inventory as they think the writer of the text would, that would provide a very clear measure of how accurate their inferences were.

CONCLUSIONS

A relatively straightforward study of the detection of forged signatures has been used to illustrate an experimental research design. Throughout this book the ways of collecting and summarising the data is demonstrated. Consequently, in this chapter, as in all the others, the details of the statistical calculations that could be used to test the 'significance' of the results have not been described. There are libraries of books describing those procedures as well as many excellent websites. Nonetheless, the illustrative examples provided in this chapter have demonstrated that a very interesting study can be carried out that opens the way to many considerations about cognitive processes in pattern recognition and potential biases in experimental procedures. The results of the study of signature identification also carries practical implications, suggesting, among other things, that reliance on signatures (autographs) for unique identification may be misplaced. With the emergence of 'deep fakes' the same may soon be true for selfies with famous people.[1]

QUESTIONS FOR DISCUSSION

1. How could this experiment be made more realistic?

2. What did you learn from this experiment?

3. How could you set up this study to get the results you wanted?

4. What measure of personality would be interesting to add to test hypotheses about ability to identify genuine signatures?

[1] See https://deepfakedetectionchallenge.ai.

5. What measure of personality would be interesting to add to test hypotheses about ability to forge signatures?

6. What measure of individual differences would you use to test the claims of graphologists?

NOTES

....

1   See, for instance, https://tinyurl.com/y5urdlcd as a typical of set of claims for the ability to determine a person's character from their signature.
2   This is not my usual signature for signing important documents or cheques! The correct answer can be found in Table 1.2.

FURTHER READING

....

A recent publication shows the potential of signature identification as a tool for learning about research in practice:

Cadola, L., Hochholdinger, S., Bannwarth, A., Voisard, R., Marquis, R., & Weyermann, C. (2020). The potential of collaborative learning as a tool for forensic students: Application to signature examination. *Science and Justice*, 60(3), 273–283.

A legal consideration of the significance of a signature is available at:
    www.landmarkchambers.co.uk/wp-content/uploads/2018/07/TW-reliance-on-documents-2015.pdf.

REFERENCES

....

Beyerstein, B.L., & Beyerstein, D.F. (Eds.) (1992). *The write stuff: Evaluations of graphology, the study of handwriting analysis.* Amherst, NY: Prometheus Books

Canter, D., Grieve N., Nicol, C., & Benneworth, K. (2003). Narrative plausibility: The impact of sequence and anchoring. Behavioral Sciences and the Law, 21(2), 251–267.

Canter, D., Youngs, D., & Hammond, L. (2012). Cognitive bias in line-up identifications: The impact of administrator knowledge, *Science and Justice*, 53(2), 83–88. http://dx.doi.org/10.1016/j.scijus.2012.12.001.

Dey, S. (2019). Signature fraud detection: An advanced analytics approach. *Towards Data Science*, 26 June. Retrieved from https://towardsdatascience.com/signature-fraud-detection-an-advanced-analytics-approach-10c810cda26e.

Hamilton, C. (1991). *The Hitler diaries: Fakes that fooled the world.* Lexington: University of Kentucky Press.

Harrison, W.R. (1981). *Suspect documents: Their scientific examination.* Lanham, MD: Burnham.

Hollinshead, J. (2014). *Administrator effects on respondent choice* (PhD thesis, University of Huddersfield, UK). Retrieved from http://eprints.hud.ac.uk/id/eprint/24473/1/Master_Revised_Final_Jemma_Hollinshead_July_2014.pdf.

Knight, P., & Long, J. (2004). *Fakes and forgeries.* Newcastle upon Tyne, UK: Cambridge Scholars Press.

Kukucka, J., & Kassin, S.M. (2013). Do confessions taint perceptions of handwriting evidence? An empirical test of the forensic confirmation. *Bias Law and Human Behavior*, 38(3), 256–270. doi: 10.1037/lhb0000066.

Negi, R. (2018). Graphology in staff selection: How to use graphology in recruitment (Kindle ed.). Retrieved from Livewell.com.

Neisser, U., & Weene, P. (1967). *Cognitive psychology.* New York, NY: Appleton-Century-Crofts.

Oliveira, L.S., Justino, E., Freitas, C., & Sabourin, R. (2005). The graphology applied to signature verification. Paper presented at the 12th Conference of the International Graphonomics Society (IGS), Salerno, Italy, 26–29 June, pp. 286–290.

Olsson, J. (2018). More word crime: Solving crime with linguistics. London: Bloomsbury Academic.

Orne, M.T. (1962). On the social psychology of the psychological experiment: With particular reference to demand characteristics and their implications. American Psychologist, 17(11), 776–783.https://doi.org/10.1037/h0043424.

Orne, M.T., Dinges, D.F., & Orne, E.C. (1984). On the differential diagnosis of multiple personality in the forensic context. International Journal of Clinical and Experimental Hypnosis, 32(2), 118–169. doi: 10.1080/00207148408416007.

Perry, G. (2012). Behind the shock machine: The untold story of the notorious Milgram psychology experiments. New York, NY: New Press.

Piegorsch, W.W. (1986). The Gregor Mendel controversy: Early issues of goodness-of-fit and recent issues of genetic linkage. History of Science, 24, 173–182.

Reed, S.K. (1973). Psychological processes in pattern recognition. New York, NY: Academic Press.

Rosenthal, R., & Fode, K.L. (1963). The effect of experimenter bias on the performance of the albino rat. Systems Research and Behavioral Science, 8, 183–189. doi:10.1002/bs.3830080302.

Sekular, W.R., & Abrams, M. (1968). Visual sameness: A choice time analysis of pattern recognition processes. Journal of Experimental Psychology, 77(2), 232–238.

Watkin, J.G. (1984). The Bianchi (L.A. hillside strangler) case: Sociopath or multiple personality? International Journal of Clinical and Experimental Hypnosis, 32(2), 67–101. doi: 10.1080/00207148408416005.

DECEPTION

STUDY 2
Detecting deception

SYNOPSIS

The different approaches to determining if someone is lying are briefly examined. Two studies are proposed that test the possibility of detecting deception, drawing directly on the laboratory experiment framework. As such they consist, essentially, of generating, or finding, genuine and false accounts and exploring the possible processes for telling one from the other, as well as assessing how accurately people can distinguish between the two. This is part of a large and complex variety of studies that have been conducted starting early in the twentieth century, but with precursors that can be found in the Bible and in all early cultures.

The chapter emphasises psychological accounts of the cognitive demands made when not telling the truth and how they can be utilised to develop techniques for detecting deception. In one study true and false accounts are generated and then a criteria-based content analysis (CBCA) system is used to determine if that process can detect deceit. The second study utilises available videos of people making appeals to the public when their loved ones have disappeared. In some cases, the people making the appeal are the actual culprits. Aspects of their utterances are examined as a way of establishing who is lying.

The context in which accounts are generated are considered throughout. They are an integral part of understanding how lies are uncovered. This may be the artificiality of the academic laboratory, or real events in which determining truth is crucial. It may be focused questioning or freely given accounts. All of these are relevant to the processes of detecting lying and truthfulness.

Some Key Concepts
....

- psychophysiological indicators

- non-verbal indicators

- criteria-based content analysis (CBCA)

- ecological validity

- high-stakes events.

Background
....

There is a fundamental challenge inherent in deciding whether someone is telling the truth or not. A great deal of research has shown that most people are not very good at it, as is explored, for example, by Bond and DePaulo (2006) and Street, Bischof, Vadillo, and Kingstone (2015). It is also a common experience that most people do not always tell the truth, as DePaulo, Kashy, Kirkendol, Wyer, and Epstein (1996) and Bond, Howard, Hutchinson, and Masip (2013) discuss. Lying can therefore be regarded as a natural part of social interactions. It must also be the case that, from time to time, people have to decide how plausible an utterance is. Detecting deception may consequently be regarded as a natural part of being human. Indeed, many people make a living from presenting themselves as what they are not, actors, or writing something that is not the truth, novelists.

In the context of a criminal investigation, disentangling the truth from lies is an important part of the job. It is quite possible that not only suspects, but also witnesses and even victims may not always tell the truth. False allegations (Lisak, Gardinier, Nicksa, & Cote, 2010) and even false confessions are known to happen (Garrett, 2010). These are all forms of deception. This makes the study of the information the police work with rather different from typical psychological research. Perhaps naively, psychologists usually assume the information they obtain from surveys, or in other interactions with participants in their research, is honestly the case as the respondent sees it. The study of deception has therefore been focused on the context of police interviews.

Besides the clear practical value of revealing how to tell truth from lies, there is another reason why there are so many studies of the topic (a Google search for 'detecting deception' gives well over 2 million hits and Amazon UK over 60 books). The study of this lends itself very well to the sort of manageable laboratory experiment, so favoured by psychologists and feasible for students to carry out. All that is needed are examples of truthful and not truthful material that is then offered to people to see how readily they can determine the difference. These 'judges' can be given various strategies to use and their effectiveness is measured. There is also the possibility of varying the conditions under which the material is generated.

The material used in these studies covers the full range of possible communications. Written accounts, verbatim transcripts, audio and video recordings. Innovative research from Hjelmsäter, Öhman, Granhag, and Vrij (2012) has even added to this with ideas such as getting people to carry out a spatial drawing exercise as part of describing the events. Another approach is to increase the intellectual demands, for example by getting people to say what happened in reverse chronological order (Vrij, Mann, Fisher, Leal, Milne, & Bull, 2008). There are even interesting results from interviewing people in pairs (Vrij, 2015) rather than the time-honoured approach of interviewing each member of a criminal duo separately.

Exploring what people say and do and how that may be evaluated for its truthfulness is only one aspect of the process. There is also the context that is created for generating the account given. In most cases this is an interview. How an interview is set up, the questions asked, and any interventions such as offering evidence, is a further possibility for studying the how lies may be revealed (Hartwig et al., 2006). In the more public context of television interviews, or notably the broadcast appeals that relatives of a victim may make, there are interesting research possibilities for establishing what might reveal whether the appeal is genuine or not (Ng & Youngs, 2015).

Converting all the possibilities for developing ways of detecting deception into tidy laboratory experiments suffers from one major drawback. Ethics (and indeed ethics committees) do not allow serious, especially high-stakes, events to be the basis of lies or telling the truth. There is an important difference between someone denying a murder, or claiming in front of a television camera that their loved one has been abducted, and lying in a laboratory experiment about what you had for breakfast, or even whether you stole the blue envelope from the office, which was the task being studied.

In situations not manufactured for their study there is not only a commitment to be as convincing as possible, but also, typically, opportunity to prepare for giving the account. It is also often feasible in real situations to be able to draw on things that actually occurred, as well as genuine emotions relevant to the current situation, or remembered from earlier situations. In recent years a number of researchers have tried to tackle these differences either by creating experimental conditions that are as realistic as possible, or by studying actual accounts given in real situations, such as the television appeals mentioned (Vrij, 2008).

In order to create scientifically pure experiments which reflect natural, or realistic situations, the challenge is to set up effective comparison or control groups. These are the hallmark of scientific experimental studies. It is essential, in this context, to demonstrate that analysis procedures do clearly distinguish between genuine and false material. It may be interesting to claim, for example, that a particular twitch or verbalisation is typical of a given person lying – say in a television interview. But if it cannot be demonstrated that there are situations where that person is telling the truth, in which such twitches or verbalisations are never present, then the hypothesis is not really being tested at all. This is an important point because there are many claims of techniques to reveal deception that fail this all-important scientific test.

Difficulty of detecting deception

One of the recurrent findings of studies in this area is how difficult it is for most people in most situations to tell if someone is telling the truth or not. There is even a very popular, funny BBC television game show called *Would I lie to You?* that is based on the assumption that people can invent convincing stories very quickly that will confuse their opponents. There is also a BBC radio show called *The Unbelievable Truth* that works on the principle that people cannot tell if actual truth has been embedded in an otherwise bizarre story.

Best, Hodgson, and Street (2019) have explored why people have such difficulty in detecting deception. They claim that there is a natural bias to assuming an account is truthful, unless the source of the account is doubted. There are other more immediate reasons. One is that we all are untruthful some of the time, for many different reasons. Another is that a lie can be built around something that actually happened, giving it many real components. A third is that a person may convince themselves that they are actually telling the truth, even though it's a lie. With preparation and rehearsal, it is possible to be prepared to lie without it causing the person any stress.

Challenges to being deceptive

All of this is relevant when considering any procedure for detecting deception. All such procedures derive, one way or another, from the challenges to being deceptive that are not present when telling the truth. The lie has to be invented because it did not happen as claimed. That is different from just recounting what actually happened. There is also the potential stress of being caught out, although many people would feel stress from being closely questioned. There is therefore a possible 'cognitive load' that comes from the need to be inventive, as well as likely emotional reactions. It is these issues that lay the foundation for theories about how deception can be detected, which have generated many different lie-detecting procedures.

Table 2.1 Decision matrix

		Told	
		truth	lie
Decision	was true	correct	incorrect
	was lie	incorrect	correct

Deciding on truth/lies

Before reviewing approaches to detecting deception it is useful to be aware that there are actually four different judgements that can be made with regard to determining whether the truth is being told or not (see Table 2.1).

Table 2.1 shows the various combinations of the correct recognitions of truthfulness or determining whether someone is lying. Determining truthfulness is distinctly different from deciding lies are being told. Some techniques, notably those relying on **psychophysiological indicators**, are better at determining whether someone is telling the truth rather than indicating that a lie is being told. Also consider the situation in which it is assumed lies are being perpetrated. In those circumstances lies will be correctly recognised more often than when the assumption of truth is the dominant perspective.

False negatives are those decisions that claim a person is lying when they are not. False positives are the reverse, deciding utterances are truthful when they are lies. The balance between false positives and false negatives can be an important issue to consider. In some circumstances, for example when the risk is great of assuming truth when a person is lying, as may be the case when interviewing a known terrorist, the balance will be towards false positives. In other cases, for instance when the risk is of claiming an innocent person is guilty, and thereby causing social discomfort, the balance may shift towards false negatives.

All this just goes to show that the judgement of veracity is not necessarily a simple one. There are many aspects of the circumstances that need to be considered. The outcome of any technique therefore has to be evaluated in relation to the details of the context of its use.

SOURCES OF INFORMATION THAT MAY REVEAL LYING

There is such a plethora of ways that have been claimed to assist in distinguishing truth from lying that it is helpful to have at least a brief summary of them and the basis of their claims.

Psychophysiological measures

The widely discussed 'polygraph' is the most well-known procedure that claims to detect the stress a liar experiences, which is then revealed through physiological responses. These usually consist of measures of how sweaty the palms are (the 'galvanic skin response'), blood pressure, and often heart rate, and sometimes even aspects of fidgeting. These different measures can interfere with each other and it is possible that the very act of being wired up to a device with so many wires is a source of anxiety,

One crucial aspect of the polygraph procedure is that is takes place within the context of an interview. There are many different ways of conducting that interview and there is no internationally recognised standard procedure. However, Granhag and Strömwall (2004), as well as others, have shown that under special circumstances, when the process is carried out very carefully, this can support the possibility that the respondent is innocent. It is less effective in demonstrating the person is guilty.

The most effective procedure is offering a mixture of information only the guilty person would know compared with neutral questions – 'the guilty knowledge test'. The idea is that responses to questions that only the guilty person would realise were significant would be expected to generate anxiety, or mild stress, when compared with non-stressful questions. In the majority of actual cases it is difficult to frame questions that draw on such specific information. Therefore a procedure in which responses to normally stressful questions, such as, "Have you ever hurt someone accidentally?" are compared with neutral 'control' questions. The variation in responses are thought to distinguish truth from lies. However, the evidence for this approach is not at all strong. It also tends to bias interpretations towards assuming lying.

In keeping with these findings, it is interesting to note that in the United Kingdom the polygraph is not allowed as evidence in court. It is allowed in some US states, but only if the defendant agrees to be tested. In other words, people may be allowed to volunteer to take the test to prove their innocence. Even this, however, is very controversial. A very thorough challenge to the validity of the polygraph is provided in an extensive review by Maschke and Scalabrini (2018) under the title *The Lie Behind the Lie Detector*. This provides accounts of many studies to show how misleading a polygraph test can be. This has not stopped its increasing use with sex offenders, notably to see if they've broken the conditions of their parole, and there are plans to use it with suspected or convicted terrorists who are being considered for parole.

Voice stress analysis (VSA)

Another attempt to create a lie detector from measures of psychophysiological reactions is the gadgetry known as 'voice stress analysis' (VSA). This reputedly analyses the sounds of a person speaking in order to determine if there is any indication of stress in the voice. I mention this because many companies still buy this kit thinking it will help them to detect lying. The Wikipedia article about it quite appropriately calls it 'pseudoscience'.[1] There are many systematic studies testing the effectiveness of VSA. For example, Hollien, Geison, and Hicks (1987) concluded that the system only had a chance-level detection of stress and a chance-level detection of lies. McShane (2013) helpfully reviews a number of studies, all of which come to the conclusion that VSA has no value.

The morals of this example are twofold. One is that although the idea that someone lying may be stressed about what they are saying has some merit, this does not mean that any claim to be measuring a person's stress will inevitably lead to detecting lying. The other is that many devices and procedures that claim to detect deception are presented, and indeed sold, with examples of them 'working'. In other words, the promoters of these obtain an example of someone not telling the truth. They demonstrate that their system reveals that person is lying, thereby claiming they have the method to distinguish truthfulness from lying. However, it is only by tests in which truths and lies are both examined using the procedure, without foreknowledge of which is which, that the real power, or otherwise, of the procedure can be revealed.

In recent years the advent of various forms of brain scans have been explored to determine if there are aspects of neurological activity that will indicate a person is not telling the truth. Ganis (2015) proposes that there is some potential in this approach. However, its use on a day-to-day basis is not feasible at the moment.

Non-verbal indicators

Vrij (2008) refers to what he calls 'objective' aspects of a person's behaviour. These are what an observer can monitor without needing to make sense of, or interpret what the person is claiming. He distinguishes between 'vocal cues' and 'visual cues'. The former are aspects of the way the person speaks. The latter are what can be seen of the person's actions. I prefer to think of the visual cues as those that do not rely on utterances. In this sense they are 'non-verbal'.

In any social interaction there are aspects of body movement and gestures that contribute to the flow and meaning of the conversation. These are often erroneously called 'body language'. The term is misleading because language has a structure. It has syntax and grammar and is made up of words that have distinct, even if ambiguous, meaning. By contrast, gestures and other body movements vary between individuals, do not usually have general meanings, although a few – such as the V-sign – are like words, and obtain their significance from the particular context in which they are used. This has not stopped people writing popular books claiming that you can tell what a person is thinking or intends to do by reading their 'body language' (e.g. Beattie, 2016). There are also some useful findings emerging from various considerations of **non-verbal indicators**, as reviewed by Vrij, Hartwig, and Granhag (2018).

It is therefore not surprising that no general indicators of whether a person is telling the truth or not can be gleaned solely from their body movements. This is often referred to as the lack of a 'Pinocchio's nose', which in the fairy tale grew longer whenever Pinocchio did not tell the truth. But many gestures have been explored as possible indicators. These include 'scratching', 'movements of the leg and feet', 'blinking', 'head nods and shakes', and many others. When Vrij (2008) reviewed 132 studies exploring many aspects of both verbal and non-verbal cues to deception he came to the conclusion that there were lots of contradictions in the findings. However, many people, especially police officers, believe there are cues to deception. This has led to the study of what people believe becoming a lively area of research in its own right.

One particularly intriguing aspect of non-verbal behaviour is what Ekman (2009) has called the 'micro-expression'. Micro-expressions are typically small facial muscle movements that can only be identified by very close examination, usually in slowed-down videos. Ekman's claims do not seem to be available in actual scientific studies published in academic journals. They grew out of his earlier studies of the way people express various emotions (interestingly, a development of Darwin's seminal book *The Expression of Emotions in Man and Animals*, published in 1872). Ekman argues that it is difficult to hide real emotions even when feigning some other emotion. Consequently, there is 'non-verbal leakage' that can be recognised by an experienced careful observer. Although there do not appear to be any peer-reviewed publications supporting this, the idea has been taken up by many security and law enforcement agencies, including screening of passengers at airports. But as Bradshaw (2008) has reported, Ekman himself admits that nine out of ten people, stopped because of their apparent non-verbal leakage, are innocent. A very large proportion of false positives. This raises civil liberty questions as well as the possibility that a random selection of passengers may reveal 10% are worthy of suspicion?

There is a lot to consider here. Therefore, you may want to explore the possibility of detecting deception using 'objective' indicators by adding these to the procedure for Study B described later in this chapter.

Indicators within aspects of utterances

The consideration of 'vocal cues' could possibly be divided into two aspects. One is *how* a person speaks, the other is *what* they say. I'll come to the latter in a moment. Many different aspects of the way in which utterances are made have been studied (Vrij, 2008). They include the rhythms of speech, the patterns of stresses, and intonations – often called *prosody*. Frequency and duration of pauses, hesitations, self-interruptions, and voice pitch are all features that have been explored to see if they help detection of deception. These are possibly more use because they can indicate 'cognitive load'. That is the challenge of having to make things up when the truth is not available. Of course, having rehearsed what you are going to say, or building fiction on what has actually happened, reduces the intellectual demands.

Vrij (2008) claims that when these vocal aspects are combined with watching gestures there is an increase in being able to tell if someone is deceitful. But as O'Sullivan and Ekman (2004), among others, have emphasised there are big differences between people in their ability to detect deception. They claim some people are 'wizards' at it. This does point to the need in any experiment to make sure to be able to distinguish the effectiveness of different respondents and establish if you can work out what makes them more effective than others.

Actual content

It may come as a surprise after all the consideration of physiology, behaviour, and aspects of speech that by far the best way to detect deception is to listen carefully to what a person actually says. When creating a detailed lie, there are two crucial issues that have to be dealt with. One is inventing enough convincing detail, which incorporates many aspects of an actual experience. Another is putting the narrative together in a way that fits with what people know is likely and possible. In other words, making the account

Table 2.2 CBCA criteria

General characteristics
1. Logical structure
2. Unstructured production
3. Quantity of details

Specific contents
4. Contextual embedding
5. Descriptions of interactions
6. Reproduction of conversation
7. Unexpected complications during the incident
8. Unusual details
9. Superfluous details
10. Accurately reported details misunderstood
11. Related external associations
12. Accounts of subjective mental state
13. Attribution of perpetrator's mental state

Motivation-related contents
14. Spontaneous corrections
15. Admitting lack of memory
16. Raising doubts about one's own testimony
17. Self-deprecation
18. Pardoning the perpetrator

Offence-specific elements
19. Details characteristic of the offence

Source: After Steller and Köhnken (1989).

plausible. Many attempts at detecting deception have therefore focused on the inherent weaknesses that are probable when a person does not deal with these challenges effectively.

The central idea is a simple one. Invention of a plausible story requires imagination to provide convincing details. As Nahari, Vrij, and Fisher (2014) have explored, the strategies that liars use can be the basis for considering how to verify the details of what they say. The hypothesis is that a liar would be hard-pressed to come up with as much, or as rich, detail as someone recounting what they actually experienced. This would include difficulties in creating subtle or apparently irrelevant details, such as unexpected aspects of the event being described, or vivid, colourful aspects of what was felt or seen. It is also hypothesised that a liar will avoid giving any information that may be open to dispute or reveal features that could indicate the truth was not being told. These aspects that are thought to distinguish genuine from false accounts were codified by Undeutsch (1989) and elaborated by Köhnken (2004). They are now usually referred to as **criteria-based content analysis (CBCA)**. Although originally developed for evaluating children's statements about abuse, apparently the use of this framework is allowed as evidence in courts in Germany and other countries for evaluating statements from adults as well as children. A summary of these criteria is given in Table 2.2.

DIFFICULTIES OF DOING RESEARCH ON DETECTING DECEPTION

Achieving 'ecological validity'

The biggest challenge to carrying out experiments in this area is obtaining lies in a context where the liar is seriously trying to be convincing. This is an aspect of **'ecological validity'** – the idea that the experimental conditions are close enough to reality so that there is a real possibility of the results being generalisable outside of the laboratory. Many strategies have been developed to achieve this, notably by Vrij et al. (2008), more recently reviewed by Granhag and Hartwig (2015). They typically consist of creating a situation in which people are randomly assigned to at least two conditions: one in which they experience an actual event, the other in which they are told to lie about an event they did not experience. A very clear and detailed example of this sort of study is given by Vrij and Mann (2006). Participants in both conditions are then required to be interviewed about the experience. A transcript of this interview is then the basis for analysis. Although video and/or audio recording can also be used.

Establishing 'ground truth'

If more natural situations are used as the basis for detecting deceit it is crucial to determine what the actual, or 'ground' truth is. This is not always as easy as it might seem. There may be ambiguities about what really happened, or even difference of opinion about the circumstances of the events. Even in an experimental set-up it is crucial to be clear about precisely what the circumstances were.

Ethical issues

As with all the studies in this book, there are genuine concerns about what it is acceptable to tell participants and what it is appropriate to call on them to do. Careful study of the experiments carried out by Aldert Vrij and Pär Anders Granhag (2012) demonstrate the inventive and effective ways of creating situations that support motivation to be untruthful, while still carrying out a process acceptable to an ethical committee.

ISSUES TO CONSIDER WHEN SETTING UP STUDIES OF TRUTHFULNESS

Before proposing an illustrative study, it is worth mentioning a variety of issues that the study of deception and its detection have dealt with. Any of these on their own or in combination with others can be the basis of a fascinating research project. But they cannot all be combined in a manageable project. It is best to take one or two issues and study them carefully rather than design some complex study that includes so many variables that you will lose track of them in your analysis and find it difficult to report your work.

Sources of information

As already mentioned, there are many different sources of information that can be examined to see if they indicate truthfulness or deceit. They are summarised here for convenience.

(a) *Observations* of the person making the statement. This includes gestures and body movements, as well as objective aspects of utterances, such as umms and ehhs, pauses, and repetitions. This material is of course available from video and audio recordings, but can also be derived from very detailed linguistically sophisticated transcripts.

(b) Examination of the *content* of what is said. This includes consideration of the detail and richness of what is contained in statements as well as what is not said or avoided from comment, aspects of plausibility and how well the claims fit any known facts, or what is usually assumed to be likely to happen.

Research design

Controlled experiments have been carried out for many years. They consist of creating situations in which people can lie or tell the truth. The studies then search for differences between the accounts given by individuals in the different situations. Obtaining high-stakes lying in these experiments is difficult for both ethical and practical reasons. Paying people to be as convincing as possible is one mechanism used to increase participants' motivation to lie as effectively as possible. But they are still not at risk for being unconvincing in the same way as an actual criminal, such as a murderer, would be.

Naturally occurring situations in which some people have told the truth and others have been untruthful provide different opportunities for research. There is also the fundamental issue of determining what the actual truth – the 'ground truth' – of the situation is. Neither are the conditions under which they speak and act managed by the researcher. Some material may be generated in very formal circumstances, others in a casual interview. Although they have much higher ecological validity, they are much less controlled. The liars and truth tellers have not been randomly assigned to different conditions, as they would be in a 'laboratory' experiment. There are therefore likely to be aspects of their differences that are relevant to what they say or do, which make it more difficult to be sure exactly what is generating the differences between the liars and truthtellers.

There is also the matter of how *serious*, and/or *complex* the lies are that are being considered. Describing the theft of a wallet from a table is likely to make quite different demands on a person's cognitive processes than giving an account of a journey they are planning to make, while hiding the intention that they are planning some nefarious activity.

There are also the characteristics of the *person* being interviewed. Are there gender or personality differences? It is also important to consider any aspect of their experience of being deceptive, or indeed the amount of preparation they have had before giving their account.

Judgements made

When it comes to the decisions made by 'judges' about the truthfulness, or otherwise, of the material generated for the study, there are a variety of different possibilities to choose from, each of which has its own strengths and weakness.

(a) The decision can be a straightforward *categorical* one that makes the binary choice of true or false. This does not allow people's doubts or confusions to be expressed, although a 'don't know' category is possible. However, these judgements are similar to those that might be made by a jury or police officer and thus have some merit in their realism.

(b) *Probabilistic* judgements about how likely it is that a truth/falsehood is being offered allows for a more nuanced exploration of judges' decisions. If these are broken into aspects of the decision, such as how plausible, how detailed, how emotionally convincing the material is, then it is possible to explore further the basis on which veracity is being determined.

(c) It is also important to *distinguish* between deciding whether a statement is truthful or is false. Many studies reveal that people can be more accurate in relation to one than the other. Part of this could be an assumption on the part of the participants that everyone they are dealing with is likely to be lying – a lying bias – or conversely a bias towards truthfulness. Each of these biases will favour an increased accuracy in the direction of the bias. But it is also likely that people use different criteria for deciding on truth telling from those they draw on to decide if someone is a liar.

Areas of research

For completeness it is useful to list briefly the many different areas of research that explore detecting deception. Some excellent major books reviewing these are listed at the end of this chapter.

(a) The *interview process* has been subject to a great deal of research. In more recent times attention has been paid to how an interview can be shaped to increase the likelihood of detecting deception. The use of evidence in a strategic way is one aspect of that, which has been considered. The general strategy of getting the interviewee to give as much detail as possible in an open, free-flowing account has also been emphasised. The cognitive load of having to create detail in this situation may reveal weaknesses in the story a liar offers, as well as other indicators of stress.

As mentioned, an interesting development has been to challenge the conventional wisdom of interviewing each person in a joint venture on their own. Vrij (2008) and others have demonstrated that pairs who have concocted a lie behave somewhat differently when interviewed together when compared with truthtellers.

A further development, explored by Granhag and Hartwig (2015), Vrij and Granhag (2012), and Vrij (2015) is to move beyond direct verbal interactions and to get suspects to draw maps or describe the geography of whatever they claim to have happened. This is all about increasing the cognitive demands on the respondent. A further step in this direction is to require respondents to do something else while recounting an event, such as physical exercise.

In the context of an interview there is also the possibility of the strategic use of evidence. This can encourage suspects to provide the truth (Granhag & Hartwig, 2015). Such an approach emphasises the way in which an interview is conducted, this crucially includes what and how questions are asked (Vrij & Granhag, 2012).

(b) Beyond the nature of the interview there are also aspects of the *interviewers* to consider. Their *experience* and *characteristics* have been explored. It certainly seems likely that some people are much better interviewers than others. They can draw on aspects of questioning and use of evidence that are more likely to reveal if an individual is lying.

(c) *Assumptions about deception detection* is an emerging area of research. (Masip, Alonso, Garrido, & Herrero, 2009: Masip & Herrero, 2017; Meissner & Kassin, 2002). This looks at myths and expectations that people, notably police officers and others involved in law enforcement, have about the clues to deception. It is important to study these because they do influence how people react in crucial situations. They consequently may underlie miscarriages of justice.

PROPOSED STUDIES

It is clear from the great variety of studies that have been carried out concerning deception and its detection that there are virtually limitless projects that can be designed and developed around this fascinating topic. As indicated earlier, this is also an excellent arena in which to explore the processes of experimental studies in psychology. Therefore, what is proposed here are two different examples that highlight the experimental possibilities.

The first (Study A) deals with written material specially created for the research. In this regard it can be seen as an example of a carefully *controlled laboratory experiment*. There are many processes that have been proposed to determine if an account is the truth or not. For the present study two different procedures are described. One is a general global judgement of whether the material is truthful or not. This may be called an 'intuitive' decision. Although respondents will be encouraged to explain how they came to that decision. The second is to use the detailed set of guidelines known as criteria-based content analysis (CBCA). This is part of careful considerations of how the content of utterances can be examined, as discussed and evaluated by Vrij (2015).

The second proposed project (Study B) recommends the study of widely available video recordings of people making appeals for loved ones who have disappeared. These are naturally occurring events and consequently take the form of what might be thought of as *field experiments*. There is the added issue of whether participants in the studies make judgement about whether people are lying or not, or the more nuanced decision of how plausible the account is. This latter consideration opens up the broader question of how plausibility is determined.

Study A: testing CBCA

Aim

To examine the effectiveness of the CBCA approach to detecting deception in written material. In terms of a formal hypothesis: "To test whether CBCA will help to distinguish between false and genuine statements".

Method

The exact number of respondents involved depends on the precision and detail required for the analysis. A minimum of 20 is recommended to ensure interpretable results. However, what is known as 'statistical power' would require many more respondents. This relates to the need to have large enough samples to be able effectively to test hypotheses.

Equipment

The crucial aspect of this project is obtaining genuine and false accounts. Preferably you need a few of each in order to generate enough data to make useful comparisons. There are many ways of generating these. At the simplest level you could divide ten people randomly into two groups. You ask one group each to describe what they had for breakfast – the 'truth' group. You ask the other group to invent an account of their breakfast – the 'lie' group. A shopping trip, a visit to the theatre, or any of a range of other activities could be chosen. Professor Vrij has helpfully pointed out that a more powerful requirement is asking people to tell the truth or lie about (i) a trip they recently made or (ii) a recent memorable event that was out of the ordinary.

You could take this a stage further in a more elaborate and personally relevant process by asking people to think of an event they remember and to think of something that did not happen to them that they believe they could lie convincingly about. You then ask them to write an account of each.

In order to have more control over the actual event you can do what Vrij and Mann (2006) did. They went to a lot of trouble to create a situation in which people either told the truth or lied about the theft of money from a wallet. The participants were not aware at the time of the event that this was going to be what they would be called upon to give a convincing account of.

Another example of this approach is illustrated by the subtle process set up by Elaad (1999). He was actually creating a situation that he could use to test the effectiveness of the polygraph. He had people go to a room and take a blue envelope from a desk. In the proposed project here, the 'lying' group could invent an account of what they were doing during the time that they were carrying out this activity. The 'truth' group would just describe what they did.

Process

In the Vrij and Mann (2006) study, each of the participants was interviewed and a transcript produced for examination. Although that is closer to the process used in law enforcement, it is suggested that for the proposed project all participants are required to produce a written account in relation to the instructions they have been given. This account is then analysed using CBCA.

Using CBCA

In most studies of CBCA it is the effectiveness of the approach that is being tested. There is therefore considerable effort put into ensuring that the person using that coding framework is thoroughly trained in its use. However, the present project is an illustration of the approach and the way of setting up and carrying out a controlled experiment. The extent to which the people using CBCA familiarise themselves with it is therefore dependent on the time and resources available. There are detailed explanations of the criteria in Vrij (2008, p. 209 ff.), Granhag and Strömwall (2004, p. 48 ff.), or in a variety of publications readily available on the Internet (e.g. Roma, Martini, Sabatello, Tatarelli, & Ferracuti, 2011). The 19 criteria listed in Table 2.2 are to be used in the present study.

Rating the transcripts

Two or more raters should familiarise themselves with the 19 CBCA criteria. They will then each independently rate the transcripts on each of the criteria using the 5-point Likert scale that Vrij and Mann (2006) used, ranging from 1 for the criterion was absent to 5 the criterion was strongly present. Participants are also asked to simply indicate whether the statement was true or not.

Recording the results

This provides a set of tables of scores, one table for each statement for each criterion for each person rating, as in Table 2.3.

Analysis

Inter-rater reliability

The first stage is to examine how much the people doing the rating agree with each other. This is an aspect of reliability, discussed in more detail in Study 5. There are various ways of measuring the amount of agreement. The simplest would be to calculate how often they assigned the same rating to each of their assessments. More complex statistics such as correlations and Cronbach's alpha (described in Study 5) are also possible. More generally, intraclass correlations (ICC) can be used.

Table 2.3 Example of comparison of two sets of ratings on all 19 criteria across all the statements (the values in the cells of the table range from 1 to 5 using the Likert scale described)

Criterion	Rater 1	Rater 2	Truth/lie
Statement A			Here an indication is given of whether the statement is truthful or not
1	Here the score from 1 to 5 that the rater gave for this criterion	Here the score from 1 to 5 that the rater gave for this criterion	
2			
3			
Etc.			
Statement B			Here an indication is given of whether the statement is truthful or not
1			
2			
3			
Etc.			
Statement C			
Etc.			

Many studies find reasonably high, although not perfect, levels of agreement between people on these ratings. It is also possible to look at the levels of agreement for individual criterion. These provide the basis for discussion and clarification between those carrying out the rating, which can result in adjustment of the assessments.

Effectiveness of CBCA

Once the ratings have been agreed it is then possible to determine if there is any difference of the scores between the true and false accounts. This can be carried out using a total score derived by adding up all 19 values for each statement. Considering the differences between truthful and lying statements on each of the 19 criteria also allows a more nuanced examination of what aspects of CBCA are of value (Landers 2015). However, generally the total score is a more reliable indicator.

Considerations

The systematic nature of CBCA enables careful research to be conducted using it. As a consequence, there are many studies of its utility in many different settings. For example, Amado, Arce, Fariña, and Vilariño (2016) reviewed 39 studies of its use with statements from adults. These studies are far from uniform in finding support for CBCA. In his extensive book and in an earlier journal article, Vrij (2005, 2008) concludes that the approach is not reliable or valid enough to be used as evidence in court, but may be of value in police investigations.

Various authorities seek to add or modify the original CBCA criteria presented in this chapter as well as considering them as part of a more thorough examination of the interview process and the broader approach of statement validity analysis (SVA). SVA is not to be confused with scientific content analysis (SCAN), which is a procedure drawing on aspects of the use of language that has not survived detailed systematic evaluation, as Vrij (2008) discusses in detail.

It is therefore important to emphasise that the proposed study here of CBCA is just a toe in the water. The exploration of what it is about the content of an account that can reveal whether it is truthful or not is a large area of research. As in most developing areas of research, the more studies that are carried out the more complex the issues become. It is doubtless a fascinating topic and well worth the effort of studying it.

Study B: judgement of veracity in high-stakes situations

Aim

(a) Determine which aspects of a person's reactions to a television appeal from people whose loved ones have disappeared most influences their judgement of the plausibility of the appeals.

(b) Examine whether appeals in which only audio information was available produced differences in ratings of veracity of the appeal when compared with both audio and visual information.

This is a study of television appeals made by relatives of victims who have disappeared or been found murdered.

Purpose

This study explores the opinions the public have about those who make such appeals and has two crucial aspects, compared with many studies of veracity judgements. The first is that this has some 'ecological validity' in that they are actual events, not accounts created for the purpose of the research. The second is that they are significant events for the people generating the account. They are **'high-stakes' events** of importance for the person making the appeal to ensure they are believed. As ten Brinke and Porter (2012) have argued, there are real penalties for not being believed in high-stakes situations.

Table 2.4 Possible design of experiment

	Genuine	False
Male	a	b
Female	c	d

There is a great deal of interest in these television appeals because they show relatives of victims in a vulnerable situation seeking help. In some cases, these relatives have later been found to be the culprits so the public is often sceptical of the appealer. This study therefore examines the judgements made by the public and what influences those judgements.

The judgements the public make are of great importance because the whole point of the television appeal is to seek help and support from those watching.

Equipment

Television appeals are widely available to view on the Internet. It is interesting to select them to fit a factorial design. For example, you could select two appeals made by women, one being genuine and one false, then two by men, one genuine and one false. This gives you a 2 x 2 matrix, as in Table 2.4.

The four conditions, a, b, c, d, are the four videos. They can be shown to your respondents with the sound only or with sound and vision, giving you eight conditions in total.

One crucial point is to be sure you have 'ground truth' for each of the videos; that is, clear indication of whether the person in the video is guilty or not. This does require some background research to determine what the legal judgement was.

Another consideration is that the videos are comparable in how they are recorded. For example, a person being interviewed standing outside her house is not the same as someone making a statement at a press conference organised by the police. Where a couple is involved, having two people talking on the video adds complications for comparison with a person being interviewed on his own. The selection of the examples therefore has to be done very carefully.

Procedure

Four short clips of people making appeals on television are available to look at. After watching each clip, the respondent is asked to answer a few questions about the appealer. There are then a few questions about the background of the respondent.

If everyone looks at every video there is the issue of the order in which the videos are presented. It is always possible that having seen one video will influence judgements about the next. One way of dealing with this is to only get each person to see one video. This adds extra time to running the experiment and increases the possibility of variations between people introducing more unwanted variation into the study.

A more common way of dealing with this issue in most psychology experiments is to vary the order in which people view/listen to the videos. If you were to get each person to view/listen to all eight videos then you have a large number of possible sequences for them to make judgements. My calculation is that there are over 40,000 permutations of the different sequences possible ($8 \times 7 \times 6 \times 5 \times 4 \times 3 \times 2 \times 1$). You could just generate, say, half a dozen random sequences, but there is a risk then of something about the sequences you end up with having an unwanted influence. That is probably a risk worth taking.

A compromise between the single and all eight viewing is to divide the study up into sections. Watching/listening to eight examples may tax the concentration of many participants, so for instance identifying two sets of four examples as two distinct studies would be more manageable both for organising the study and for those giving responses. I suggest one set are audio only and the other set are audio and video. This still gives a sequence of four to be organised. That would be 24 different sequences, which is manageable but it is probably best to select a subset of these and check later whether the order of presentations has any effect. For example, making each of the four the first in the sequence and keeping the others in the same order. This discussion, however, does show the complexity of having fully controlled laboratory studies.

There are further issues that arise from the mechanics of exactly how the material is handled by the respondents. If this is an online survey people could have control over how long they watched the video and whether they watched it a number of times. This would be possible to monitor. On the other hand, if the material was played to a class and they were then asked to respond it would be possible to ensure that every example was presented for the same length of time.

Instructions

Appendix 2B provides an example of the sort of questionnaire that could be used for this project. Although, remember, an ethical approval committee may want more information, such as the informed consent form given in Appendix 2A. You will also require a debrief process, as illustrated in Appendix 2C.

Number of respondents

The number of people you get to view/listen to the videos depends both on the opportunities you have available and how much detail you want to explore in subsequent analyses. As a very loose rule of thumb you need at least ten people to respond to each video, so that you get enough information to reveal patterns in the results. However, as already mentioned, because of the issue of the 'power' of your results, if you want to do a study that would get through the journal review process you would probably need at least 25 people for each of your four conditions.

Analyses

There are a variety of statistical procedures that can be applied to the data collected in this study, ranging from χ^2 (chi-square), to analysis of variance (ANOVA), multivariate analysis of variance (MANOVA), to various forms of regression and multiple regression analyses. In keeping with the rest of this book, and the very many other excellent books and websites that provide details of these procedures and their associated inferential statistics, I will not mention them further here. I will just provide simple examples of the sorts of tables that are the basis of these calculations. These are based on the first-rate PhD thesis of Magdalene Y.L. Ng (2016), which I supervised.

First just working with the answers to the first question about guilt or innocence in the different conditions, in order to determine how accurate people are, the first step is to remove all those judgements that were unsure. Examining the conditions under which people were unsure is another aspect of the study that can be carried out separately. In Ng's (2016) case this was part of a much larger study so it is a little complicated to indicate the actual frequencies, but in order to carry out effective statistical analysis the original frequencies in relation to the sample sizes would be best to work with.

Table 2.5 gives the percentages of correct answers in this particular case. They reveal some intriguing results. A random judgement of guilt or innocence would be 50%. Therefore the accuracy percentages for the audio-visual condition are only marginally above the chance level. Nonetheless, there are slightly more correct judgements for the true appeals than the false ones, 55% compared with 52%.

Table 2.5 Percentage of correct judgements in the four conditions

Appeal	Audio only (%)	Audio-visual (%)
True	66	55
False	73	52

One concern always in studies such as this is whether respondents have a tendency, or bias, to assume guilt or innocence. If they did have such a bias it would distort the results. Consequently, it is encouraging to see that the accuracy rates hovering around 50% for the audio-visual conditions do not suggest any strong bias.

For the audio-only condition respondents are overall more accurate than for the audio-visual condition. Their accuracy judgements are notably above chance levels. That is an unexpected finding. It might have been thought that the more information available to respondents the better they would be at determining truthfulness. The opposite seems to be the case in this example. The visual information would seem to mask the audio material. This is especially true of the accuracy of judging false appeals, which reaches the impressive figure of nearly three-quarters of the assessments being correct. Further research would be necessary to explore the reasons for this and to determine if the result can be replicated in further studies. It does, however, accord with published research reviewed by Bond and DePaulo (2006). Furthermore, intriguingly, when I ran a pilot version of this in which there was one blind respondent, he was very good at detecting deception. This opens another possibility for research of testing blind and sighted people's ability to detect deception in audio-only material.

One aspect of responses that could throw light on this finding is that derived from the other four questions asked. These questions are drawn from the growing amount of research that has explored what it is about an utterance that leads an observer to believe it or not (Strömwall, Granhag, & Hartwig, 2004). They draw on the empathy that the appeal generates: "I felt sympathy for the appealer". This includes an assessment of the emotion the speaker seems to be expressing: "The appealer seems sad". There is also research that shows attractive people are more likely to be believed than unattractive people. Hence the statement: "The appealer is quite attractive". Finally, there is the cognitive assessment of the plausibility of the account (Canter, Nicol, & Benneworth, 2003). Does it fit with what is known about how things happen? "The appealer's account makes sense".

There are various ways of using the responses to these questions in order to determine their influence on judgements of veracity. One common practice is to divide respondents up into two groups on the basis of their answers to each of the questions. For example, one group would be those who felt sympathy for the appealer. The other group would be those who did not. Then the relative proportions for each group of those who thought the appealer was genuine would be compared. These relative proportions can then be compared to determine which of the comparisons has the greatest impact. For example, consider Table 2.6

Table 2.6 indicates that the greatest influence on respondents correctly deciding the truthfulness of the appeals was how much sense the description given by the appealer made. However, whether the appealer was attractive or not made no difference to accuracy of judgements.

A more subtle analysis is to use multivariate statistics to relate aspects of the videos to their veracity. This was the sophisticated analysis carried out, for example, by Wright, Wagstaff, and Wheatcroft (2014). The technical details of this are beyond the current book, but broadly speaking they found that deceptive appeals contained more equivocal language, gaze aversion, head shaking, and speech errors, and honest appeals contained more references to norms of emotion/behaviour, more expressions of hope of finding the missing relative alive, more expressions of positive emotion towards the relative, more expressions of concern/pain, and an avoidance of brutal language.

Table 2.6 Percentage of people in each subgroup correctly determining truthfulness

Question	High (%)	Low (%)	Difference (%)
Felt sympathy	62	38	24
Seemed sad	78	22	56
Was attractive	56	58	2
Made sense	82	10	72

CONCLUSIONS

The studies of deception, how to detect it, and what people believe about how to detect it is now a vast area of psychological research. It touches on many aspects of human social interaction, cognitive processes, and criminal activity. The essence of this area of research is quite straightforward – the binary distinction between deceit and truthfulness. It therefore lends itself to tidy experimental procedures. As such it is an excellent vehicle for learning how to carry out psychological experiments. Two different studies have been described, one working with material generated for research, the other using naturally occurring accounts that are truthful or not.

Unlike the previous chapter elaborating an experiment on detecting which signatures are forged, for which there is not a large literature or detailed theoretical bases on which to form hypotheses, detecting deception has a library of research all its own. This provides rich models and hypotheses to form the foundation of any experiments.

OTHER STUDIES THAT COULD USE THIS RESEARCH DESIGN

A central hypothesis about the challenge of lying is that it produces a 'cognitive load'. One development of Study A is therefore to explore directly whether the cognitive load is experienced more by liars than truthful participants. Further, to examine whether those who do experience the intellectual challenge of lying give rise to more CBCA indicators than those who do not. In the Vrij and Mann (2006) study, from which the proposed project was derived, those creating the accounts were also asked a set of questions to indicate how much effort was involved in the creating of the account. Scores derived from their answers were then related to their CBCA scores.

In Study B only audio and audio-visual presentations were compared. Of course, a third comparison of only visual information is possible. The details of that possibility have not been given here because it adds a further complication. This would mean three comparisons rather than two:

audio with audio-visual;

audio with visual only;

visual with audio-visual.

With the four conditions of male, female, combined with genuine and false that gives 12 comparisons to make in total. Quite a challenging number to find participants for, then to make sense of the results, and present in an organised way. I always think it is better to carry out a series of small studies, rather than one big complicated one. That way you can learn from each study and use it to improve the next.

In all of the possible studies there is the possibility of considering different types of individuals, as liars or those trying to detect deceit. For instance, are children different from adults in this regard? Are there really expert deceit detectors, as O'Sullivan and Ekman (2004) claim? The books listed in the references at the end of this chapter consider these issues as well.

One intriguing area is whether people are any better at detecting lying in those who they know well (Bond & DePaulo, 2006; DePaulo et al., 1996). An illustration of this would be whether parents can tell if their own children are being untruthful better than other people's children. Of course, the age of the children involved would be crucial. The real test would be with teenagers!

A Note on 'Authorship'

There is one other area of research that overlaps with the considerations here. That is the determination of the authorship of a piece of text. This has practical importance when a document is contested, with claims it was not authored by who it is claimed to have written, or spoken, it. The clearest example of this is when suspects insist that the confession attributed to them was created by the police. The authorship of anonymous offensive texts is also a matter that can have legal implications. Whether a suicide note really was written by the deceased is another example of potential legal significance (Canter, 2005). In a literary context, authorship attribution has an academic interest, exemplified by issues such as whether Shakespeare was the playwright for all the plays that bear his name.

An area of research known as forensic linguistics (Coulthard & Johnson, 2007) has grown up around authorship, and related questions. As, sadly, is so often the case when a matter of legal significance may have a scientific resolution, often the initial proposals find currency long before they have any established scientific validity. One such example was the claim that a relatively straightforward arithmetical calculation would indicate whether a text was the work of one or more than one author; a procedure known as cumulative summation (CUSUM), promulgated by Morton and Farringdon (1992).

This is relevant for the present chapter on experimental tests of deception detection because it was only by systematic, conventional experimental testing (Canter & Chester, 1997) that it was possible to demonstrate that the procedure generated random results. If the results accorded with what the CUSUM researcher was trying to claim then they were presented as proof that it worked. If they did not, they were not mentioned. Unfortunately, CUSUM found its way into court proceedings before the experimental studies demonstrated its worthlessness.

That is not to say that the advent of massive databases and information technology that allows the searching and systematisation of large amounts of text is not opening up the possibility, when there is a lot of material to work with, to throw light on questions that have puzzled literary scholars for years. Although, as Olsson (2018) shows in his interesting case studies in forensic linguistics, it is still often the case today that an expert in language and how it is used, especially if well informed about differences between languages and contexts, may be able to elucidate the meaning and authorship of challenged texts without the need for computer analyses.

Questions for Discussion

1. Are there situations you can think of where it is not a straightforward matter to determine what is actually the truth (the 'ground truth')?

2. What are the civil liberties, ethical, and judicial issues raised by using a procedure like CBCA to determine whether a statement is truthful or not, in comparison with the extent to which the statement fits the facts?

3. The police claim they never use appeals from relatives of missing or murdered victims to determine if the relative may be involved in the crime in some way. Is that sensible or could they use appeals to indicate the guilt of the person making the appeal?

4. If the power of the polygraph is in the belief people have that it is a lie detector, how can that be utilised in other areas of detecting deceit?

5. What are the dangers of people holding false beliefs about ways of detecting deception?

NOTE

1   See https://en.wikipedia.org/wiki/Voice_stress_analysis.

FURTHER READING

There are two researchers who have devoted their academic careers to studies around police interviewing and the detection of deception. A search on Google Scholar reveals many relevant publications for Aldert Vrij and Pär Anders Granhag. Many of their publications are available online, especially through their university repositories. The books they've written or edited, which I have drawn on particularly are:

Granhag, P.A., & Strömwall, L.A. (Eds.) (2004). *The detection of deception in forensic contexts.* Cambridge, UK: Cambridge University Press.
Vrij, A. (2008). *Detecting lies and deceit: Pitfalls and opportunities* (2nd ed.). Chichester, UK: Wiley.
Vrij, A. (2018). Verbal lie detection tools from an applied perspective. In J.P. Rosenfeld (Ed.), *Detecting concealed information and deception: Recent developments* (pp. 297–321). San Diego, CA: Elsevier: Academic Press.

Some forensic psychology textbooks also have detailed chapters on detecting deception and related areas, notably:

Howitt, D. (2018). *Introduction to forensic and criminal psychology* (6th ed.). Harlow, UK: Pearson.

REFERENCES

Amado, B.G., Arce, R., Fariña, F., & Vilariño, M. (2016). Criteria-based content analysis (CBCA) reality criteria in adults: A meta-analytic review. *International Journal of Clinical and Health Psychology*, 16(2), 201–210. https://doi.org/10.1016/j.ijchp.2016.01.002.
Beattie, G. (2016). *Rethinking body language: How hand movements reveal hidden thoughts.* London: Routledge.
Best, G., Hodgeon, J., & Street, C. (2019). How contemporary theory informs lie detection accuracy and bias. *Crime Security and Society*, 1(2). doi: https://doi.org/10.5920/css.555.
Bond, C.F., & DePaulo, B.M. (2006). Accuracy of deception judgments. *Personality and Social Psychology Review*, 10, 214–234.
Bond, C.F., Howard, A.R., Hutchison, J.L., & Masip, J. (2013). Overlooking the obvious: Incentives to lie. *Basic and Applied Social Psychology*, 35, 212–221.
Bradshaw, J. (2008). Behavioral detectives patrol airports. *National Psychologist*, July/August, p. 10
Canter, D. (2005). Suicide or murder. In L. Alison (Ed.), *The forensic psychologist's casebook* (pp. 315–333). Devon, UK: Willan Publishing.
Canter, D., & Chester, J. (1997). Investigation into the claim of weighted CUSUM in authorship attribution studies. *Journal of Forensic Linguistics*, 4(2), 252–261.
Canter, D., Nicol, C., & Benneworth, K. (2003). Narrative plausibility: The impact of sequence and anchoring. *Behavioural Sciences & the Law*, 21(2), 251–267.
Coulthard, M., & Johnson, A. (2007). *An introduction to forensic linguistics language in evidence.* London: Routledge. Retrieved from https://tinyurl.com/s8cclzb.
DePaulo, B.M., Kashy, D., Kirkendol, S.E., Wyer, M.M., & Epstein, J.A. (1996). Lying in everyday life. *Journal of Personality and Social Psychology*, 70, 979–995.
Ekman, O. (2009). Lie catching and micro-expressions. In C. Martin (Ed.), The philosophy of deception (pp. 118–138). Oxford: Oxford University Press.

Elaad, E. (1999). A comparative study of polygraph tests and other forensic methods. In D. Canter & L. Alison (Eds.), Interviewing and deception (pp. 209–231). Dartmouth, UK: Ashgate.

Ganis, G. (2015). Investigating deception and deception detection with brain stimulation methods. In P.A. Granhag, A. Vrig, & B. Verschuere (Eds.), *Detecting deception: Current challenges and cognitive approaches* (pp. 253–268). Chichester, UK: Wiley

Garrett, B.L. (2010). The substance of false confessions. *Stanford Law Review*, 62(4), 1051.

Granhag, P.A., & Hartwig, M. (2015). The strategic use of evidence (SUE) technique: A conceptual overview. In P.A. Granhag, A. Vrij, & B. Verschuere (Eds.), *Deception detection: Current challenges and new approaches* (pp. 231–251). Chichester, UK: Wiley.

Granhag, P.A., & Strömwall, L.A. (Eds.) (2004). *The detection of deception in forensic contexts.* Cambridge, UK: Cambridge University Press.

Hartwig, M., Granhag, P.A., Strömwall, L.A., & Kronkvist, O. (2006). Strategic use of evidence during police interviews: When training to detect deception works. Law and Human Behavior, 30(5), 603–619. doi: 10.1007/s10979-006-9053-9.

Hjelmsäter, E.R., Öhman, L. Granhag, P.A., & Vrij, A. (2012). Mapping deception in adolescents: Eliciting cues to deceit through an unanticipated spatial drawing task. *Legal and Criminological Psychology*, 19(1), 179–188. https://doi.org/10.1111/j.2044-8333.2012.02068.x.

Hollien, H., Geison, L., & Hicks, J.W. Jr. (1987). Voice stress analysis and lie detection. *Journal of Forensic Sciences*, 32(2), 405–418.

Köhnken, G. (2004). Statement validity analysis and the 'detection of the truth'. In P.A. Granhag & L.A. Strömwall (Eds.), *The detection of deception in forensic contexts* (pp. 41–63). Cambridge, UK: Cambridge University Press.

Landers, R.N. (2015). Computing intraclass correlations (ICC) as estimates of interrater reliability in SPSS. *The Winnower*, 7, e143518.81744. doi: 10.15200/winn.143518.81744.

Lisak, D., Gardinier, L.,. Nicksa, S.C., & Cote, A.M. (2010). False allegations of sexual assault: An analysis of ten years of reported cases. *Violence Against Women*, 16, 1318–1334. https://doi.org/10.1177/1077801210387747.

McShane, J.J. (2013). Voice stress analysis challenges. *The Truth About Forensic Science*, 19 December. Retrieved from https://thetruthaboutforensicscience.com/voice-stress-analysis-challenges.

Maschke. G.W., & Scalabrini, G.J. (2018). *The lie behind the lie detector* (5th ed.). Retrieved from https://antipolygraph.org/pubs.shtml.

Masip, J., Alonso, H., Garrido, E., & Herrero, C. (2009). Training to detect what? The biasing effects of training on veracity judgments. *Applied Cognitive Psychology*, 23, 1282–1296.

Masip, J., & Herrero, C. (2017). Examining police officers' response bias in judging veracity. *Psichothema*, 29, 490–495.

Meissner, C.A., & Kassin, S.M. (2002). "He's guilty!": Investigator bias in judgments of truth and deception. *Law and Human Behavior*, 26, 469–480.

Morton A.Q., & Farringdon, M.G. (1992). Identifying utterance. *Expert Evidence*, 1(3), 84–92.

Nahari, G., Vrij, A., & Fisher, R.P. (2014). Exploiting liars' verbal strategies by examining the verifiability of details. *Legal and Criminological Psychology*, 19, 227–239.

Ng, M. (2016). *Innocence and guilt detection in high-stakes television appeals* (PhD thesis, University of Huddersfield, UK). Retrieved from http://eprints.hud.ac.uk/id/eprint/32621.

Ng, M., & Youngs, D. (2015). Veracity assessment: Aspects of the account, the source and the judge that influence judgements of plausibility. *Crime Psychology Review*, 1(1), 135–154. doi: 10.1080/23744006.2016.1177946.

Olsson, J. (2018). *More word crime.* London: Bloomsbury Academic.

O'Sullivan, M., & Ekman, O. (2004). The wizards of deception detection. In P.A. Granhag & L.A. Strömwall (Eds.), The detection of deception in forensic contexts (pp. 269–286). Cambridge, UK: Cambridge University Press.

Roma, P., Martini, P.S., Sabatello, U., Tatarelli, R., & Ferracuti, S. (2011). Validity of criteria-based content analysis (CBCA) at trial in free-narrative interviews. *Child Abuse and Neglect*, 35(8), 613–620. doi: 10.1016/j.chiabu.2011.04.004.

Steller, M., & Köhnken, G. (1989). Criteria-based statement analysis. In D.C. Raskin (Ed.), Psychological methods for investigation and evidence (pp. 217–245). New York, NY: Springer.

Street, C., Bischof, W., Vadillo, M., & Kingstone, A. (2015). Inferring others' hidden thoughts: Smart guesses in a low diagnostic world. *Journal of Behavioral Decision Making*, 29(5), 539–549. https://doi.org/10.1002/bdm.1904.

Strömwall, L.A., Granhag, P.A., & Hartwig, M. (2004). Practitioners' beliefs about deception. In P.A. Granhag & L.A. Strömwall (Eds.), *Deception detection in forensic contexts* (pp. 229–250). Cambridge, UK: Cambridge University Press.

ten Brinke, L., & Porter, S. (2012). Cry me a river: Identifying the behavioral consequences of extremely high-stakes interpersonal deception. *Law and Human Behavior*, 36, 469–477.

Undeutsch, U. (1989). The development of statement reality analysis. In J.C. Yuille (Ed.), Nato Advanced Institute series. Series D: Behavioural and Social Sciences (vol. 47, pp. 101–119). Dordrecht, the Netherlands: Kluwer Academic/Plenum. https://psycnet.apa.org/doi/10.1007/978-94-015-7856-1_6.

Vrij, A. (2005). Criteria-based content analysis: A qualitative review of the first 37 studies psychology. *Public Policy, and Law*, 11(1), 3–41.

Vrij, A. (2008). *Detecting lies and deceit: Pitfalls and opportunities* (2nd ed.). Chichester, UK: Wiley.

Vrij, A. (2015). Verbal lie detection tools: Statement validity analysis, reality monitoring and scientific content analysis. In P.A. Granhag, A. Vrij, & B. Verschuere (Eds.), *Detection deception: Current challenges and cognitive approaches* (pp. 3–36). Chichester, UK: Wiley.

Vrij, A., & Granhag, P.A. (2012). Eliciting cues to deception and truth: What matters are the questions asked. *Journal of Applied Research in Memory and Cognition*, 1, 110–117. doi.org/10.1016/j.jarmac.2012.02.004.

Vrij, A., Hartwig, M., & Granhag, P.A. (2018). Reading lies: Nonverbal communication and deception. *Annual Review of Psychology*, 70, 295–317. doi: 10.1146/annurev-psych-010418-103135.

Vrij, A., & Mann, S.A. (2006). Criteria-based content analysis: An empirical test of its underlying processes. Psychology, Crime & Law, 12(4), 337–349. doi: 10.1080/10683160500129007.

Vrij, A., Mann, S.A., Fisher, R.P., Leal, S., Milne, R., & Bull, R. (2008). Increasing cognitive load to facilitate lie detection: The benefit of recalling an event in reverse order. *Law and Human Behavior*, 32, 253. https://doi.org/10.1007/s10979-007-9103.

Wright, W.C., Wagstaff, G.F., & Wheatcroft, J. (2014). Highstakes lies: Verbal and nonverbal cues to deception in public appeals for help with missing or murdered relatives. *Psychiatry, Psychology and Law*, 21(4), 523–537.

Appendix 2A   Consent Form for Study B

As part of a study of people making appeals or interviews on television where their loved ones have disappeared or been killed, I will show you four short films taken from actual televised appeals. Some of them are guilty and some of them are not. I would then like you to answer some questions about each film. It should all take less than 30 minutes.

There is no right or wrong answer. It is your own personal opinion that is wanted.

We do not need to know your name, so the whole study is anonymous and your responses will be confidential to the research team.

Some people may find these short videos distressing. If, at any time for whatever reason, you feel like you wish to stop taking part just let me know and we'll stop the experiment and you can leave without any consequences. You can withdraw from this experiment at any time but once the questionnaire is handed in it is subject to analysis and your name will be replaced by a code number so all anonymity is ensured. If you feel you have been affected by any of the issues surrounding this experiment you can approach the Samaritans for emotional support; alternatively, you can access the counselling service offered by Careline and Victim Support. My name is Magdalene Ng. I am supervised by Professor David Canter and Dr Donna Youngs. If you would like any further information regarding the study please contact Dr Youngs at d.youngs@hud.ac.uk.

If you do wish to continue with the experiment please sign this consent form below.

Thank you for your time and agreement to take part in this study.

Signature: ....

Date: ....

APPENDIX 2B   QUESTIONNAIRE FOR STUDY B

This is a study of people making appeals on television where their loved ones have disappeared or been killed.

There are four very short videos, each of a different person making an actual television appeal.

We would like you to answer a few questions about each video. At the end we would like you to give us a few details about yourself. We do not need to know your name, so the whole study is anonymous and your responses will be confidential to the research team.

There are no right or wrong answers. It is your own personal opinion that is wanted.

Some people may find these short videos distressing. So, if at any time for whatever reason, you feel like you wish to stop taking part that is fine.

Please <u>do not</u> begin answering the questions until each appeal has been played. It is also important that you answer every question, <u>missing any questions makes your responses invalid.</u>

First [some identifier needs to be recorded here to identify the material being presented] video/audio:

Key question: Do you think the appealer was innocent?   Yes/ No/Not sure

Do you think the appealer was guilty?   Yes/No/Not sure

Please indicate the extent to which you agree or disagree with the following statements about the video selecting a number from 1 to 5.

1   indicates 'strongly disagree'

2   indicates 'disagree'

3   indicates 'undecided'

4   indicates 'agree'

5   indicates 'strongly agree'

    A.   "I felt sympathy for the appealer"

    B.   "The appealer is quite attractive"

    C.   "The appealer's account makes sense"

    D.   "The appealer seems sad"

Do you know anything about the case you have just watched or the appealer?

Yes/No

If yes what was the outcome? S/he was innocent/guilty

[This set of questions needs to be repeated a further three times, for each of the other videos/audios.]

Finally, please answer the following questions about yourself:

(a) What is your gender?

(b) What is your age?

(c) What is your occupation?

This is the end of the questionnaire. Thank you for your participation.

Appendix 2C Debrief Form

Thank you very much for taking the time to complete this experiment. The aim of this experiment was to investigate the phenomena of lying and telling the truth behaviours specifically in the context of false appeals from the receiver's end. A false appeal is where a family member or partner of a person who has gone missing or has been injured or murdered publicly appeals for information regarding the crime either in a press conference or while being interviewed by a journalist. However, this person is either involved in the disappearance or is complicit in it but pretends not to know anything about it and deceives both the investigating police officers and attempts to extend this to the general public. In order to explore false appeals I found cases of false appeals and matched them with true appeals for participants to watch and/or listen to them to see whether they could decide whether the person speaking in each case was lying or telling the truth. I also matched these appeals according to other variables such as age and attractiveness, as well as the narrative contents and roles. The study aims to explore whether people typically perceive certain characteristics in true and false appeals and whether these impact on their judgment of veracity. If you were not able to correctly decide whether they were lying or telling the truth you must not worry. Detecting lies in other people is a notoriously difficult task and that is why psychology and other disciplines have for many decades now been trying to explore ways to detect lies and identify the verbal and non-verbal behaviour that may signal deceit. If you feel you would like more information on any of the issues this experiment addresses, or on the experiment in general, you can contact my supervisor [supervisor name here]. Or alternatively you could contact me at [your email address here]. If you feel you have been affected by any of the issues surrounding this experiment you can call the Samaritans for emotional support on [phone no.]. Alternatively, you could call the counselling service Careline on [phone no.] or Victim Support [phone no.].

PROFILING

STUDY 3
Profiling serial killers

SYNOPSIS

As an introduction to the idea of 'offender profiling' a study is proposed in which descriptions of crimes are to be related to background information about perpetrators. This highlights the task of developing inferences about the characteristics of offenders from the details of their criminal activities. The task of creating such 'profiles' is so bound up in mythology and fiction that the task provides a context in which to explore the challenges of this process and to briefly review the development of a scientific approach to creating 'profiles'.

The curious fascination with, and many publications about, serial killers provides a viable context for the proposed study. The distinctions between various forms of multiple homicide are considered, as well as approaches to distinguishing between different themes in serial killing. These differentiations are crucial for making any inferences about those who commit a number of murders.

SOME KEY CONCEPTS

- profiling equation
- salience
- consistency
- behavioural investigative advisor (BIA)
- types of multiple murderers.

BACKGROUND

Criminal profiling has become a recurring aspect of crime fiction ever since Clarice Starling interviewed Hannibal Lector in Thomas Harris's engrossing book *The Silence of the Lambs*. Whole series of television fiction, such as *Cracker*, *Criminal Minds*, and *Mindhunter* have emerged, built around the exploits of characters who offer 'profiles' that help move the plot on. This really is little more than an updated version of Sherlock Holmes and subsequent sleuths who have special insights that enable them to solve crimes.

The problem is that these fictional accounts have given the notion of producing a 'criminal profile' an almost mythical character. Such psychological descriptions of an unknown offender (usually in fiction a serial killer) seem to come out of the profound intuitions of very special people – the fictional 'profilers'. In practice the descriptions are intended to give guidance to an investigation. They may do this by indicating where possible suspects may be found in police records, or other means, helping to prioritise those suspects who emerge in an investigation so that police resources can be appropriately focused, and sometimes opening up interview strategies for key suspects.

All of this is not that dissimilar from what experienced detectives would do without the assistance of a 'profile'. The difference is partly the idea that the profiler offers additional insights not normally available. It is also that the suggestions about the characteristics of the criminal emerge out of some overt logic and possibly research background. The truth is that there is no standard process for drawing up a 'profile', nor about what it should or normally describes. The proposed study therefore draws attention to the central issue of how inferences may be made about an offender from what is known about his crimes.

Yet at the heart of the idea of generating a 'profile' of an unknown person is an attempt to make inferences about the characteristics of a person by drawing on the details of their crime(s). I have called this inference process a **'profiling equation'** (Canter, 2011). This equation consists of relating details of the **A**ctions in a crime to **C**haracteristics of the offender, summarised as A→C, where the arrow is the inference process. Contrary to what might be thought from fictional accounts, this inference process is not nearly as easy as you might think. There are many reasons why any specific aspect of a crime may be related to many different features of the criminal. Youngs (2008) has elaborated these complexities. These can be summarised as four features that have to be managed:

- *Pertinence*. Essentially this is the challenge of determining what aspect of a crime is relevant to form inferences about the offender. For example, in a stranger rape is it the nature of the sexual behaviour, the way the victim was controlled, how the offender made a getaway, or some other aspects of the criminal activities? More generally, how is the 'style' of an offence to be determined?

- **Salience**. Beyond identifying the style of an offender's actions there is the associated challenge of being able to distinguish that style from that of other offenders. Many studies of actions in many different types of crime demonstrate that for any crime type, whether it be, for instance, arson, burglary, murder or rape, there will be some actions that are typical of all the crimes of that type. Those general actions help to define what type of crime it is. There will also be some actions that are very rare indeed, they may even only occur in the crimes of a particular individual. These very rare actions are sometimes, rather inappropriately, called 'signatures'.

The police also use the somewhat ambiguous term modus operandi (MO) to indicate characteristic actions of a particular offender. However, without knowing the frequency distribution of actions across offence types it is difficult to be sure what is unique to an offender and what is just unusual. Creating models of the frequency of co-occurrence of criminal actions therefore helps to indicate what is salient for any particular set of crimes. This approach is reviewed in detail in Canter and Youngs (2009).

Interestingly, Fox, Farrington, Kapardis, and Hambly (2020) have defined offender profiling more in terms of specifying *types* of offences that can be related to *types* of offenders. This is an elaboration of the very useful book by Miethe and McCorkle (1998), which summarised the published descriptions of offenders across a range of different crimes. Fox et al. (2020) have given their approach the label of 'evidence based offender profiling', which provides the jolly acronym EBOP. This approach gives pride of place to large-scale number crunching in which relationships between variables are searched for statistical significance. For example, after sophisticated statistical analysis of a large dataset of burglaries, Fox et al. (2020) identified four types of burglar and four offence styles. This enabled them to present results such that 41% of 'opportunistic' burglars were of the subtype 'peer influenced'. By contrast an 'interpersonal' offence style was found in 64% of 'impulsive' type of offenders (Fox et al., 2020, p. 35).

These statistical relationships seem to be presented without any attempt to produce general explanations, theories, or models of what gives rise to them. They are just pragmatic findings. However, Fox and Farrington (2015) do report successful application of such relationships to active police investigations.

- *Contingencies.* How do the actions relate to each other and the contexts in which they occur? Smashing a window to gain entry at night carries different implication from doing that in the daytime. If a burglar, happy to climb up a drainpipe and in through a window, first discovers a door has been left open, then the door will be used rather than the window. These features will also vary as criminals learn or develop over time.

- *Canonical relationships.* The EBOP approach uses advanced statistics to reveal distinct types of actions and characteristics and then reveals the patterns of relationships between them. The results, however, do reveal an issue that I referred to some time ago as a 'canonical correlation' (Canter, 2011). This draws on an algebraic idea that a mixture of actions can relate to a mixture of characteristics. There is no reason to assume the one-to-one association so beloved by crime novelists, ever since Conan Doyle first wrote, between a clue and its implications. Although there are some general, loose relationships between some actions and some characteristics, no one has yet discovered the sort of wonderful connections so beloved by fiction writers.

Behaviour is not like a fingerprint. There is a mixture of actions that can combine in different ways to have a variety of implications. For instance, an intelligent serial killer who has access to a vehicle may target young women on the streets in certain parts of the city. But the same person who can use public transport may target other potential victims in other contexts.

The table Fox et al. (2020) produce of the relationships between offence styles and offender subtypes show this complexity, even when only utilising four distinct styles of criminal actions. The style they refer to as 'organised', is related to 29% 'impulsive' offenders, 14% 'peer influenced', 9% substance abusers, and 48% 'career criminals' (Fox et al., 2020, p. 35). Consequently, although a high proportion are 'career criminals' there are still plenty of 'impulsive' criminals and not a few 'peer influenced' ones in their sample. There is no one A that can be uniquely used to infer a distinct set of Cs.

The scientific approach explored by Youngs (2008) and many other studies in this tradition, as well as the EBOP approach, all of which are examined in Canter and Youngs (2009) and in Fox et al. (2020), tends to be contrasted with what is usually called, nowadays, a 'clinical' approach to profiling. This attempts to develop accounts of relevant features of unknown offenders on a case-by-case basis. The development of such features relies heavily on the experience, knowledge, and skills of a particular individual – the 'psychiatric Sherlock Holmes' as James Brussel, one of the first people in modern times to produce 'profiles' for major police investigations, called himself in his 1968 autobiography.

An interesting aspect of the clinical approach to profiling, in comparison with the statistical EBOP strategy, is that it has to draw on explicit or implicit theories about what allows inferences to be drawn from actions to imply characteristics. These may be derived from Freudian theories such as displacement, whereby a person attacks others because he cannot attack some target of his hatred. The clichéd example of this is the henpecked husband who cannot stand up to his wife, so attacks other women.

Another idea for elaborating the → in the A→C equation, is that of **'consistency'**. From this perspective the criminal actions are seen as a reflection of how the offender would act in a non-criminal context. I drew on this for the first major police enquiry I contributed to (Canter, 1994) by reversing the basic psychological idea that the best predictor of future behaviour is previous behaviour. In other words, the actions in crime will have precursors in the offender's earlier behaviour. In that case the offender approached women and started to talk to them before he attacked them. I therefore proposed that he had in the past had an established relationship with a woman. But he did attack his victims so the argument followed that he would have some known history of attacking the woman with whom he had had a relationship. It turned out that the person convicted of the attacks was known to the police because of a violent assault on his estranged wife.

A more general clinical framework may draw on ideas about the mental disturbances and personality disorders that are apparent in the actions in a crime. A stark illustration of this are those killers who mutilate the bodies of their victims. This is often characteristic of a person who is out of touch with reality, having some form of psychotic illness, unable to relate to others as sentient human beings. Such inference models may draw on years of experience with forensic patients, but they are extremely difficult to substantiate on statistically based samples because of the difficulty of obtaining really clear data.

One way in which the statistical and clinical perspectives apparently overlaps is the widely quoted dichotomy offered by special agents from the Federal Bureau of Investigation (FBI) (Douglas, Ressler, & Hartman, 1986). They claim that serial killers are either 'organised' or 'disorganised'. The former are carefully planned crimes, carried out methodically, destroying or concealing forensic evidence. By contrast 'disorganised' crimes are opportunistic and chaotic. The inferences drawn from this distinction are really a distillation of the 'consistency' hypothesis already mentioned. Organised crimes will be committed by organised offenders. These individuals will consequently be expected to be intelligent with good interpersonal skills, living apparently effective lives. Those who carry out disorganised crimes are hypothesised to be reckless and inexperienced.

The underlying argument behind the inference process for the FBI dichotomy seems reasonable. We all know people whose activities reflect how careful and well organised they are or how messy and confused they are. I suspect this is why this idea has gained such a following, being quoted in textbooks and even finding its way into Hollywood films such as the brilliant *Seven*. However, a particular advantage of these speculations by FBI agents is that they are specific enough to be open to empirical test. When such tests are carried out, they fail, as I have shown (Canter, Alison, Alison, & Wentink, 2004). What emerges is that in order to be able to kill without getting caught so that you can kill again, the villain has to be reasonably organised. All serial killers therefore have many characteristics of the 'organised' type. It is the variety of ways of being disorganised on top of these characteristics, which distinguishes serial killers from each other.

In a comprehensive review of serial killer investigations, Morton, Tillman, and Gaines (2014, p. 5) made clear that

> applying the organized/disorganized dichotomy to active serial murder cases has limited utility in serial investigations. Further, the NCAVC [National Center for the Analysis of Violent Crime] has not embraced the organized/disorganized dichotomy for over 10 years and does not currently utilize the typology when reviewing cases in day-to-day operations.

Intriguingly Holmes and Holmes (1998) offer a more detailed, seven-fold typology of serial killers. But on closer examination this is just an elaboration of the FBI dichotomy. The overlap between the different 'types' is considerable, which makes it rather ambiguous to actually apply to any case. It also fails to be substantiated when actual data is tested (Canter & Wentink, 2004).

The message that emerges from the scientific tests of these proposed typologies is that there are indeed a set of statistical assumptions underlying the proposed categories. This is that the actions, or characteristics, which are used to specify any particular type are (a) more likely to co-occur with each other in any actual crime than with other features, and (b) there will be little overlap between the aspects used to describe any particular type and those of other types. For example, if not leaving any forensic evidence at the crime scene is taken to be characteristic of an 'organised' killer and leaving the crime scene in a chaotic mess is taken as definitive of a 'disorganised' killer, then it would not be expected that all forensic evidence had been removed from a chaotic crime scene. Many such relationships, and lack of them, can be statistically tested and the overall pattern of actions and characteristics revealed. It is these studies that show the weaknesses of the typologies proposed by FBI agents and Holmes and Holmes. It is perhaps not surprising that these typologies fail empirically based statistical tests. The authors of these typologies clearly knew nothing of psychometrics. They based their proposals on little more than anecdotes.

THE CHALLENGE OF MAKING PROFILING INFERENCES

I will be frank. As far as I can tell from published accounts, no one has been able to develop a convincing, empirically based model that allows reliable inferences to be made about offenders from their criminal actions. Those few people around the world who do offer 'profiles' to investigations draw on whatever research they consider relevant and their own knowledge and experience. Increasingly, those who understand the challenges of drawing these inferences have moved away from calling themselves 'profilers'. The agents of the FBI who provide guidance to law enforcement organisations call their work 'criminal investigative analysis'. That handful of erstwhile students of mine who operate within the UK National Crime Faculty call themselves **'behavioural investigative advisors'** (BIAs).

Those working as BIAs have now been contributing to police investigations for over 20 years. In that time, they have broadened the range, style, and variety of contributions beyond the original notion of creating a 'pen picture' that describes an unknown assailant. This includes contributions from specialists about the likely location of an offender's base – geographical offender profiling – described in Study 4. As the head of the BIA unit Lee Rainbow puts it when describing how their role has evolved:

> [They] are no longer isolated experts restricted to generating inferences about offenders in an isolated void … BIAs can offer senior investigating officers an additional perspective and decision support throughout a serious crime investigation through pragmatic application of behavioural science theory, research and experience … and the overall philosophy of providing an enhanced understanding of the criminal event.
>
> (Rainbow & Gregory, 2011, p. 33)

Of note in this account is the "enhanced understanding of the criminal event". This implies developing a view of what the criminal might have been doing before, during, and after the crime, and what psychological processes might have been involved. For example, being aware that a person who rapes strangers often spends a lot of time looking for vulnerable victims, draws attention to what opportunity a crime scene may reveal about where an offender may wait for a suitable moment and person to attack. With their background in psychology, the BIA may also augment the knowledge and understanding of police investigators about unusual types of criminals, for instance those who violently mutilate their victims.

The insights offered by a BIA are therefore derived partly from a knowledge of the research available and partly from their experience of contributing to many investigations. All this is combined with an intelligent understanding of criminality and what sort of information law enforcement agencies can deal with. This leads the way to a realisation, as with all the studies in this book, that making inferences about the relationship between an offence and offender is an area of great interest and challenge. How can a process be developed that will allow useful inferences to be reliably and validly made about an offender from what information is available about a crime they have committed? It is useful to note that this can be regarded as reverse engineering the task psychologists usually face.

Usually psychologists have a person in front of them, who they can interview or test in various ways. That is, they establish the characteristics of that individual. What they then try to do is make some inference about what the person will do in the future. How well they will do at school, what job they'd be good at, and so on; their future actions. The profiling challenge is the opposite. The actions are known, but it is the characteristics that are to be inferred. It may therefore be possible to utilise some psychological theories. But before considering one possibility of doing that, which I find very interesting, it is useful to consider how crimes are usually solved.

How Crimes are Solved

Crimes are usually solved by one or more of the following routes:

- Offenders confess. Many murderers call the police and admit to what they've done.

- Someone recognises, or knows, the culprit and reports him/her to the police

- Criminals are caught in the act.

- Forensic evidence, such as fingerprints, DNA, fibres, and/or CCTV recordings link a suspect to the crime scene.

- Detectives know who has committed one crime and link other crimes to that (Fox et al., 2020).

It is in the absence of any of this evidence that investigators have to trawl through possible suspects. The list of these is drawn from people in police records who have committed similar crimes in the past, names offered by members of the public, especially police informers, and those that emerge as suspicious in house-to-house enquiries. In a major police investigation into a serious crime such as a murder or a series of stranger rapes, many hundreds of potential suspects may be elicited. It is when there is none of the sort of evidence listed above that investigators may turn to 'profilers' for assistance. This may be either to help indicate how to elicit potential suspects, or to prioritise those identified in order to focus police resources on the most likely suspects.

How Useful are 'Offender Profiles'?

An important aspect of this much broader range of contributions to investigations from behavioural science is that the question of the value of these is not an easy one to answer. It is certainly never the case, as portrayed in some fiction, that a psychological profile solves a crime. There may be an aspect of the investigation that is stimulated by a suggestion from what is known about the actions of certain types of criminals. It may even be that the contribution of a 'profiler' indicates new lines of enquiry that enables the senior investigating officer to get support to continue the investigation. It is also inevitable that an intelligent, informed person who has been contributing to a variety of investigations into serious crimes for over 20 years has a lot of useful experience to draw upon. In effect, such people become knowledgeable detectives, whose scientific, psychological background gives them a rational perspective that can be of great utility.

Types of Multiple Murderers

It is also important to distinguish between very different **types of multiple murderers** – people who kill more than one person. These are usually very different from people who kill just one person. Those 'one-off' killers typically kill someone they know in an outburst, as interestingly reviewed by Miethe and Regoeczi (2004). Although these one-off killers may have a history of violence, they often do not go on to kill other people. Indeed, if they are arrested for that one killing then their imprisonment will limit the possibility of their killing again. It is therefore likely that the arrest and conviction of some 'one-off' killers does stop them becoming serial killers. These people may therefore be similar to others who do go on to kill, not get caught, and kill again.

People who kill a number of people fall into rather distinct subsets:

- *Spree killers* are those who kill a number of people in a great outburst in one short period of time. They are usually driven by anger against an institution or a particular group of people. The horrific school shootings that are almost endemic in the United States fall into this category. I think many outrages that are given the label 'terrorist', such as Brenton Tarrant in Christchurch, New Zealand in 2019, or Anders Breivik in Oslo in July 2011, are of this form. I've likened these attacks to the biblical account of Samson pulling down the temple on himself to destroy his enemy, the Philistines (Canter, 2006). In other words, these outbursts can be understood as a form of suicide. In the United States, people who get themselves into a shoot-out by the police are sometimes described as creating 'suicide by cop'.

- *Contract killers*, or 'hit men', are people employed by a third party to murder an individual. The glamorisation of such people in the very popular *Killing Eve* television series is a totally inaccurate representation of such murderers. Various studies (notably Crumplin, 2009) have revealed that people 'contracted' to carry out a murder usually have some relationship or acquaintance with the person contracting them. The target is consequently often someone known by the person issuing the contract. Within a criminal organisation the process may be a little more distant, but still operates within the world of the criminals. I like to mention the description of such killers in the fascinating book *Tough Jews* (Cohen, 1999) about Jewish gangsters, in which one religious Jew, who is a contract killer, is described as refusing to kill anyone on the Sabbath because that is a day on which work is forbidden!

- *Killers for profit* are a relatively unusual group these days, but did exist in the past, as described by Bolitho (1926). These were people who set up processes whereby they could get financial benefit from the death of their victims. In the 1890s, serial killer H.H. Holmes even built special aspects of a building that became known as Murder Castle to be able to move the bodies. There are even cases of men and women who marry a number of times. Each time they murder their partner to obtain their wealth.

- *Serial killers* are usually specified as people who kill three or more people over a period of time with some form of interval (sometimes called a 'cooling-off period') between each killing. They prey on vulnerable victims, such as those who are homeless, street sex workers, or youngsters away from home who will not be missed. The crucial aspect is that the murders occur in episodes rather than in one outpouring of violence. Consequently, even a person who kills two people at different points in time may be given the label 'serial killer'.

All these types of multiple killers vary within each subset. It is therefore misleading to think of one 'profile' for any given type, although as noted, there will be some general characteristics that each subset has in common. In this study it is possible to explore the ways in which serial killers differ from each other.

A NARRATIVE APPROACH

I come back to the central, fascinating question of what psychological processes can be drawn on to facilitate the association of actions with characteristics. These may help to explain why the statistical results of EBOP occur, or in the absence of such data and findings provide the basis for hypotheses that elaborate the profiling equation. Various models of how profiling inferences can be made have been published. The most direct is presented in Canter and Youngs (2009).

The first issue discussed there, as mentioned earlier, is the need to identify what is 'salient' about the actions in a crime. Many things can happen in even a brief, straightforward crime, like, say, a street mugging. In rapes and murders there is the possibility of even more variation. It is the variations that provide the basis for any inference. For illustration, in a rape the sexual activity is what defines it as rape. Just indicating there was sexual activity is not providing much basis, therefore, for distinguishing one rapist from another. But how the sexual acts were carried out and all the actions surrounding them, such as how the victim was approached or controlled, can vary considerably. It is therefore these variations that provide an indication of what is salient in the crime.

Beyond identifying what is distinguishing about a set of offence activities there are a number of processes that can be drawn on to provide the bases for linking actions and characteristics. The following list is drawn from Canter and Youngs (2009, p. 163).

1. *Intellect.* What intelligence level is indicated by the way the crimes are committed? This can lead to inferences about previous education or possible employment.

2. *Familiarity.* What do the actions indicate about what or who, when or where the offender is aware of and familiar with?

3. *Skills.* What particular skills does the offender have, such as the use of a firearm or other weapons?

4. *Knowledge.* Do the actions reveal any special knowledge of people or circumstances?

5. *Emotionality.* How much is the offender in control of their emotions? Do they exhibit rage or a very calm way of dealing with victims?

6. *Social interactions.* How readily does the offender engage with victims? Does the approach and contact with the victims indicate a facility with social interaction or a lack of it?

7. *Predilections.* What do particular aspects of any deviant activity reveal about preferences for certain activities or victims? The most obvious of these are sexual preferences and victim ages.

It has to be borne in mind that there is not usually simple consistency in an offender's actions over a series of crimes. Summaries of crimes, often over a long period of time – many years in some cases – mask information about the developmental aspects. However, the way a serial killer may change activities has always to be taken into account, as skills are developed and how to reduce the risks taken in earlier crimes are thought about. The other question that needs to be considered is how did serial offenders get away with so many crimes?

There is a theoretically rich approach to developing inferences to link actions and characteristics that I have been exploring for some time now (Canter & Youngs, 2012a, 2012b, 2015; Youngs, Canter, & Carthy, 2016). That is, to consider the 'implicit personal narrative' the offender may be living out. This is an approach that brings together many different aspects of the criminal's psychology – their distorted ways of justifying their crimes to themselves, the nature of their emotional disturbance, the ways in which they see themselves and others, as well as the psychological and social aspects of their experiences. For the present study, a summary of four dominant narratives have been identified in a number of different studies (best summarised in Canter & Youngs, 2009, chap. 6; 2015; and more recently elaborated by Yaneva, Ioannou, Hammond, & Synnot, 2018), and is listed below as a basis for consideration and discussion when carrying out the proposed study.

•   *A hero's expressive quest.* This a person for whom the actions reveal directly the sort of person he is and the intellectual abilities that guide his actions.

•   *A professional's adaptive adventure.* Here the particular interpersonal skills and other abilities are harnessed to generate controlled, determined actions that reflect his professionalism in other contexts.

•   *A revenger's conservative tragedy.* The anger, reflected in dealing with the victim as some sort of representation of a particular subset of people the offender wishes to annihilate, indicates aspects of the killer's background and previous relationships.

•   *A victim's integrative irony.* The aspects of the individual's predilections and distinct characteristics that give rise to the crimes. They are understood as the direct causes of the criminal actions.

PROPOSED STUDY: MATCHING ACTIONS AND CHARACTERISTICS

For the present study, examples drawn from serial killers are chosen. This is because of the general fascination with these crimes and murderers – a cliché in many crime dramas. It is also because there is a lot of information about these readily available. But with more intensive searches any other types of crimes could be used in a similar study.

It is important to emphasise that in an actual investigation the actions are those features of a crime that would be known before the offender is identified. The killers' reasons for the killing may be surmised but are not overtly available. The nature of the victims, however, for instance, their age and gender would be crucial information. The method of killing and disposing of the bodies, or keeping things (or body parts) of the victims would be another aspect that may be regarded as distinguishing. The activities surrounding the killing, such as torture and/or sexual activity would all be relevant. Some of these facts would, of course, only be available once the bodies of the victims have been found. For the examples in the appendix at the end of this chapter, I have tried to keep the information as overt as possible.

It is important to emphasise again that in an actual investigation the linking of crimes to one offender, identifying a crime series, would draw heavily on the actions in the crime. Are they similar enough to indicate it is a 'style' or 'theme' of one person's crimes? This makes many assumptions about the consistency of an offender. But it has to be said, that in many countries, where violent crime is relatively rare, if a number of relatively similar attacks on strangers, whether murder or rape, occur in a particular area over a distinct period of time, then they are likely to have been committed by the same person. In the proposed study I am assuming the crimes have already been linked. Only a general description of the crimes is given, not accounts of different crimes in a linked series.

The time frame and locations of the crimes, where the victims disappeared from, and the actual places where the bodies were discovered are all very important for a real investigation. But that information would distort the linking of crimes to offenders in the present study, so it has been left out.

The characteristics that are of use to detectives seeking possible suspects are also those that are overtly available. They can be used to search through criminal records, from suggested suspects that come from the public or informants, to elicit people who can be considered. If there are many possibilities, then putting them in some sort of order of priority to focus police resources on can be assisted by considering the likely characteristics of the offender.

In the British context where the police have a number of possible suspects in a major enquiry, especially of a serial killer, then they carry out what is known as a TIE. That is, they **T**race the suspect. They **I**dentify the person they've traced to ensure they are who they say they are. Finally, they explore that person's alibis or other reasons why the person can be **E**liminated from the investigation. This process usually reduces the number of suspects to a handful that can be carefully focused on to obtain evidence for a conviction, which may include an intensive interview, DNA samples, and related forensic considerations.

It can be seen that in the investigative process of eliciting suspects, prioritising them, and then focusing on the those prioritised more closely, inner thought processes of the criminals, or subtle aspects of their personality are more difficult to utilise. Their skills and well-known aspects of their relationships could be used to filter the many possible suspects. But crucial information is where to look in criminal records, if it is assumed the offender has been arrested before.

The present study explores the challenge of the profiling equation in an experimental set-up. Sets of details of crimes are presented and sets of information about offenders. The participants' task is to match the correct characteristics to the crimes. As in all experiments, there are many aspects of this study that are artificial. Only a limited number of murders and killers can be made available. The information about the offences and offenders is already available in a digested form. Perhaps the aspect of the material available that is most different from a real investigation is that crimes have already been linked to the same offender. Determining which crimes form part of a series, in the absence of clear forensic evidence linking them, is often a crucial part of the detective work.

Objectives

The central purpose of the study is to open up discussion about what is involved in offender profiling, the challenges of carrying it out, and the bases on which it can be done. The study also illustrates a common form of experimental procedure.

Method

The exact number of participants and cases to be used depends on the resources you have available. I would suggest that half a dozen serial killer details with a dozen or more participants will give you enough details as an exploratory study to understand how this experimental design works and to get some interesting results.

Equipment

You need to obtain details of the backgrounds and characteristics of serial killers and their crimes. There are many such details available on the Internet. Just use the search term 'serial killers' and you will find a plethora of material. The record of court cases and other legal information called *Westlaw* is also an excellent resource, usually available through university law departments.

Divide this material into two sets:

- *One deals with the details of the crimes: the actions.* Remove from these any identifying features, such as exactly when and where the crimes took place, any names of people involved, or other information that would give direct clues to the perpetrators.

- *The other provides details of the killers: the characteristics.* These need to provide information on the background of the killers and any other general information that does not have an obvious link to, for example, where the crimes occurred, or when they happened.

The artificiality of these creations will be clear. In an actual investigation, where and when the crimes occur are crucial to eliciting suspects and then checking their alibis, eventually seeking evidence to obtain a conviction. In this experiment the focus is on the possibility of linking details of what happens in a crime to the characteristics of the offender in the absence of any forensic evidence or other information pointing to a specific culprit. Such association between crime details and features of the offender provides the basis for considering the inferences that allow those associations to be proposed.

Some examples of the material that can be used are given in the appendix at the end of this chapter. I have deliberately arranged the material so that the actions listed 1 to 4 do not map directly on to the characteristics A to D. This is how you should organise your material so that respondents do not get any clues from the set-up as to which goes with which. I've given the actual relationships in the appendix at the end of this chapter.

Process

The study consists essentially of giving participants the full set of actions and characteristics to read through, preferably each presented on a separate card or piece of paper. They are then asked to match the characteristics to the appropriate actions. It would also be very instructive to ask them to make a note of what the basis was for their assignment of a particular action set to a particular characteristic set. A possible pro forma for them to complete is given in Table 3.1.

One of the weaknesses of the simple approach of assigning one action set to one characteristics set is that participants are choosing between the examples given. Once they've chosen one set, it is excluded from the possibility of being related to anything else. In this way they are not really looking for the inherent link between any pair of sets. They are seeing which of the sets on offer is most plausibly linked to which other set. It is not a direct exploration of A → C inferences, but a comparison of the most likely links. That is still interesting to explore but if you used a more quantitative approach you could examine how much each action set seemed to link to each characteristic set. This can be done by asking people to give a number between 1 and 10 for how likely they think each set of actions matches each set of characteristics: 1 would indicate no match at all, 10 means they are certainly matched. That way you could explore whether there were some characteristics that seemed to fit all the action sets, or some none. An example of a possible pro forma for them to complete is given in Table 3.2.

One other check you need to make is whether any participant recognises any of the descriptions and therefore may have some prior knowledge to use when making a decision. These people should be analysed separately. They could be wrong! But they are likely to distort the results so should not be included in the general mix of data.

Recording the results

Table 3.1 Example of completed response form to be filled in by each person for the straightforward linking assignment

Participant (name or code number)				
Which set of characteristics do you think is associated with the following action sets?	1	2	3	4
Action set choice	A	C	D	B
Could you please indicate why you made that decision	He seemed to be gay and his victims were boys	Not sure, but keeping the body parts was odd	Wasn't he just very violent throughout his life?	This was the only match left
If you recognised any of the descriptions please indicate here				

Table 3.2 Example of completed response form to be filled in by each person in the quantitative assessment procedure

Participant (name or code number)																
How likely do you think it is that this set of actions were carried out by the person described in this set of characteristics? Use numbers from 1 to 10, with 1 meaning very unlikely indeed and 10 meaning almost certainly	A1	A2	A3	A4	B1	B2	B3	B4	C1	C2	C3	C4	D1	D2	D3	D4

Table 3.3 Possible frequency with which characteristics could be linked to actions for 20 respondents using the four sets of material in the appendix

Characteristics / Actions	A	B	C	D	Totals
1	0	10*	5	5	20
2	6	4	5*	5	20
3	12*	2	6	0	20
4	2	4	4	10*	20
Totals	20	20	20	20	80

* Indicates the correct match of the material in the appendix.

Analyses

For the responses collected in the 'simple' choice from Table 3.1 the frequency with which each action is linked to each characteristic could then be calculated, as in Table 3.3. This table assumes you have 20 participants.

If these were actual results, they indicate some interesting findings.

- *How good are people at matching the material from these rather denuded examples?* The frequencies in the cells with an * are the frequencies of correct judgements. In this case there are 37 correct judgements out of the 80 possible correct. That is 46% correct. You could calculate the probability of getting correct assignments by chance (25%?) and then calculate the statistical probability of this being above chance, for example by using the chi-square inferential statistic.

- *Which correct links are people best at?* In Table 3.3 it is A3 that has the highest number of correct hits (Dennis Rader in our examples). Why might that be? By looking at respondents' explanations it may be possible to see the basis of their inferences.

- *What do people make most mistakes about?* In Table 3.3 it is serial killer C (John Wayne Gacy) who is most often mistakenly assigned. Only 5 people got this right out of 20 – approximately chance level.

Exploring the bases of respondents' inferences

The statements people make about how/why they made the links they did are examples of what might be thought of a 'naive profiling'. Unless, of course, respondents have studied the topic. Do such 'experts' do any better? Comparing experts and non-experts in their judgements would be an interesting study. Even a comparison of psychology and non-psychology students would be informative.

The reasons people give for their links open up the possibility of content analysis, as discussed in Study 7. There are more details in that chapter, so only a brief outline of the potential process will be described here.

Analysis of the quantitative version of this study

Table 3.2 provides scores, ranging from 1 to 10 for all respondents across the 16 possible combinations of actions and characteristics. The means of these scores can be inserted into a similar table to that in Table 3.3. Because they are means rather than frequencies, they can be analysed using more sophisticated statistics. This can allow more subtle exploration of the relationships people assign and which actions or characteristics are most readily dealt with. You might find, for instance, that some actions or some characteristics are not used at all, presumably because respondents cannot make any sense of them and how inferences may be derived from them. This in turn could help to reveal what it is that people draw on to make inferences. How do these relate to the arguments of the psychological bases for inferences indicated above and in the 'profiling' literature.

One issue that discussion of the results of this study is likely to give rise to are all the other aspects of the crimes and criminals that are not mentioned in the examples I've prepared here. At the very least, this indicates the inevitable limitations of any 'tidy' experiment. For the examples here, if the dates of the crimes and their locations had been included, as well as the ages of the killers and where they lived, it would have been very easy to link the actions to the characteristics. Indeed, if you explore how these killers were eventually caught you will discover that it was invariably through 'good conventional police work'. Details of where victims were last seen, suspicions offered by members of the public, forensic evidence such as DNA or fibres, and many other day-to-day aspects of detective work without any intervention of a 'profiler'. This does not invalidate the value of this study though. The study opens up the consideration of what it is about the behaviour of offenders that relates to their psychology.

The study also allows consideration of how people make inferences about the characteristics of offenders. This can open up many issues about the assumptions that are commonly made about the possibilities of 'profiling'. Also, by comparing the judgements of men with those of women, experienced investigators with members of the public, older people with younger, those with different personalities, or any combination of these, and more, a framework could be built of what it is about the people acting as 'profilers' in your study that influences how they make their decisions.

One further aspect of the exploration of the basis for making inferences about offenders is to consider the four dominant narratives that were outlined earlier. Do these relate in any ways to the offenders and their characteristics as revealed in the summaries you have available? By getting participants to verbalise their thought processes, known as verbal protocol analysis (see, for example, Austin & Delaney, 1998), will also help to reveal the way they are making their inferences.

OTHER STUDIES THAT COULD USE THIS RESEARCH DESIGN

The present study has focused on serial killers, but as mentioned earlier, any type of criminal activity is potentially open to this form of study. The challenge is getting the examples of actions and characteristics to create the study. There is a lot of information on the Internet about one-off murders and other types of multiple killers. There are also some details about serious crimes such as bank robbery or even contract killers. Accounts of who is involved, and what they do, for more common crimes such as burglary and car theft are less frequently available.

QUESTIONS FOR DISCUSSION

1. What do you take 'profiling' to mean? How might it be useful in a criminal investigation?

2. What limitations do you think 'offender profiling' has?

3. Consider your actions in specific situations (e.g. when shopping for shoes, or preparing for a meeting). Do you think your actions in those situations are consistent enough to be used to infer your characteristics? What do you think the actions reveal about you?

4. What circumstances could reduce the relationship between a person's actions and their characteristics?

5. Find an example of a 'profile' in use in crime fiction, or factual accounts. What evidence does the 'profiler' draw on (if any). How plausible are the 'profiler's' claims?

FURTHER READING

An early book that tries to summarise what was known about psychological profiling, covering arson, rape, and paedophilia is:

Holmes, R.M., & Holmes, S.T. (1996). *Profiling violent crimes: An investigative tool.* London: Sage.

Since then there have been many other books and sections in major forensic psychology textbooks. Amazon gives 146 books in a search for 'offender profiling'. Most of these are summaries of other books or personal accounts of working with offenders or in police investigations.

Something very different (if you can get hold of a second-hand copy) is the summary of a major study of over 1,500 men convicted of a wide variety of sex offences:

Genhard, P.H., Gagnon, J.H., Pomeroy, W.B., & Christenson, C.V. (1965). *Sex offenders: An analysis of types.* New York, NY: Harper & Row.

An overview of criminals' accounts, covering a very wide range of offences, also of relevance to Study 8, is:

Pogrebin, M. (Ed.) (2004). About criminals: A view of the offender's world. London: Sage.

REFERENCES

Austin, J., & Delaney, P.F. (1998). Protocol analysis as a tool for behavior analysis. *Analysis of Verbal Behavior*, 15, 41–56. https://doi.org/10.1007/BF03392922.

Bolitho, W. (1926). *Murder for profit.* New York, NY: Garden City.

Canter, D. (1994). Criminal shadows: Inside the mind of the serial killer. London: HarperCollins.

Canter, D. (2006). The Samson syndrome: Is there a kamikaze psychology? *21st Century Society*, 1(2), 107–127.

Canter, D. (2011). Resolving the offender 'profiling equations' and the emergence of an investigative psychology. *Current Directions in Psychological Science*, 20(1), 5–10.

Canter, D., Alison, L.J., Alison, E., & Wentink, N. (2004). The organized/disorganized typology of serial murder: Myth or model? *Psychology, Public Policy, and Law*, 10(3), 293–320.

Canter, D., & Wentink, N. (2004). An empirical test of the Holmes and Holmes serial murder typology. *Criminal Justice and Behavior*, 31(4), 489–515.

Canter, D., & Youngs, D. (2009). *Investigative psychology: Offender profiling and the analysis of criminal action.* Chichester, UK: Wiley.

Canter, D. & Youngs, D. (2012a). Narratives of criminal action and forensic psychology. *Legal and Criminological Psychology*, 17, 262–272. doi: 10.1111/j.2044-8333.2012.02050.x.

Canter, D. & Youngs, D. (2012b). Sexual and violent offenders' victim role assignment: A general model of offending style. *Journal of Forensic Psychiatry & Psychology*, 23(3), 297–326. doi: 10.1080/14789949.2012.690102.

Canter, D., & Youngs, D. (2015). The LAAF procedure for exploring offenders' narrative. *Howard Journal of Criminal Justice*, 54(3), 219–236.

Cohen, R. (1999). *Tough Jews.* New York, NY: Random House.

Crumplin, P. (2009). *Contract murder, in profiling violent crime* (D. Canter & D. Youngs, Eds.). Aldershot, UK: Ashgate.

Douglas, J.E., Ressler, R.K., & Hartman, C.R. (1986). Criminal profiling from crime scene analysis. Behavioral Sciences and the Law, 4(4), 401–421.

Fox, B.H., & Farrington, D.P. (2015). An experimental evaluation on the utility of burglary profiles applied in active police investigations. Criminal Justice and Behavior, 42(2), 156–175. https://doi.org/10.1177/0093854814548446.

Fox, B., Farrington, D.P., Kapardis, A., & Hambly, O.C. (2020). *Evidence-based offender profiling.* London: Routledge.

Holmes, R.M., & Holmes, S.T. (1998). *Serial murder* (2nd ed.). Thousand Oaks, CA: Sage.

Miethe, T.D., & McCorkle, R. (1998). *Crime profiles: The anatomy of dangerous persons, places, and situations.* Los Angeles, CA: Roxbury.

Miethe, T.D., & Regoeczi, W.C. (2004). *Rethinking homicide*. Cambridge, UK: University Press.

Morton, R.J., Tillman, J.M., & Gaines, S.J. (2014). *Serial murder: Pathways for investigations*. Washington, DC: Federal Bureau of Investigation, National Center for the Analysis of Violent Crime.

Rainbow, L., & Gregory, A. (2011). What behavioural investigative advisors actually do. In L. Alison & L. Rainbow (Eds.), Professionalizing offender profiling (pp. 18–34). New York, NY: Routledge.

Yaneva, M., Ioannou, M., Hammond, L., & Synnot, J. (2018). Differentiating contract killers: A narrative-based approach. *Howard Journal of Crime and Justice*, 57(1), 107–123. https://doi.org/10.1111/hojo.12243.

Youngs, D. (2008). Contemporary challenges in investigative psychology: Revisiting the canter offender profiling equations. In D. Canter & R. Zukauskiene (Eds.), *Psychology and law: Bridging the gap* (pp. 23–30). Aldershot, UK: Ashgate.

Youngs, D.E., Canter, D., & Carthy, N. (2016). The offender's narrative: Unresolved dissonance in life as a film (LAAF) responses. *Legal and Criminological Psychology*, 21(2), 251–265.

Appendix: Examples of Actions and Characteristics of Serial Killers

Four Sets of Actions

1

Committed the rape, murder, and dismemberment of men and boys. Many of his murders involved necrophilia, cannibalism, and the permanent preservation of body parts – typically all or part of the skeleton. In on murder he bludgeoned his victim with a 10 lb dumb-bell. While the victim was unconscious, he strangled him to death with the bar of the dumb-bell, then stripped the clothes from his body before masturbating as he stood above the corpse. The following day he dissected the body in his basement; he later buried the remains in a shallow grave in his backyard before, several weeks later, unearthing the remains and paring the flesh from the bones. He dissolved the flesh in acid before flushing the solution down the toilet; he crushed the bones with a sledgehammer and scattered them in the woodland behind the family home.

2

He raped, tortured, and murdered many teenage boys and young men. His first victim was stabbed to death, all the others were murdered by either asphyxiation or strangulation with a makeshift garrotte. He buried most of his victims in the crawl space of his home. Three other victims were buried elsewhere on his property, while the bodies of his last four known victims were discarded in the local river.

3

Killed ten people. He sent taunting letters to police and newspapers describing the details of his crimes. After a decade-long hiatus he resumed sending letters, leading to his arrest and subsequent guilty plea. The murders were carried out by strangling or suffocating his victims, although in one case he stabbed the victim to death. In another he hung the victim from a drainpipe. He killed four members of one family: two parents aged 38 and 33, and two children aged 9 and 11. One woman he murdered was 53 years old. He left her body in a ditch. His victims were often found bound with tape or ropes. He stabbed and strangled a young college student and shot her brother. One victim was raped and choked.

4

He kidnapped, raped, and murdered numerous young women and girls. He would typically approach his victims in public places, feigning injury or disability, or impersonating an authority figure, before overpowering, raping, and killing them in secluded locations. He sometimes revisited his secondary crime scenes, grooming and performing sexual acts with the decomposing corpses until putrefaction and destruction by wild animals made any further interactions impossible. He decapitated many victims and kept some of the severed heads as mementos in his apartment. On a few occasions, he broke into dwellings at night and bludgeoned his victims as they slept.

Four Sets of Characteristics

A

From a young age, he had sadistic sexual fantasies involving bondage and torture, and exhibited zoosadism by torturing, killing, and hanging small animals. He also acted out sexual fetishes for autoerotic asphyxiation and cross-dressing, and would often spy on female neighbours while dressed in women's clothing and masturbate with a rope around his neck. He spent four years in the air force. He worked in the meat department of a supermarket where his mother was a bookkeeper. He married and they had two children. He obtained a qualification in electronics and a bachelor's degree in administration of justice. He installed security alarms as part of his job and was census field operations supervisor before the national census. He became a dogcatcher and compliance officer. In this position, neighbours recalled him as being sometimes overzealous and extremely strict. One neighbour complained he killed her dog for no reason. He was a member of the Christ Lutheran Church and had been elected president of the church council.

B

He was described as an energetic and happy child until the age of 4, when surgery to correct a double hernia seemed to effect a change in him. Noticeably subdued, he became increasingly withdrawn following the birth of his younger brother and the family's frequent moves. By his early teens, he was disengaged, tense, and largely friendless. By his early twenties he was an alcoholic. He dropped out of university after half a semester, and his recently remarried father insisted that he join the army. He enlisted, and was posted to Germany. His drinking persisted, so he was discharged. Following his discharge, he was arrested for disorderly conduct and subsequently for indecent exposure. Then again when two boys accused him of masturbating in front of them. Although he was diagnosed with borderline personality disorder, schizotypal personality disorder, and a psychotic disorder, he was found to be legally sane at his trial.

C

As a child, he was overweight and not athletic. He was close to his two sisters and mother but endured a difficult relationship with his father, an alcoholic who was physically abusive to his wife and children. Throughout his childhood, he strove to make his stern father proud of him, but seldom received his approval. When he was 7 his father was informed that his son and another boy had been caught sexually fondling a young girl. He's father whipped him with a razor strop as punishment. The same year he was molested by a family friend. At the age of 18, he worked as an assistant for a local politician. The same year he became a Democratic candidate. He left the family home for three months and found work within the ambulance service before he was transferred to work as a mortuary attendant. Upon his return home he graduated from a business school and took a job as a management trainee and them as a salesman, eventually being promoted to manager. He married a co-worker. Her father subsequently bought three fast-food restaurants that he managed. He was very active in a local charitable organisation. He dressed up as a clown at charitable services, at fund-raising events, parades, and children's parties.

D

After graduating from high school, he spent a year at one university before he transferred to another to study Chinese. He had a relationship with young woman before dropping out of college and working at a series of minimum-wage jobs. He briefly worked as a driver and bodyguard for a politician campaigning to be a lieutenant governor. He later enrolled as a psychology major, becoming an honour's student, subsequently he worked on a suicide hotline, where he was described as kind, solicitous, and empathetic. He later attended law school but never completed. He had some intense relationships with women that he suddenly ended without explanation.

MATCHES

A is Dennis Rader 3 are his crimes.

B is Jeffrey Dahmer 1 are his crimes.

C is John Wayne Gacy 2 are his crimes.

D is Ted Bundy 4 are his crimes.

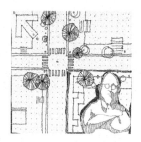

STUDY 4
Geographical offender profiling

SYNOPSIS

A study is proposed of how the locations where crimes are committed can be used to indicate where the offender may have a base, and other aspects of their criminality. This illustrates the design of a 'field experiment'. In this case the experiment consists of a comparison between urban and rural areas of patterns of criminal spatial activity. The empirical background to this is described, drawing on what is known of the typical distances offenders travel from their home, as well as a common spatial formation of crimes around the home. Theories explaining these findings are considered, notably cognitive representations of places. Ways of evaluating the effectiveness of any geographical profiling method are discussed.

SOME KEY CONCEPTS

- field experiment
- journey to crime
- marauder
- decay functions
- buffer zone
- mental maps
- routine activity theory
- propinquity
- morphology
- domocentricity.

OVERVIEW

Over the past quarter of a century there has been a considerable amount of research on where serial offenders commit their crimes. In particular the significance of where the offender has a base has been found often, but not always, to relate in a predictable way to where the crimes are committed. This in turn carries the possibility of indicating the area in which an offender may reside by studying the locations of a linked series of crimes. Using the process of examining crime locations to indicate the area of an offender's base has become known as 'geographical profiling' (in North America 'geographic profiling' or sometimes 'geoprofiling').

This is now a very large area of research, in part because law enforcement agencies around the world now systematically collect information about where crimes occur and where convicted offenders live. Although police were very reluctant to make such information available to me when I first became involved in contributing to investigations (Canter, 1994), that has changed considerably over recent years. Many researchers in different countries now get access, under appropriate confidentiality and security conditions, to police databases.

The access to actual offence and offender locations is crucial for this area of research. Crime locations and the places associated with the criminals who commit those crimes cannot be simulated in a laboratory. There have been some studies using data generated by various random number procedures, notably Bernasco (2007), but although the results are sometimes intriguing their application to real-world events is not very convincing.

The study proposed in this chapter is an introduction to the processes of geographical profiling and considers the psychological mechanisms that are hypothesised to generate the results that have been found. Most notably, models of cognitive representations of places are considered (drawing on the area of study known as environmental psychology) as ways of explaining why crime locations relate to where an offender has a base.

As well as the significance of an offender's base for understanding where crimes occur, there is also the opportunity for considering the spatial nature of criminal activity in any given area. Where the population is dense there are more possible targets for crime, and criminals can often move around without much notice being taken of them. Where there is only a sparse population there are fewer targets and people are less anonymous. This allows a **field experiment** to be conducted, in which the distribution of crimes, the distances offenders travel, and the effectiveness of geographical profiling can be compared between different situations. One such direct comparison is between crimes committed in an urban area and those in a rural area. In effect, urban/rural are similar to two experimental conditions (an independent variable, with the dependent variables being measures drawn from where the crimes are committed).

This study could have many different areas as independent variables, of different densities, different mixes of possible target (e.g. domestic or industrial, having different transport routes, and so on). For the present chapter I'll keep it simple with just two 'experimental' conditions: urban and rural.

This is not a 'pure' field experiment, though. That would require the random assignment of criminals to different areas! Not really a possibility.

FUNDAMENTAL CONCEPTS

Figure 4.1 is derived from the locations of an aggressive intruder who disturbed a number of households in a major city. Where do you think the offender lived? More importantly, how would you go about determining the area where he[1] had a base?

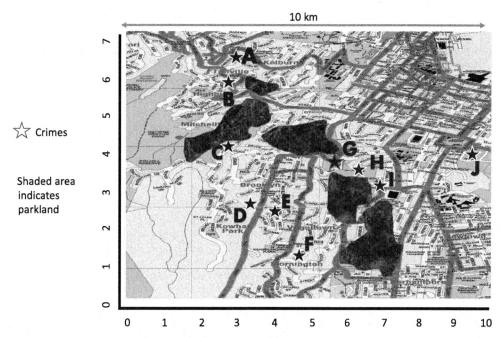

Figure 4.1 The locations where an aggressive intruder was seen. Can you guess where his base was?

To hypothesise where the intruder had a base you have to start by making some assumptions. Any scientific theory or model is built upon assumptions. For example, laws in physics assume that what is being described is not moving close to the speed of light, or near to a temperature of absolute zero, because in those extreme situations other laws are likely to be relevant. The definition of the circumstances under which any scientific principle applies is crucial.

The following assumptions, relevant to estimating where an offender is likely to live, are drawn from an extensive literature (e.g. Hammond, 2014; Laukkanen & Santtila, 2006; or the books listed in the references at the end of this chapter).

Domocentricity

The term '**domocentricity**' means that the home operates as a centre for activity. Somewhat more generally the assumption is that there is some sort of fixed location (a 'base') from which the criminal sets out to commit crimes. If the criminal is travelling, for instance if he has a job as a delivery driver, a very different pattern might be expected.

What is an offender's 'base'?

It is worth clarifying what is meant by a 'base'. Unless he is wandering around, 'of no fixed abode' as it is often called – in which case the geographical distribution of his crime will be very different – an offender will need to have somewhere as a starting point for his 'journey to crime'. This, most typically, is where he sleeps, because that is the most private and vulnerable location. He could set out to offend from a pub or other recreational base, or even where his girlfriend lives, or where he used to live. It could even be where he gets off from a public transport stop or station. This complexity is why I'm using the word 'base' – some researchers call it an 'anchor point', but let's think of it as where he lives.

Morphology

There is a recognisable spatial structure to the distribution of crimes. This derives from the possibility that the opportunities for crimes, such as possible victims, or houses with wealthy objects worth burgling, are distributed around the criminal's base.

It is important to emphasise that these are assumptions to help get started on working out how to decide the area in which an offender may be living. Such assumptions are not likely to be valid for all criminals. For example, it is more than likely that in many situations criminal opportunities are not evenly spread around a home. There may be parks, rivers, or transport routes, for example, that distort the distribution of possible targets. There are also likely to be uneven distributions of particular types of target. If a serial killer wants to find street-level sex workers, or homeless people, he needs to go the places he knows they will be.

However, many studies have shown that the following three assumptions are valid for a remarkably high proportion of many different types of crime, such as cybercrime (Butkovic, Mrdovic, Uludag, & Tanovic, 2019), serial killers (Canter, Coffey, Huntley, & Missen, 2000; Lundrigan & Canter, 2001), serial arson (Tamura & Suzuki, 1997), serial burglars in India (Sarangi & Youngs, 2006), serial rape (Santtila, Zappalà, Laukkanen, & Picozzi, 2003), and obscene phone calls (Ebberline, 2008):

(a) that the offender has a distinct base;

(b) that the home acts as a focus for criminal activity; and

(c) that the opportunities for crime are distributed around the home.

It has even been applied to locating the nests of bumble bees (Suzuki-Ohno, Inoue, & Ohno, 2010).

The idea is that an offender moves out from a base to commit a crime then returns, only to move out a similar distance from his base in a different direction, and so on, which maps out an area of criminal activity within which he lives. To give this some sort of identifying label I called this a **marauder** pattern, as illustrated in Figure 4.2. The intriguing hypothesis that arises from this is that a spatial pattern of crimes, as illustrated in Figure 4.2, may reveal the offender's base being within the area circumscribed by the crimes.

This idea of crimes being round a base can be converted into a number of different mathematical models allowing a direct test of hypotheses about how to locate the area where an offender is living. One of the first people to realise this was Stuart Kind, when he was head of the UK forensic science service. He looked at the series of rapes and some murders in Yorkshire in the early 1980s, referred to as the work of the 'Yorkshire Ripper'. Kind describes how he drew on his experience as an air force navigator during World War II (Kind, 1987). He proposed that the locations the Ripper selected were analogous to where fuel dumps would be left for aeroplanes to refuel. The objective was to make the overall average flight distance as small as possible. To estimate this the centre of gravity was calculated (an explanation of how to do this simple calculation is given in the appendix at the end of this chapter). Kind did, indeed, do this calculation for the location of the crimes of the Yorkshire Ripper. When the culprit was caught it turned out that he lived in the village indicated by that centre of gravity. The Ripper had been caught, though, before anyone took any notice of Kind's report.

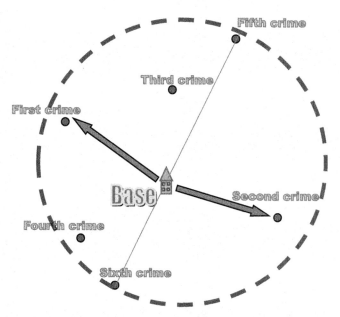

Figure 4.2 Marauder pattern of crime locations, illustrating the circle hypothesis

When I was asked by police officers from Scotland Yard, a few years after the Yorkshire Ripper investigation, to help catch the person responsible for a number of rapes and two murders around London (known as the 'Railways Rapist'), I was not told anything about Kind's work, which had not yet been published. I therefore worked from my own first principles. In this case the crimes moved further and further out over time, combined with it being clear that the offence activity was becoming more determined and carefully planned. This seemed to me to indicate that the early crimes were around the offender's home (Canter, 1994). That turned out to be very useful for the investigation. It helped the police to narrow their search of the people who had come to their notice to the one person who lived in the area circumscribed by those early crimes.

The success of my contribution to solving the Railway Rapist investigation opened the doors to police data so that I could start studying the frequency with which various models of offenders' crime location choice were valid. Still unaware of Kind's gravitational model, I decided to use the simplest way possible of calculating where an offender may be based. Working on the **morphology** assumption that the crimes would be spread around where the criminal lived, I proposed that one way of defining the area in which the base would be was to draw a circle to include all the crimes. My hypothesis was that the offender would live within that circle. But how can that circle be drawn? There are some complex geometries that will allow the smallest possible circle to be calculated, but the simplest way to do this is to select the two furthest crimes and use these as the diameter of a circle. In Figure 4.2 this is the line drawn from the fifth to the sixth crime. The dashed line defines the resulting circle.

As is clear in Figure 4.2, the crimes are not laid out in any sort of a circle. The circle is just the most elementary way to define the area. Such a circle has many weaknesses, not least that any crime at an extreme distance from a group of others will lead to a very wide area being defined by the circle.

The hypothesis then is that the base will be within this circle, probably closer to the centre of the circle than its circumference (as illustrated in Figure 4.2). To my surprise when this model was tested on various data sets it was found that well over half of offenders did indeed live within the circle (Canter & Larkin, 1993).

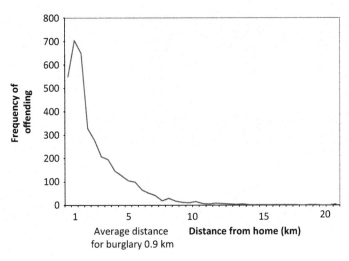

Figure 4.3 Typical decay function – here for burglaries

The existence of this process, a morphology of crimes around a base, raises the question of what psychological process gives rise to it. Two issues seem to me to help explain it.

Propinquity

The tendency for many criminals not to travel far to commit their crimes is the notion of '**propinquity**'. Figure 4.3 shows the typical pattern of distances that offenders tend to travel from their home to the crime scene. In this case it is based on a very large sample of burglars. This is often called the **journey to crime**. Typically, it tails off the further away the crime is from home – rather than being a straight-line reduction, it 'decays'. For this reason, it is known as a **decay function**. Various mathematical formulae can be applied to the shape of this curve and used in probabilistic calculations of likely home location derived from crime locations (Canter et al., 2000).

Note also that there is a dip at the start of the curve. This shows the reluctance of some offenders to commit crimes very close to where they live, often referred to as a **buffer zone** (Warren et al., 1998). This is more likely to be found in those crimes where the offender may be seen. An example would be a distraction burglary in which the offender may knock on a door and ask for help, then once inside the house take the opportunity to steal something. Such an offender would be recognised if he lived nearby. But there are certainly plenty of other sorts of crimes where the offender will, for example, steal from other people living in the same house as him, where the offender is not seen. In these sorts of crimes there would be no obvious 'buffer zone'.

Also, where the target of the crime is known to the criminal, as most obviously in domestic violence, no decay function would be expected. It also has to be emphasised that the decay function is an aggregate of distances across a whole sample. There are important studies, notably that of van Koppen and De Keijser (1997), which show that individuals tend to have an optimum distance they travel, rather than a general decay. Consequently, decay functions tend not to occur for individuals. One study developed estimates of optimum distances for each series, rather than using aggregate information (Canter, Hammond, Youngs, & Juszcza, 2013). This was found to be more successful than using aggregate decay functions.

Familiarity

Many offenders operate in areas they know well, or at least places where they know there is an opportunity for the sort of criminal activity they want to carry out. This is interesting to explore

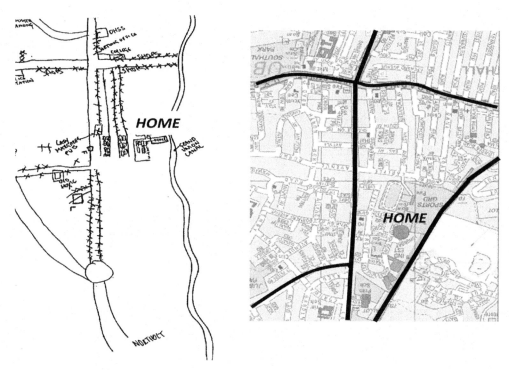

Figure 4.4 A burglar's 'mental map'. The crosses indicate the places he burgled, compared with an actual map

following ideas from environmental psychology (Canter, 1977). Drawing on a cognitive perspective of how people make sense of their surroundings, it is proposed that some sort of mental representation of what is where is created. This is often referred to as a **mental map**. This is not an entirely accurate label because our internal representation is not what would be produced by a cartographer. However, if people are asked to draw a sketch map of an area, from memory, it does give some indication of their knowledge of that area. Distortions in the sketch, when compared with an actual map, are also revealing.

Figure 4.4 is a 'mental map' drawn by a prolific burglar, when asked to draw a sketch of where he broke into properties. The little crosses on the map indicate what a busy chap he was. Of particular interest is how the location of his burglaries are all to the left of the canal. The right side was an area he did not go to and with which he was not familiar. Comparing his sketch with an actual map, given in Figure 4.4, it is clear that on the right side of the canal is a very different sort of property. Also, of interest is the comparison of the major details of his sketch, when compared with reality. The canal and the main road running from top to bottom are not actually parallel to each other. They diverge considerably at the top, forming more of a V shape. But the consequence of this distortion is to make the area of the burglaries more compact and distinct. The sketch helps to show how he thinks of his home area, his 'comfort zone', which radiates out from his home. Taken together with the details on the sketch this one example helps to illustrate the idea that series of crimes often occur in an area that is very familiar to the criminal.

There is also a more behaviourally oriented explanation that complements the power of familiarity and mental maps. This is the idea that many crime locations are a product of the non-criminal day-to-day activities of an offender, what is known as their routine activity (Clarke & Felson, 1993; Felson, 2002). In their daily life, socialising, going to work, or shopping, offenders become aware of the opportunities for criminal activity. They also have a reason for being in a potential crime location without arising suspicion. Furthermore, their actions will follow general patterns of non-criminal movements, for example, moving in and out of a town centre rather than across its periphery.

Two weaknesses in **routine activity theory** and the mental map approach are that committed (professional) offenders may seek out areas for their crimes and become familiar with them independently of any other activity. The other is that they can find out about offending opportunities from secondary sources. This could be other criminals or published details. One burglar I interviewed, who stole golfing equipment from golf courses around the country, told me he just acquired a map, as any golfer would, of where the golf courses were located.

The findings that support the marauder model of criminal activity lead to a challenging question. For any series of crimes, for which the offender is unknown, do the patterns of crimes reveal them being generated by a 'marauder' or not? As yet there is no clear way of determining from crime locations whether they are. That is a rich area for future research.

Criminal range

Another intriguing consequence of routine activity, familiarity, and domocentricity, as well as the resources of time and mobility, is that criminals are likely to have a characteristic range over which they operate (Canter & Larkin, 1993). Those whose crimes are near their home will have their nearest crimes relatively close and their furthest relatively close. In other words, the hypothesis is that there will be a correlation between the distance to their nearest crime and the distance to their most distant. This hypothesis is straightforward to test as part of the proposed field experiment.

Sequence of crimes

The first contribution I made to a major police investigation (Canter, 1994) made use of the indication that as the crime series continued the location of the offences moved further and further away from the area where they started. This also coincided with indications that the offenders were more committed to their violent crimes, planning them more carefully. I used that to hypothesise that they were moving out from the area where they had an original base. This turned out to be pivotal for the police investigation. Curiously though, in all the studies I've read about and conducted since then I have never found such a clear developmental sequence. Quite the opposite in fact. Criminals are familiar with an area and tend to offend within that area. They may move to other areas and then their offences are based around that new location. Nonetheless, the sequence of locations of crimes are worthy of consideration. If you can get those details then you can study any differences that may be related.

There is a caveat, nonetheless, when using the sequence or dates of crimes recorded in police data. There are plenty of good (and some poor) reasons why this information may not be accurate. One inaccuracy comes from nobody knowing exactly when a crime was committed (even the offender may have forgotten). If someone goes on holiday for a couple of weeks and comes back to find their house has been burgled, it could be very difficult to determine exactly when it happened. If a body is found it can be difficult to determine when it was left at the place it was discovered or where or when the death occurred. The fictional 'time of death' given by forensic pathologists is very unusual indeed in reality. The time of death is usually calculated from the time the victim was last seen. Even if these details of when the crime happened can be established, they may be wrongly recorded. Typically, crimes in a series are numbered by the police in relation to when they are reported, not when they took place. Therefore, police records have to be carefully examined to determine what the actual sequence of the offences was.

One aspect of crime sequence that has revealed some interesting and useful patterns is the difference between alternating and sequential crimes. Drawing on the model outlined above, it seems likely that a serial offender may try not to return to the area of a crime soon after that crime has been committed, especially if it is possible he may have been seen, or there is as a result a lot more surveillance and police presence. This is illustrated in the sequence of crimes in Figure 4.2. They move across the area in which they are occurring. The second crime is diagonally opposite the first; the sixth opposite the fifth.

If this process of keeping away from a previous crime area is the case, then it would be hypothesised that the distance between consecutive crimes would be further than the distance between alternate crimes (i.e. the first and second crimes), and the third and fourth would be further apart than the first and third and the second and fourth. One study did support this hypothesis for serial killers (Lundrigan & Canter, 2001), but many more studies are possible.

One intriguing possibility that develops this idea is that after an offender has committed a few crimes, if he wishes to carry on within the same area, then he may return to the locality of an earlier crime. I have seen anecdotal examples of this but no careful study.

Travelling offenders

The contrast to the marauder is the travelling offender (Meaney, 2004). These are criminals who move out to a location to commit perhaps a number of crimes, then return back to their base. I initially suggested these were rather like commuters going to work and the distinction between 'commuters' and 'marauders' found its way into the crime psychology literature. But those who do not fit the marauder pattern are much more varied then the notion of 'commuting' would suggest. They can be travelling offenders who probably have some sort of job that takes them to many places, like the delivery man Robert Black, who kidnapped young girls along his delivery routes.

HOW MANY CRIMES ARE NEEDED?

In general, geographical profiling is carried out on a series of linked crimes, although some of the basic ideas are relevant to any single crime. The typical distance any type of offender travels to the crime scene, for instance, is relevant to a one-off crime. There is some discussion about how many crimes are needed before geographical profiling will be of any value. My own studies indicate that even with just two crimes the results are meaningful. I've also found that beyond about five crimes the results do not improve greatly. The suggestion has gained currency that you need about five crimes to get useful results, but this really depends on the nature of the crimes and the area(s) in which they are taking place.

One curious claim promulgated by some researchers is that a full set of most crimes in a series is necessary to apply geographical profiling to their analysis. This would only make sense if the location of the linked crimes varied in some significant way during the series. In other words, if the crimes being taken to characterise a series were biased in some way. This could be due, for example, to the offender changing the mode of transport to get to crime locations. Or radically changing the targets, say from domestic to business premises. But if the selection of crimes is reasonably representative of a series then it is not essential to have all of them for any given geographical profiling analysis.

PRACTICAL APPLICATIONS

There are a number of practical benefits to geographical profiling, although it has to be emphasised that it is still very rare for the police anywhere to use geographical profiling regularly, or in any strategic way. One of the few examples where the ideas from geographical profiling are applied in actual investigations is when DNA samples are to be collected from a community to identify the culprit. In these cases, ideas from geographical profiling are combined with other constraints, notably the probable age and gender of the culprit, to draw up a list of people to be tested (Gregory & Rainbow, 2011). In other circumstances they may explore the principles behind geographical profiling in individual serious cases.

Some practical applications of geographical profiling

- *Eliciting suspects.* Pointing to areas where a search for suspects through house-to-house enquiries or from informants would be fruitful.
- *Prioritising suspects.* Helping to rank suspects, identified from criminal records or other sources, by considering where they are based in relation to crime locations, in order to focus resources on more detailed examination of the most likely culprit.
- *Linking crimes.* Checking whether crimes are likely to have been committed by the same person. If unusual crimes, like stranger murder, happen in a distinct area they are likely to be committed by the same individual or group.
- *Taken into consideration (TICs).* A basis for discussing with known criminals other crimes that they may also have committed because of where they are located and where the criminal has a base.
- *Predicting crime locations.* Examining crime series to determine where (and when) future crimes may occur.

DEVELOPING GEOGRAPHICAL PROFILING MODELS

Beyond the centre of gravity (often called a 'centroid') and the centre of the circle models, more sophisticated calculations can be made incorporating the frequency distribution of distances of crimes from home. The idea is that every point in an area can be given a probability of it being the offender's base. A decay function indicates what proportion of offenders live at each distance from a crime. These proportions can then be used to calculate the probability, for each crime, of the home being at different distances from a crime location. When these probabilities are added together for every linked crime a distribution of base location probabilities can be produced across the area. To carry out these calculations assistance is needed from computer algorithms, such as the software I developed called Dragnet (Canter et al., 2000), or Rossmo's (2000) system known as Rigel. These algorithms rely on aggregate decay functions, which can be calculated from crime in an area. However, it is possible to estimate the probability distribution for individual offenders, which does give more accurate results (Canter et al., 2013). Making use of such software takes us beyond the remit for the current book.

PROPOSED GEOGRAPHICAL PROFILING STUDY

Objectives

As an illustration of the study of crime location choice this project examines the following:

1. The distances offenders travel from their base to commit crimes and how this differs between types of area in which crime series occur.

2. The role criminals' bases play in influencing where they commit their crimes.

3. Testing two simple models that indicate the general location in which an offender is likely to have a base:

   (a) the 'centre of the circle' model; and

   (b) the centroid model.

Sources of data

Unless you have a good working relationship with a police force, obtaining details of where a series of crimes occur, and the residential location of the culprit, is not readily available. Plenty of researchers have passed this barrier in the last decade, as the extensive literature around the topic of geographical profiling now shows.

The reticence of the police to make this information available is slightly odd. Many police forces now publish details of where crimes have occurred. Once a serial offender is brought to court and convicted many of the details about him and his crimes are public knowledge. For more serious cases the locations of crimes may actually be published on a map in newspapers. There are also many examples of maps of crime and offender location in both the academic and the popular 'true-crime' literature.

Although it may take some effort to amass enough details for a study of the form described here it is very possible. However, to enable me to illustrate the workings of the study I have provided some examples from research in which I have been involved. This consists of the location co-ordinates of solved crime series drawn from two different areas, one rural and one metropolitan. It also includes the residential co-ordinates of the offenders convicted for each crime series.

Process

For each set of crime series, urban and rural, there are a set of proposed calculations. Details of how to carry out these calculations are given in the appendix to this chapter.

1. Calculate *distances from home to crime sites* for each of the crime series.

    (a) Prepare a frequency distribution for each data set.

    (b) Compare the mean and ranges for each data set.

2. Locate the *centre of the crime circle* for each of the crime series.

    (a) In how many cases is the home within the crime circle?

    (b) Compare the frequency of cases for each data set.

    (c) Calculate distances from home to centre of circle.

    (d) Prepare frequency distribution for each data set.

    (e) Compare the mean and ranges for each data set to establish the typical ranges for each data set.

3. Locate the *centroid* of each crime series.

    (a) Calculate distances from home to centroid.

    (b) Prepare frequency distribution for each data set.

    (c) Compare the mean and ranges of these distances for each data set.

4. Examine the *range* over which crimes occur.

    (a) Calculate the distance from home to each crime for all crimes in a series.

    (b) Determine the distance of the nearest, and of the furthest crime from home for each series.

    (c) Produce a scatter plot (and correlation) of the distances of the nearest against the distance of the furthest for all the series.

Analyses

Converting crime locations into co-ordinates ready for analysis is a crucial stage. Once that is done many of the calculations can be built into spreadsheets or statistical programs so that a number of analyses can be carried out automatically. Then the results can be summarised in various forms and inferential statistical calculations carried out. Comparison of published results for different crimes in different contexts will be of interest (see, for example, the papers in Canter & Youngs, 2008a, 2008b).

A further refinement of the test of the centre of gravity and the circle centre models is to calculate the distance from the centre points produced by the models to the actual location of known offenders.

OTHER STUDIES THAT COULD USE THIS RESEARCH DESIGN

Geographical offender profiling is now a large area of study with a wide range and considerable number of publications. Just about every type of crime has been subjected to this sort of spatial scrutiny, as listed in the references at the end of this chapter. Ever more sophisticated algorithms are being developed to model criminals' spatial activity, working with the large amounts of data that law enforcement agencies now have available. Consequently, in this short chapter only a very small part of the possible research that can be, and is being, carried out in this area has been touched on.

It is also worth noting that the issues outlined here have a relevance way beyond crime. An increasing number of biological studies, beyond the bumble bees mentioned earlier, are using geographical profiling. Examples include the locations of the prey of leopards (Mizutani & Jewell, 2006), or the foraging of bats (Le Comber, Nicholls, Rossmo, & Racey, 2006). There are doubtless also closely guarded algorithms used by large-scale retailers to identify where to locate shops and by traffic engineers planning road systems. As I write, most of the world is in lockdown because of COVID-19. This virus spreads through various forms of physical contact. There is therefore inevitably a geographical profile to the unfolding distribution of people suffering from the disease. So far, though, I have not come across any reference to the nature of this profile. Apparently, there is fascinating research going on that distinguished between different strains of the virus, using RNA and DNA analyses. This enables the location of different outbursts of the disease to be identified.

The reference to COVID-19 connects with one of the first demonstrations of the utility of modelling incident locations. This was carried out in 1850 when the queen's physician John Snow mapped the location of cholera victims as a way of demonstrating the location of the water source where the infection was picked up (Snow, 1855). When he removed the handle of the pump that he hypothesised was the source of the cholera outbreak, the incidence of the disease subsided. This was a key moment in the development of the science of epidemiology.

The limit on the studies that can be done in this area is mainly determined by access to suitable data. As already mentioned, there is a lot of open-source material on the Internet and in various publications that can be trawled to obtain crime location details. Offender base details are more difficult to find, but not impossible, especially in true-crime publications. The seven questions listed earlier in Study 3 (see p. 82) are relevant to any criminal activity, or comparisons between types of crimes or types of offender.

QUESTIONS FOR DISCUSSION

1. Why do you think that research into geographical profiling has been so prevalent over the past few years and produced so many clear and useful results, especially compared with other areas of crime psychology?

2. What are the difficulties of comparing crime series of different lengths? How can you overcome them?

3. What are the challenges of working with crime location information?

4. How would you explain the results you get when comparing the distances of metropolitan and rural burglary data sets?

5. Do you have any evidence that criminals have characteristic ranges?

Notes

1 All the data and studies of which I am aware deal exclusively with male offenders. I will therefore stay with this somewhat biased reference for this chapter.

2 If you don't enjoy doing this calculation yourself there are websites that will do it for you, such as www. calculator.net. For Excel, the formula I used is =SQRT(A10–A1)^2+(B10–B1)^2 where A10, and B10 are the x and y co-ordinates for the home and A1 and B1 are the x and y co-ordinates for location 1.

Further Reading

There is now a considerable amount published on geographical profiling, often in readily accessible popular forms. Two books bring together most of the original key papers on geographical profiling:

Canter, D., & Youngs, D. (2008). *Applications of geographical profiling*. Aldershot, UK: Ashgate.
Canter, D., & Youngs, D. (2008). *Principles of geographical profiling*. Aldershot, UK: Ashgate.

Chapter 8 in the following book gives a useful overview:

Canter, D., & Youngs, D. (2009). *Investigative psychology*. Chichester, UK: Wiley.

A useful general review is:

van der Kemp, J.J., & van Kopppen, P.J. (2007). Fine-tuning geographical profiling. In Kocsis, R.N. (Ed.), *Criminal profiling: International theory, research, and practice* (pp. 347–364). | Totowa, NJ: Humana Press.

My popular book is available as an eBook and an audiobook:

Canter, D. (2007). *Mapping murder: The secrets of geographical profiling*. London: Virgin Books.

The six-part TV documentary series that I wrote and presented, *Mapping Murder*, is available as a box set from Demand DVD.

References

Bernasco, W. (2007). The usefulness of measuring spatial opportunity structures for tracking down offenders: A theoretical analysis of geographic offender profiling using simulation studies. *Psychology, Crime & Law*, 13(2), 155–171. doi: 10.1080/10683160600558402.
Butkovic, A., Mrdovic, S., Uludag, S., & Tanovic, A. (2019). Geographic profiling for serial cybercrime investigation. *Digital Investigation*, 28, 176–182. https://doi.org/10.1016/j.diin.2018.12.001.
Canter, D. (1977). The psychology of place. London: Architectural Press.
Canter, D. (1994). Criminal shadows: Inside the mind of the serial killer. London: HarperCollins.
Canter, D., & Youngs, D. (2008a). *Applications of geographical profiling*. Aldershot, UK: Ashgate.
Canter, D., & Youngs, D. (2008b). *Principles of geographical profiling*. Aldershot, UK: Ashgate.
Canter, D., Coffey, T., Huntley, M., & Missen, C. (2000). Predicting serial killers' home base using a decision support system. *Journal of Quantitative Criminology*, 16, 457–478.

Canter, D., Hammond. L., Youngs, D., & Juszcza, P. (2013). The efficacy of ideographic models for geographical offender profiling. *Journal of Quantitative Criminology*, 29, 423–446. doi: 10.1007/s10940-012-9186-6.

Canter, D., & Larkin, P. (1993). The environmental range of serial rapists. *Journal of Environmental Psychology*, 13, 63–69.

Clarke, R.V., & Felson, M. (Eds.) (1993). *Routine activity and rational choice*. New Brunswick, NJ: Transaction.

Ebberline, J. (2008). Geographical profiling obscene phone calls: A case study. *Journal of Investigative Psychology and Offender Profiling*, 5(1–2), 93–105.

Felson, M. (2002). Crime and everyday life (3rd ed.). Thousand Oaks, CA: Sage & Pine Forge Press.

Gregory, A., & Rainbow, L. (2011). Familial DNA prioritization. In L. Alison & L. Rainbow (Eds.), *Professionalizing offender profiling* (pp. 160–177). London: Routledge.

Hammond, L. (2014). Geographical profiling in a novel context: Prioritising the search for New Zealand sex offenders. *Psychology, Crime & Law*, 20(4), 358–371. doi: 10.1080/1068316X.2013.793331.

Kind, S. (1987). *The scientific investigation of crime*. London: Forensic Science Services.

Laukkanen, M., & Santtila, P. (2006). Predicting the residential location of a serial commercial robber. *Forensic Science International*, 157(1), 71–82. https://doi.org/10.1016/j.forsciint.2005.03.020.

Le Comber, S.C., Nicholls, B., Rossmo, D.K., & Racey, P.A. (2006). Geographic profiling and animal foraging. *Journal of Theoretical Biology*, 240(2), 233–240. https://doi.org/10.1016/j.jtbi.2005.09.012.

Lundrigan, S., & Canter, D. (2001). A multivariate analysis of serial murderers' disposal site location choice. *Journal of Environmental Psychology*, 21, 423–432.

Meaney, R. (2004). Commuters and marauders: An examination of the spatial behaviour of serial criminals. *Journal of Investigative Psychology and Offender Profiling*, 1(2), 121–137.

Mizutani, F., & Jewell, P.A. (2006). Home-range and movements of leopards (Panthera pardus) on a livestock ranch in Kenya. Journal of Zoology, 244(2). https://doi.org/10.1111/j.1469-7998.1998.tb00031.x.

Rossmo, D.K. (2000). *Geographic profiling*. Boca Raton, FL: CRC.

Santtila, P., Zappalà, A., Laukkanen, M., & Picozzi, M. (2003). Testing the utility of a geographical profiling approach in three rape series of a single offender: A case study. *Forensic Science International*, 131(1), 42–52. https://doi.org/10.1016/S0379-0738(02)00385-7.

Sarangi, S., & Youngs, D. (2006). Spatial patterns of Indian serial burglars with relevance to geographical profiling. *Journal of Investigative Psychology and Offender Profiling*, 3(2), 105–115. https://doi.org/10.1002/jip.38.

Snow, J. (1855). *On the mode of communication of cholera* (2nd ed.). London: John Churchill. Retrieved from https://collections.nlm.nih.gov/ext/cholera/PDF/0050707.pdf.

Suzuki-Ohno, Y., Inoue, M.N., & Ohno, K. (2010). Applying geographic profiling used in the field of criminology for predicting the nest locations of bumble bees. *Journal of Theoretical Biology*, 265(2), 211–217. https://doi.org/10.1016/j.jtbi.2010.04.010.

Tamura, M., & Suzuki, M. (1997). Criminal profiling research on serial arson: Examinations of the circle hypothesis estimating offenders' residential area. *Research into Prevention of Crime and Delinquency*, 38, 13–25.

van Koppen, P.J., & De Keijser, J.W. (1997). Desisting distance decay: On the aggregation of individual crime trips. *Criminology*, 35, 505–515.

Warren, J.I., Reboussin, R.R., Hazelwood, R.R., Cummings, A., Gibbs, N., & Trumbetta, S. (1998). Crime scene and distance correlates of serial rape. *Journal of Quantitative Criminology*, 14, 35–60.

Appendix: Data and Calculations

The following tables list the geographical co-ordinates for the burglary crime locations and home locations of the offenders for each of ten crime series for two different samples, one metropolitan, the other rural. The co-ordinates are the X and Y (horizontal and vertical) values in an abstract geometry, although they are real distances in kilometres. They have been taken from actual map locations, but to maintain privacy and confidentiality the map details have been converted into values that have no immediate relationship to a particular map. Of course, in providing the data in this way a lot of information that would be useful to an investigation, such as the location of roads, open ground, and so on is not available. However, for this study it is interesting how successful an analysis of even such limited material can be.

The actual location of the home of the aggressive intruder is given in Figure 4.5

To illustrate how the co-ordinates are calculated, Table 4.1 provides them for the crime and offender home location and of the aggressive intruder in Figure 4.1.

Calculating the Centre of Gravity (Centroid) of a Number of Locations

Calculate the average co-ordinate for the horizontal and for the vertical axes from Table 4.1.

In this example the average for the horizontal axis is 4.7. and for the vertical axis is 3.9. This centroid location is marked on Figure 4.6.

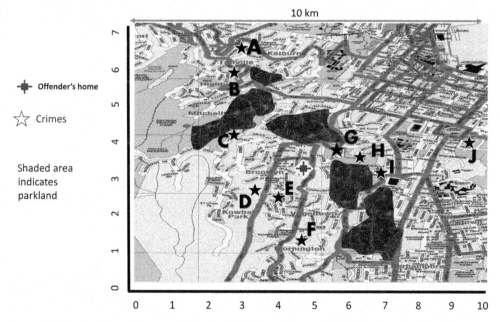

Figure 4.5 The locations where an aggressive intruder was seen, indicating where he lived

Table 4.1 Co-ordinates for the ten crime locations and home in Figure 4.1 and the calculated centroid

Crime	Horizontal	Vertical
A	3.0	6.5
B	2.9	6.0
C	2.9	4.3
D	3.3	2.9
E	4.0	2.8
F	4.6	1.5
G	5.6	4.0
H	6.6	3.8
I	6.8	3.5
J	9.5	4.1
Home	4.9	3.2
Centroid	4.7	3.9
Circle centre	6.0	4.2

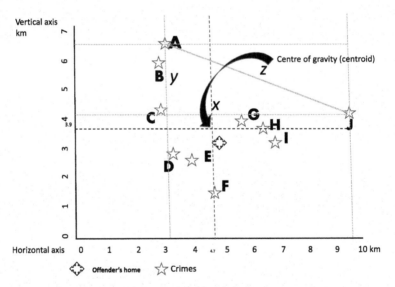

Figure 4.6 Geometry for calculating distances between locations

CALCULATING THE DISTANCE BETWEEN TWO POINTS

To calculate the distance between any two points, the high school Pythagoras theorem will do the job.[2] The well-tried formula is $x^2 + y^2 = z^2$. An illustration of this is given in Figure 4.6, taking the example of the distance from A to J. It is first necessary to work out the distances of the vertical side of the triangle, y. This is $6.8 - 4.1 = 2.7$ km. x is $9.8 - 3.1 = 6.7$. Applying the values of 2.7 and 6.7 to the formula gives 7.29 + 44.89 = 52.18. The square root of 52.18 = 7.2 km. Therefore, the distance y, between A and J.

With a little ingenuity the formula can be put into a spreadsheet, such as Excel, so that all the relevant distances can be calculated automatically.

A further example, calculating the distance between the centroid and the home location is given in Figure 4.6

Looking at Table 4.1, it can be seen that the distance between the horizontal location of the home and the centroid location is 4.9 − 4.7 = 0.2. For the vertical location the distance between these locations is 3.9 − 3.2 = 0.7. Applying these values to Pythagoras gives 0.73 km.

By carrying out these calculations for all the crime series in the example data, bar charts can be created for each data set. This enables the comparison of the frequency distribution of the distances from the centroid to the actual home between metropolitan and rural burglaries.

CALCULATING THE OFFENDER CIRCLE

Figure 4.7 shows a circle that encompasses the area of the crimes. It is interesting to note that some of the crimes are outside of this circle, which just shows what a crude device it is. This circle was drawn by identifying the two crimes that were furthest from each other. In this case there were a number of possible pairs that could be selected because my diagram here, presented for clarity, is not very precise. There are more sophisticated mathematics that can be applied to this task. However, a broad indication of the process the line from C to J is a reasonable approximation. Having selected this line, a circle can be put around it as the diameter. This enables the vertical, orthogonal line to that to be placed, giving a location for the centre of the circle. In this case the co-ordinates of that centre are 6.0 and 4.2.

Similar calculations to those described above give the distance from the actual home to the centre of the circle of 2.7 km, rather further than the centroid, for this data.

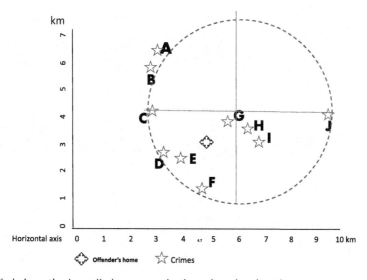

Figure 4.7 Circle hypothesis applied to aggressive intruder crime locations

CRIME LOCATION DATA

For comparison purposes two sets of data are provided. One is from a metropolitan area that I call M. The other is from a rural area that I call R. There are ten crime series for each area. The data sets are organised as follows:

9		This is the number of offence locations
1.28	1.04	These are the co-ordinates of the crime locations in km
2.85	1.29	Horizontal (x) Vertical (y)
1.80	1.83	
2.16	2.40	
2.26	1.66	
1.23	2.44	
2.09	1.68	
2.15	1.08	
1.23	2.44	
Home		
2.05	1.73	These are the co-ordinates of the home location

EXAMPLE DATA SETS

Metropolitan data sets

10	
10.517	11.454
10.551	11.433
10.348	11.547
10.632	11.332
10.24	10
10.853	10.348
10.312	10.596
11.22	10.589
11.209	10.347
10	11.293
Home	
10.97	10.294

10	
10.517	11.454
10.551	11.433
10.348	11.547
10.632	11.332
10.24	10
10.853	10.348
10.312	10.596
11.22	10.589

11.209	10.347
10	11.293
Home	
8.439	11.815

10	
10.517	11.454
10.551	11.433
10.348	11.547
10.632	11.332
10.24	10
10.853	10.348
10.312	10.596
11.22	10.589
11.209	10.347
10	11.293
Home	
8.439	11.815

7	
12.94	12.052
15.264	10.94
11.926	10
13.907	13.531
13.922	13.658
10	12.298
11.265	10.284
Home	
13.708	13.875

11	
11.848	13.07
10.581	11.78
11.684	11.401
11.684	11.401
11.484	11.683
11.296	10
11.187	10.714
11.49	10.579
11.367	10.758
10	10.617
10.078	10.65
Home	
11.473	10.931

11	
12.057	10
11.823	10.219
12.601	10.331
12.362	11.085
12.029	10.707
13.102	10.887
13.649	10.443
12.672	12.246
12.559	12.135
9.082	8.712
10	7.935
Home	
8.966	7.706

14	
11.014	363.419
11.006	363.411
12.889	365.294
12.378	364.783
12.815	365.22
12.858	365.263
12.882	365.287
12.268	364.673
12.784	365.189
9.814	362.219
9.679	362.084
10	362.405
11.981	364.386
11.996	364.401
Home	
13.454	12.688

9	
10	10.193
10.881	10
10.863	10.195
11.636	10.898
11.742	11.128
11.723	10.278
11.056	10.219
11.473	10.655
10.356	8.842
Home	
11.246	10.974

9	
10.186	11.761
10.106	11.894
10.769	11.144
10	11.687
10	11.687
10	11.687
10.076	11.911
10.179	10
10.179	10
Home	
8.558	11.092

7	
10.293	10.677
10.849	10.811
10.293	10.677
10.283	10
10.186	10.289
10.137	10.438
10	10.446
Home	
10.49	10.086

Rural data sets

(For practical reasons only the first five crimes in the burglary series are recorded here.)

5	
11.884	6.205
14.628	4.553
1.835	4.933
0.375	6.041
0.224	5.790
Home	
10.279	5.230

5	
11.081	9.873
11.301	6.181
9.321	9.052
0.07	4.064
0.691	9.520
Home	
0.70	8.803

5	
2.151	2.392
2.159	1.272
2.457	1.312
2.732	1.108
2.203	1.898
Home	
2.395	1.638

5	
10.80	19.81
11.92	13.81
12.20	3.54
12.17	3.66
11.94	6.03
Home	
13.05	6.98

5	
9.31	5.94
10.40	10.45
8.93	5.50
9.70	6.24
8.73	5.63
Home	
8.82	613

5	
40.958	29.821
40.764	29.566
41.272	30.726
41.746	30.957
40.084	30.463
Home	
5.98	26.070

5	
37.40	26.37
41.35	22.71
33.85	20.71
27.73	26.47
29.92	13.74
Home	
33.32	9.72

5	
44.11	19.49
5.05	17.80
8.50	17.99
2.79	16.88
8.12	18.36
Home	
25.56	18.53

5	
13.81	2.67
13.00	8.17
11.80	13.81
12.89	7.97
12.72	8.46
Home	
14.59	21.07

5	
47.92	12.22
51.94	17.80
42.43	6.94
51.25	19.80
54.44	16.65
Home	
4.53	45.55

Section 2
Surveys

Exploring crime seriousness

SYNOPSIS

A crucial principal of the law is that the punishment should fit the crime. If the public in general considers that punishments are too lenient or too harsh then they lose faith in the judicial system, which can undermine the rule of law. Determining what punishment a convicted offender should get draws on a view of how serious the crime is. Consequently, considerations of the seriousness of different crimes and, and how that relates to outcomes in court, are an important area of research.

The study of how serious people think any given crime is, and what the appropriate consequence should be through the sentence given for it, lends itself to the research method I have called a 'survey'. The proposed study therefore consists of obtaining ratings by people of the seriousness of various types of crime. These views can be related to the sentence that any given type of crime typically attracts, using a fairly straightforward analysis. However, the basis on which people decide how serious a crime is, and the criteria that influence the sentencing decision, are rather more complex than might appear at first sight.

SOME KEY CONCEPTS

- attitudes
- judicial guidelines
- online petition
- questionnaire formats
- multiple choice
- reliability
- validity.

OVERVIEW

A central tenet of any legal process is that the punishment should fit the crime. If the public in general considers that punishments are too lenient or too harsh then they lose faith in the judicial system, which can undermine the rule of law. Determining what punishment a convicted offender should get draws on a view of how serious the crime is. Consequently, considerations of the seriousness of different crimes and, and how that relates to outcomes in court, is an important area of research that has been studied for many years (as reviewed by Einat & Herzog, 2011). These studies raise the interesting question of whether it is the legal consequences of committing a crime that influences the public view of how serious a crime is, or vice versa, it is public opinion that shapes the judicial enactments.

Many researchers, such as Rossi, Berk, and Campbell (1997), have argued that if the legal determinants of punishment are a dominant influence on public opinion then, in general, there would be consensus across different social groups on the relationship between criminal acts and the legally specified punishments. On the other hand, if the opinions of those outside of the legal profession on crime seriousness were somewhat independent of formal punishments then variations between different groups in society would be predicted, as Miethe (1984) and O'Connell and Whelan (1996) have argued. This consequently opens up an interesting area of research comparing the **attitudes** of different groups to crime seriousness and how that relates to the punishments proposed by law.

The study of how serious people think any given crime is, and what the appropriate consequence should be through the sentence given for it, lends itself to the research method I have called a 'survey'. The essence of this is to obtain a variety of views from a designated sample of people across a range of topics. In this case the topics are types of crime. The nature of offending can vary enormously, from shoplifting to murder, from arson to terrorism. The question of the relationship between views about how serious a crime is, and the sentence any given type of crime typically attracts, is therefore an interesting and important one. It lends itself to fairly straightforward analysis. However, as we shall see, the basis on which people decide how serious a crime is, and the criteria that influence the sentencing decision, are rather more complex than might appear at first sight.

The consideration of how serious a person thinks a particular type of crime is may be usefully thought of as an 'attitude' towards different forms of criminality and what it means for crimes to vary in seriousness. There are over a century of studies covering a very wide range and variety of attitudes. This is because they are such a central, important aspect of everyone's idea of who they are. Broadly, attitudes are expressions of the amount of positive or negative feelings towards an object. They are built upon knowledge and understanding of what is implied by the object that is the target of the attitude. They also imply potential actions in relation to that object. An obvious example is that a strongly positive attitude towards religion is likely to relate to a belief in an all-powerful deity and to carry out actions that reflect a worship of that deity.

In the proposed study of views about how serious different crimes are, these attitudes draw on many different ideas about what makes a crime serious. Is the level of seriousness determined by how harmful the crime is? Or perhaps whether the target is a person or property? How much it undermines the social order? It could even relate to who commits the crime. For example, is a betrayal of trust worse than a crime against a stranger? Or is a crime committed by a woman more or less serious than the same crime committed by a man? Probably all these things come to mind. This all illustrates that attitudes are typically a bundle of related issues, each of which varies in the degree of positive or negative views. Consequently, people may form a view about how serious a crime is, but explaining the reasons for that may be quite difficult to do. Therefore, a study that explores how and why people order crimes from most to least serious can be very instructive. Such a study would probably reveal some interesting differences between

Table 5.1 Prison sentences for nudity in a public place

Location	Maximum length of imprisonment
United Kingdom	Not usually considered a criminal act
New York	90 days
Ottawa (Canada)	6 months
Brazil	1 year
Morocco	2 years

people in their assessment of seriousness. All that could be part of the study proposed, but as a starting point something a little simpler will be described.

In addition to the complexity of judging the seriousness of crimes are the subtleties of the legal process when it comes to sentencing a convicted person. There are detailed **judicial guidelines** on sentencing for every type of crime. Excellent details of the guidance for judges in England and Wales are given at www.sentencingcouncil.org.uk. There it is clear that judges have considerable discretion in the sentence to give someone. For most crimes there are minimum and maximum sentences determined by law, but the details on the website also show the range of sentences that are typically handed out for each offence. It is also worth mentioning that because of the discretion that judges have they do vary between each other in the sentence they give for similar crimes (another huge area of study).

It is therefore not possible to provide a definitive indication of what the law considers the appropriate sentence, and by implication the seriousness of any crime. A judge will take into account many details of how the crime was committed: whether the defendant admitted to it or showed remorse, whether he or she had committed other crimes, as well as the defendant's character. If we add to this the big variations between jurisdictions in what is considered an appropriate sentence then using the legal punishment as an indication of perceived seriousness gets even more complicated. For example, Table 5.1 lists just a few of the maximum punishments for public nudity in various places. Of course, in those countries with a very harsh, dogmatic religious ideology the punishments can be even more severe, such as 100 lashes, or even execution. Consequently, for any study of the relationship between attitudes towards crimes and legal punishments, some general attempt needs to be made that provides a broad indication of how grave the law seems to consider any particular crime to be.

A further point is important to clarify the sentence that is given for any crime. Sentencing is not only a punishment relating to how serious the crime is. It has other purposes as well. These are summarised in the following box, which shows that the legal process is also concerned with protecting the public from possible future actions by the criminal as well as deterring others from similar offending. As can be seen from these reasons for punishment, they are not solely related to the seriousness of a crime. For example, if a person is regarded as very dangerous, even though he has not committed the most serious of crimes, he may still get a long custodial sentence to remove him from society where he could do more harm.

There is also the interesting idea that by taking people out of society, where the temptations and influences to offend are present, provides the opportunity to retrain, re-educate, and rehabilitate criminals. Some of the earliest forms of imprisonment were set up by Quakers with these noble objectives. Prisoners were housed in single cells with a Bible to contemplate their wrongdoing, not unlike monks. Since those days the debates have raged about imprisonment, its purpose, values, and approaches to how it should be carried out. Sommer's book The End of Imprisonment (1976) is an excellent exploration of these issues, which is still as relevant today as it was 40 years ago.

The generally accepted purposes of punishment

- *Deterrence*. Discourages others from offending because they will fear the consequence.
- *Incapacitation*. Removes offenders from society so that they cannot commit more crimes.
- *Rehabilitation*. Provides an opportunity for training and education that will reduce the risk of re-offending.
- *Retribution*. Punishment for the wrongdoing.

BACKGROUND

This study provides an example of a widely used research design, often referred to as a 'questionnaire survey'. Indeed, it is worth repeating what I wrote in Part two, that over a century ago, William James, the leading psychologist of his day, said, "Because of its ease of use the survey has become the bane of modern society!" As I also mentioned in Part two, at least two very different forms of social science survey need to be distinguished.

One is the social survey in which a carefully selected sample of a given population are asked a few specific questions in order to establish the general view on a topic. This is most commonly used in 'public opinion polling' to determine, for example, people's voting intentions, or whether they believe fox hunting should be banned, or that couples of the same sex should be allowed to marry each other. Such polls are an important part of modern democracies, influencing, in some cases, the way governments act. Online systems are making such polls easier to set in motion and there are a number of online organisations (such as www.change.org) set up specifically to enable people to create opinion polls on topics of public concern. With the advent of COVID-19 online surveys are becoming even more significant when stopping people in the street to answer questions is not allowed.

In effect, these are a form of petition on a specific topic (just search for '**online petitions**'). The UK government even has its own process for creating such surveys at https://petition.parliament.uk, as do many other governments around the world. In the past, thousands of people would sign a scroll with demands on it, as in the UK Chartist movement. Nowadays hundreds of thousands of people can do that very quickly online. There are also many commercial organisations that will arrange for a sample of respondents to answer a set of questions.

There is a rather different use of the questionnaire survey that has more in-depth psychological objectives. This is the exploration of conceptions, attitudes, feelings, or intended actions across a range of issues in order to explore how these are organised in people's minds or experiences and what else they may relate to. A typical example would be exploring whether intensity of religious beliefs relate to attitudes to forms of sentencing for violent crimes, or if personality characteristics correlate with voting behaviour. In the study proposed here the intention is to explore how people make judgements of the seriousness of crimes, whether there are differences in these judgements between men and women, and the relationship that judgements of seriousness of crime have to the legal requirements for punishments for those crimes.

One crucial difference between the public opinion survey and the usual psychological questionnaire study is important to emphasise. For the former, a carefully selected representative sample of the population studied is essential. For the latter, because psychological processes within an area of research are being studied, what is needed is an identifiable set of respondents who have a recognisable relationship to the issue at hand.

Even in a psychological study the more representative a set of respondents is of a known population the more readily can the results be generalised to that population. This is revealed in a common criticism of many psychological surveys that the people chosen to respond are those readily available, usually university students. This means there are areas of psychology that may be most readily considered as the psychology of university students. However, there are many issues on which university students are either an interesting sample or they are not that different from the population at large, in which case the studies still have general value.

Determining the seriousness of crimes is an interesting topic because it does get to the heart of any justice system. How serious a crime is considered to be reflects the standards and mores of a society. This is disturbingly well illustrated by the way very strict, fundamentalist Muslim societies regard adultery or homosexual acts as requiring the death penalty. In Britain the emergence of a more civil, humanitarian society was reflected in the abolishment of the death penalty, initially for petty crimes, then altogether. Comparison of sentencing practices even between different US states show how varied views are about how serious crimes are and the appropriate punishment.

EXAMPLE STUDY OF RATINGS OF CRIME SERIOUSNESS

The present study provides experience in developing using, analysing, and reporting on the use of a questionnaire survey. It also opens up consideration of the seriousness of crimes, how they are judged, any differences between people in those judgements, and how the judgements may relate to the punishments for those crimes.

Aims

The study has two components:

1. To test the hypothesis that males will differ from females in their judgements of the seriousness of some crimes.

2. To explore the nature of the relationship between judgements of how serious crimes are and the severity of typical legal sentences for them.

Method

There are now dozens of online systems available to set up questionnaire surveys, many freely available. Just search for 'online survey software'. For the present example the details of the proposed survey will be provided, but as I hope is becoming very clear there is a great deal of flexibility and potential in this approach. Miliaikeala, Heen, Lieberman, Terance, and Miethe (2014) have published a very useful review of the different online survey systems available.

The exact number of participants included depends on the detailed objectives of the study. If an outcome is required that can be confidently generalised to a larger population then that population needs to be specified and the respondents carefully sampled from it. However, if this is an exploratory study, or one that relates to a distinct subset of individuals, then what is required is for the set of individuals who participate to be specified as clearly as possible. As in so much psychological research it is important to be clear who the participants in the experiment actually are. Always keep in mind that it is necessary to produce a written account of the research. The easier it is to describe who the participants are the easier it will be to write the report. A class of 32 pupils aged between 15 and 16 in a school in central London of whom 18 were boys and 14 were girls, is much easier to describe and understand than "I asked a few friends and some people I met in a pub".

Questionnaire creation

Approaches to developing a questionnaire

When starting a survey study there is the challenge of how to come up with the components for the questions. This can be done quite formally by specifying what the questionnaire will deal with, or even if not using a formal definition preparing a framework for generating the questions. The academic way of dealing with this challenge is to search the published literature for examples that can be drawn on or cannibalised. However, this may not be possible in a new area of research or it may be thought that the existing literature has been very myopic. A complementary approach is to carry out interviews, focus groups, and other explorations to generate a set of topics from which items for a questionnaire can be derived.

For the present study a set of crimes are required. The loose framework is to have a range of crimes that would seem to range from least to most serious. Very unusual, complex, or extremely rare crimes would probably not be good to include because respondents may not understand what they involved or may differ too much between each other in understanding what they are. For example, insider trading can mean many things, and requires some understanding of company law to appreciate its significance.

Items that have been used previously to study seriousness of crimes (Byers, 1999) and other relevant studies, notably Einat and Herzog (2011) provide a basis for the example study proposed here. As is usually the case, questions from other studies could not be used without modification – for example the Byers (1999) questionnaire has homosexuality listed as a crime, but it was decriminalised in the United Kingdom in 1967. Byers (1999) also has questions on gun ownership, which, happily, is less relevant in Britain.

Formats for psychological questionnaires

The central measuring instrument proposed here is a structured, **multiple-choice** questionnaire. This distinct from an open-ended, free-answer questionnaire. An open-ended question, for instance, would be "What do you think the most serious crime is?" There is not a yes/no answer to this, nor can a person choose from possibilities offered by the researcher. That does have the advantage of allowing respondents to generate their own ideas, which may inform or even surprise the researcher. But it has the disadvantage of providing a range of unstructured material that will take a lot of time to analyse and may be very difficult to compare between respondents.

There are also many other forms that questionnaires can take. For example, there is the process of 'sentence completion'. An illustration would be asking people to complete the sentence "A serious crime is … " This provides what might be called guided freedom. But it is difficult to determine the basis of any responses. People may interpret it as a search for definition, or a request for an example, or a desire to see what the consequences should be, or in many other ways.

A significant problem in surveys and, other forms of social science research, is 'social desirability response bias' (see, for example, Paulhus & Reid, 1991). This is the tendency for people to give the answer that they consider to be socially acceptable, or the one that they think the researcher is looking for. The legal process acknowledges this in disallowing 'leading questions', such as the classic "When did you stop beating your wife?" In a questionnaire survey there are many aspects of the process that may give respondents an indication of what answers are expected. Consider a list of crimes for which the respondent is asked to indicate seriousness, as in our current example. If the crimes are listed in the order that the researcher thinks is from the least to the most serious, then many respondents may realise this and shape their answers to fit that sequence. It is therefore essential to randomise the order of the items. The phrasing of the items can also indicate expected responses, such as "Do you think that murder is the most serious crime? Yes/No".

Another interesting device for reducing the influence of social desirability is to have two statements that have been found in pilot research to be similar in their degree of social acceptability and to require people to choose between them. This of course entails a lot of preparatory work and may be quite a challenge for respondents.

One further possibility for studying attitudes, suggested some years ago (Hammond, 1948), which I think is particularly interesting and that is also likely to reduce the impact of response bias, is to present statements as if they are facts and ask people to indicate whether they are truthful or not. This was called an indirect measure of attitudes by considering the error-choice they made. It is based on the idea that people's beliefs about the facts are influenced by their attitudes. For example, if you said to someone: "How long do you think the sentence for possession of cannabis is, 10 years, 5 years, 2 years, or 6 months?" Then the more serious a person thinks the crime is the longer the sentence they would choose. At least the more seriously they think the law considers possession of cannabis to be the longer the sentence they would choose. Of course, responses would be influenced by actual knowledge of the law, perhaps more so in this case than in other **questionnaire formats**.

There are other more complex processes available for carrying out psychological surveys, such as the *repertory grid technique* (the Wikipedia article on this is a useful starting point[1]) and *sorting tasks* (the Wikipedia article on 'cognitive flexibility'[2] gives some background to this; Canter, 2016 provides an account of it in use). More detailed considerations are beyond the scope of the present volume.

The particular format chosen depends upon the objectives of the study and the resources available. The resources include who the respondents are likely to be, how much time is available for the study, and other aspects of the management of the project. For the present example the simplest, most direct way of studying views about seriousness is proposed. The weaknesses in this approach therefore also provides a fruitful topic for discussion.

Response formats

The nature of the answers people are given to choose from, when the questionnaire allows the selection of responses from a pre-determined list, can take many forms. Broadly, there are two approaches to offering structured answers that are commonly used.

RANKING

In the current example respondents would be asked to put the crimes listed in order from the least to most serious. This has the advantage of ensuring every crime has a distinct rank and that there is a clear order to the responses. The average rank assignment can then be used as an overall indication of how seriously each crime is regarded. The disadvantage is that it is not clear if some crimes are ranked, for example, as very serious, because of their contrast with others. In other words, you are asking the respondents to make comparisons rather than a distinct reaction to each crime. The gradations between crime rankings are also typically equal. The difference between the fourth and fifth are regarded as the same as between the tenth and eleventh. This may not reflect respondents' views about differences in seriousness. They may also be uncomfortable assigning a different rank to each crime, wishing to say some are equally serious. If you allow that then the calculations become more problematic.

The values derived from rankings are not regarded as having an actual zero and it is statistically important to take account of the fact that the distinctions between values are equal. For this reason, this is regarded as an 'ordinal' measurement. That requires the application of the appropriate inferential statistics. Statistical purists, for instance, would regard deriving the arithmetic mean from ranked data as inappropriate. Instead they would recommend using the median.

RATING

A different approach is to ask people to give a distinct response for each question. This approach is usually referred to as a Likert response after Rensis Likert who was the first to promulgate this method.

In his original work he gave people five levels of response to attitudinal statements, from strongly agree to strongly disagree. Since then many different forms of these responses have been used; seven levels, three levels, and so on. The device of asking people to give a score out of 10 or some other number can be seen as a variant of this method.

The advantage of this form of multiple-choice response is that each statement or question is given a distinct answer and varying degrees of response are possible. For this reason, it is regarded as generating quite a high level of numerical sophistication. This is referred to as an 'interval' scale, although that is open to considerable debate. However, there are thousands of publications using this from of response in which averages and other forms of statistics requiring interval levels of measurement are used.

In order to generate results of interest it is necessary to obtain a range of responses. If everyone gave the same response then there would be no variation to study. Given that there are usually plenty of variations between respondents, there would be some doubt that a questionnaire was generating anything of value if there were no variations at all in the responses. This is one of the reasons why the number of options is typically an odd number. This encourages people to respond across the middle range. If they are given a choice, say, of 1 to 4 there is tendency to choose 2 and 3, moderately low and moderately high. There are many publications available that explore the many different statistical issues associated with Likert scales and also a great deal of information on the Internet, so I will not spend any more time on these considerations here. For the proposed study I am following Byers's (1999) study, in which he asked people to give a number between 1 and 100 for the seriousness of each crime. This generates a range of values that lend themselves to a variety of statistical analyses. The questionnaire used in this example study is given in the appendix to this chapter.

Developing the crime seriousness questionnaire

Developing any questionnaire, I hope is becoming clear, is like the creation of any measuring device. It is a systematic, carefully carried out process. Unfortunately, many people think they can just knock a set of questions together and find people to answer them. To get over this myth it is worth making a few general comments about the qualities scientific questionnaires are required to have.

Properties of questionnaires and other measuring instruments

Questionnaires are measuring instruments. Therefore, their properties as such need to be evaluated and, if possible, reported on. There are two key features of any measuring instrument, especially challenging for questionnaires, which are widely discussed in books on psychological assessments (see, for example, Robson & McCartan, 2017): **reliability** and **validity**.

RELIABILITY

This is how consistently the questionnaire measures whatever it is that it is measuring. A crucial aspect of this is how clear the questions are. If they are ambiguous then the same person answering the questions on a second occasion may interpret the question differently and thus give a different answer.

A common mistake that causes ambiguity is how questions are phrased. The worst error is to ask two or more different questions within a single question. For example: "How serious do you think stealing is from corner shops or supermarkets?" You don't know whether the respondent is thinking about stealing from corner shops or stealing from supermarkets, or trying to give an average assessment for both. Therefore, a person may think about corner shops on one occasion and supermarkets on another, contributing to the reduction in reliability of the question.

The problem of ambiguity and consequent unreliability, though, is always present to some degree in any questionnaire survey. It is impossible to specify exactly what a question means without going into a lot of detail, which would make the questionnaire unwieldy. Take the question in the survey proposed here: "How serious do you think murder is?" It would be possible to spend months debating this. Does it include the death penalty? What about killing by soldiers in a battle? Do you mean the murder of a stranger or a killing that occurs in bar brawl where the person who dies just happens to be the unlucky one? And so on.

This does mean that some respondents will refuse to answer or be very awkward about answering, but in the overall context of the questionnaire most people are likely to give a reasonable answer (we hope).

Another typical confusion is to provide answers that do not really fit the question. For example, in answer to the following question the following response would be illogical (but this sort of mistake is not uncommon!): "Give a value between 1 and 10 that indicates how often you think this is the case". Having a reliable measuring instrument is crucial if the results from it are to be compared with results from other measurements. Even comparing average responses between men and women would be of little value if the answers people give varied enormously. One way of assessing this possibility is the range of responses people give. There are a number of statistical measures of the range of values, such as the standard deviation and the inter-quartile range. A frequency distribution of responses would also be very revealing. These will be illustrated with the example data collected.

Another important indication of reliability is the simple expedient of giving the questionnaire out twice and seeing how closely the responses match from one administration to the next. This can be difficult to achieve, so various approximations to this can be used. In the present case the comparison of responses between two similar groups of people would indicate some aspects of reliability.

There is an interesting aspect of reliability that is sometimes overlooked in accounts devoted to questionnaire development. Some experiences of completing a questionnaire may influence a respondent's views on the topic being asked about. This would then have an effect on any subsequent answers on a second administration. The reliability of any psychological measuring instrument is therefore always a matter for consideration, being a constant part of reviewing how well it works.

VALIDITY

The usual description of the validity of a measuring instrument is the extent to which it measures what it purports to measure. Does a measure of temperature really measure that, or is it measuring pressure instead? Or perhaps the measure of temperature is distorted because it is sensitive to pressure? These questions are relatively straightforward to understand and explore in physics but are rather more problematic in psychology. How do we know, or measure, what a questionnaire, for example, is claiming to measure?

Well, *face validity*, or *content validity* is one way of answering this question. What does it look as if it's measuring? If I ask you how serious do you think theft is, as a crime, what else could I be assessing other than how serious you think it is? Well, you could be commenting on your ideas about why people thieve. Or interpreting theft as when your housemate eats your pot noodles without telling you. But at least what it seems to be measuring is a good starting point.

External validity is a way of determining validity by establishing if the responses relate to some relevant external criteria. In our case if the assessment of seriousness of each crime correlates reasonably well with the legal punishments then that does indicate that the responses have some relationship to real-world events. If there are other questionnaires that have been established as measuring something similar then any correlation with them is also support that the questionnaire is measuring what you claim it measures. The term *concurrent validity* is sometimes used to describe the relationship between two different instruments measuring similar constructs.

But, "Hold on," I hear you shout, "We're testing whether people's judgements of seriousness relate to judicial decisions". So how can any relationship we find between the two be used to demonstrate the validity of the questionnaire? Surely, we have to show that all our measurements are valid before claiming a relationship between them is meaningful? Your insightful question reveals the complexity of the concept of validity.

A questionnaire enshrines a set of hypotheses. The key to its value is whether it enables those hypotheses to be tested. This is often described as *construct validity* or *predictive validity*. Do results of using the questionnaire support hypotheses enshrined in the questionnaire constructs? Can answers to the questionnaire successfully predict outcomes in relevant studies?

The idea of a measuring an instrument's construct validity reveals that demonstrating the validity of a questionnaire is an ongoing project. Every study that uses it and obtains useful and interesting results adds a further medal to the value of the questionnaire. An important point though is that the greater the difference between the questionnaire and any outcomes or other measures not obviously measuring the same issue, that the questionnaire can be shown to relate to, the more value that particular questionnaire has. If, for instance, it can be demonstrated that judgements of how grave an action is, relate to religious beliefs, this enriches our understanding of both judgments of crime seriousness and religious beliefs.

Construct validity therefore takes us back to the original consideration of what construct the questionnaire is measuring. Findings from studies using the instrument help in clarifying what is being explored. The results point the way to new research questions.

HOMOGENEITY

The proposal that validity can be determined by relating two instruments to each other offers up a distorting, self-fulfilling hypothesis that is not uncommon in many academic publications. Think what is happening if I ask a set of questions about how serious a set of crimes are, then ask a set of questions about the punishment that people deserve for those crimes. If I get a high correlation between these two sets of answers, have I demonstrated the validity of both? Or have I just asked the same questions in two different ways?

This conundrum cannot be solved until rather more different questions are asked, say, about how destructive of the social order a crime is. This opens up the issue of what might be called *internal validity*. How well do the items in the questionnaire relate to each other? Do they all deal with the same issue? Are they homogeneous?

In deciding what it is that the questionnaire is dealing with, it is important that the questions all deal with that same issue. But besides studying them carefully, the only empirical way to do this is to look at the relationships between the answers that people give to different questions. There are ways of measuring the overall coherence, or homogeneity, of a set of questions. A commonly used such measure is Cronbach's Alpha (see, for instance, Taber, 2018). This adds together the correlations that each item has with the total addition of responses to all the times, minus that item.

But what should we make of this if it demonstrates in our case that answers to crimes against the person are correlated with each other but not with crimes against property? Well, this would support the hypothesis that personal targets are distinct from property targets when people assess crime seriousness, thereby helping to clarify what the instrument is measuring.

Homogeneity is therefore an aspect of concurrent validity. It reveals how well the relationships between different aspects of the measurement go together. It also helps to indicate whether or not the measurement is one coherent instrument or has a number of distinct but probably related components.

Have you spotted, though, something curious here? When I discussed reliability, I mentioned that one way of indicating it is to see how well it correlated with itself on different occasions. But if it is the case that items in a questionnaire measure something similar and therefore correlations between them support validity, does that not also mean those intercorrelations are an indication of reliability? The answer is yes. Homogeneity is an aspect of both internal validity and reliability. This demonstrates that these two features of a questionnaire are different faces of the same coin.

Pilot testing

If the discussion of reliability and validity has made your head spin a little then you will appreciate the importance of exploring how a questionnaire is working before you subject a serious sample to completing it. This is the need for an initial exploration, often called a 'pilot study'. The questionnaire is given out to a few brave souls who are asked to complete it and also comment on what sense the questions make and how readily they can answer them. In the light of these responses the questions may be rephrased, removed, or added to, as well as the format of the questions and how the responses are recorded. It is important to carry out a pilot study with people similar to those you intend to use in your main study because part of the purpose is to see what sense people make of the questions.

The pilot study also gives you some indication of the range and variety of responses you might expect in the main study. This is a useful indication of whether there is actually a range and variety of responses. Examination of the responses are also useful in determining if any modifications would be helpful, as well as a rough indication of the internal reliability of the questionnaire.

Recording the results

Having established that the questionnaire is likely to prove worthwhile it is then a matter of getting people to complete it. Remember that all the ethical and professional requirements that have been emphasised earlier need to be incorporated. This includes ensuring that the people find it straightforward to complete the document. The more professional the questionnaire looks the more likely people are to take it seriously. The questionnaire for the proposed study is given at the end of this chapter.

You will usually need to add an informed consent form, depending on the ethical committee that approves you carrying out this research. The instructions make clear that the form is anonymous, so you have to be sure that it maintains that and is kept confidential from anyone else. However, you do need some idea of the background of the people who are completing the questionnaire so that you can make comparisons between different subgroups.

It is easiest, and less liable to generate recording mistakes, if respondents actually fill in a copy of the form. In the questionnaire at the end of the chapter you will see I have put small numbers at the end of each question near where the answer is inserted by the respondent. This is to make it easier for you to record their answers without erroneously assigning an answer to the wrong question.

I suggest you transfer the responses to a table like that shown in Table 5.2. Write a number on each questionnaire so that you can go back to the original document if you need to check anything. To save a little trouble later, you should arrange the input so that the subgroups you want to compare are separated. For example, all the female respondents could be the top half of the table and the males the bottom half.

In order to have some example material to discuss in this chapter, a young lady called Rosie Jacobs very kindly got 39 16- and 17-year-olds in her school to complete the questionnaire, developed as an example for this project. There were 13 young men and 26 young women. Interestingly, in this pilot project the statement 'throwing away litter' was found to be confusing and was therefore left out of the calculation of the results.

Analyses

Overall ratings of the seriousness of each crime

As you are probably aware, by adding the values in each column and dividing by the number of respondents you obtain the average score for each question. This gives an interesting overview of the

Table 5.2 Example of the input table from the questionnaires

Question respondent	1	2	3	4	5	6	7	8	9	10	11	12	13	14	15	16	17	18	19	20	21	22	23	24	Age	Gender
01																										
02																										
03																										
04																										
Etc.																										
Total																										

Note: The values in the cells of the table are the numbers between 1 and 100 the respondents put in the questionnaire (this table could be put into a spread sheet, such as Excel or in a statistical package such as SPSS to facilitate subsequent calculations).

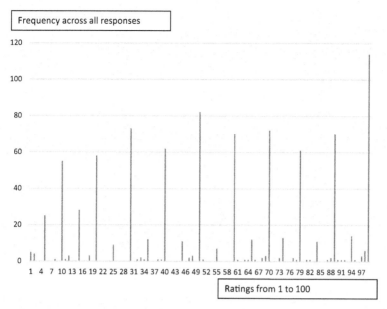

Figure 5.1 Frequency of use of each of the 1 to 100 ratings

relative weighting people give to crime seriousness. But there are other aspects of these figures that are of interest.

The first thing to consider is how the different values are used across all respondents and questions. This will help to indicate how discriminating the questions are. A bar chart that indicates the frequency distribution of the scores assigned by the respondents is given in Figure 5.1.

Looking at Figure 5.1, it can be seen that there are clear frequency peaks at 10, 20, 30, 40, 50, 60, 70, 80, 90, and 100. In other words, respondents tend not to use the finer details of the scale, but home in on the round numbers. Therefore, a scale of 1 to 10 would have been just as useful. Looking even more closely, it can be seen that the highest peaks are at 30, 50, 70, and 100. This relates to people treating this as an even cruder scale. In effect they are making a decision around the middle value, 50, then halfway between that and the extremes. A scale of 1 to 5 would pick up these responses. All of these considerations are to draw attention to the fact that the response format of a questionnaire has to be carefully considered.

One further matter to examine is the actual frequency distribution of the responses. In this case there is a very high frequency of the highest value of 100. This does indicate that there is a general tendency to consider some of the crimes very grave indeed. This makes sense and supports the possibility that people are taking the process of completing the questionnaire seriously.

Another aspect of the distribution that is worth looking at is the variation between respondents. In Table 5.3 the minimum values assigned to each crime and the maximum values are given, as well as a statistical measure of the degree of variation known as a standard deviation. It can be seen that the minimum and maximum scores for each crime vary considerably. Many crimes achieve a maximum of 100, with the lowest maximum still being 70. This shows that for some people all crimes are regarded as very serious, for others fewer are. For example, person 34 has an average rating of 37 with her lowest being 5 and her highest 70. In contrast, person 7 has an average rating of 72 with his lowest being 30 and his highest 100. Further study could explore what the basis of these differences are; perhaps religious attitudes or personal experience?

Table 5.3 Rank order with average ratings, maximum and minimum, and standard deviation for 23 crimes

Min	Max	Average	Standard Deviation	Crime	Sentence
2	70	16	15	Shoplifting something worth over £20	
1	90	24	23	Soliciting men as a sex worker	
10	60	30	15	Making off without payment	
10	70	31	17	Knowingly selling stolen goods	
10	80	38	23	Possessing heroin	
5	100	40	22	Harassing someone digitally	
5	100	41	24	Causing a violent nuisance in a public place	
10	90	47	22	Blackmail	
10	100	50	26	Carrying an offensive weapon in public	
1	100	51	28	Aiding suicide	
15	100	54	23	Planned commercial robbery	
10	100	54	26	Fraud leading to stealing over £10,000	
5	100	55	25	Practising medicine without a licence	
10	90	56	30	Threat to kill	
5	100	56	26	Polluting a river	
10	100	66	17	Collection of terrorist information	
25	25	66	20	Violently stealing £200 from a stranger	
20	20	71	21	Distributing documents that promote racial hatred	
20	20	73	11	Causing a death through dangerous driving	
60	60	86	17	Fire resulting in death	
10	10	90	9	Making sexual advances to young children	
70	70	94	5	Rape of a stranger	
80	80	96	10	Murder	

Looking further, there is considerable disagreement among responses over the statement 'threat to kill'. This has a minimum value of 10 and a maximum of 90 with a standard deviation of 30. This is a very large range of values. What might have caused this? Given this was a sample of young people, aged 16 and 17 years old, it seems likely that these differences were caused by the ambiguity of the statement. For some youngsters a casual "I'll kill you if you don't …" could be seen as almost a throwaway joke, for others it could be seen as something very serious.

Another intriguing aspect of these variations is revealed when the standard deviations are plotted against the average seriousness ratings, as in Figure 5.2. A distinct inverted J or truncated rainbow, shape can be seen. What this means is that there is a considerable agreement for the serious crimes and moderate agreement for the less serious crimes. The area of most disagreement is the middle range of seriousness. This suggests, for example, that in future studies of differences between people it is those middle-range crimes that will be most productive to explore.

The point is that the variation in responses does indicate something important. All too often researchers jump into looking at the overall results rather than exploring the nuances in the data that will help them understand the overall picture.

Comparison of women's seriousness assessments with men's

Table 5.4 give the mean scores for boys and for girls for each of the 23 crimes.

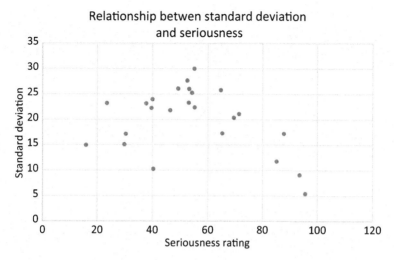

Figure 5.2 Relationship between variations in response as measured by the standard deviation and the average seriousness ratings of the crime

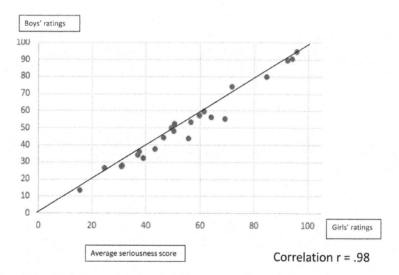

Figure 5.3 Relationship between boys' and girls' average ratings of crime seriousness

Table 5.4 Mean seriousness scores for boys and for girls for each of the 23 crimes

Girls	Boys
15.4	13.5
24.8	26.3
31.1	27.7
31.2	27.9
36.9	34.0
37.5	36.0
39.0	32.4
43.2	37.8
46.6	44.3
49.4	50.2
50.2	48.0
50.6	52.3
55.7	43.8
56.6	53.5
59.7	57.3
61.4	59.5
63.9	56.4
69.0	55.4
71.7	74.2
84.7	80.2
92.4	89.7
94.2	90.8
95.9	94.9

Figure 5.3 shows a scatter plot of the average scores for the young women against those for the young men. It is clear that the scores are very close. The correlation of 0.98 is extremely high indeed, way beyond the chance level. This can therefore be taken as an indication of a very high reliability for this scale. This means that any subsequent relationships found with this questionnaire can be considered with confidence. It also indicates that the boys do not differ very much from the girls in their ways of thinking about crime seriousness.

The diagonal line in Figure 5.3 shows the scores for which both groups would be equal. This helps to demonstrate that the ratings the girls give are slightly higher for most crimes than the boys, because most of the points are below the line. This is supported by the table of actual values. Although the differences are small, the girls' ratings are usually higher than that of the boys. They see most crimes as more serious than the boys do, as others have found, notably Sinden (1981).

Relationship to legal sentencing

Table 5.5 shows my estimates of the typical sentencing in the United Kingdom for each of the 23 crimes.

Figure 5.4 shows the overall relationship between the estimates of seriousness and the typical legal sentencing. This shows that there is a very strong relationship, almost as strong as the reliability correlation comparing boys and girls. This lends further support to the validity of the questionnaire, indicating that it makes considerable sense to the respondents and has a broad relationship to the way the legal process works. This fits the view that legal sentencing is an integral part of how people view the seriousness of crimes. Or, at least, how these young people view their seriousness.

Table 5.5 Broad indications of the legal penalties in the United Kingdom for each type of crime

Penalty	Crime
£150	Throwing away litter
£1,000	Soliciting men as a sex worker
1 year	Practising medicine without a licence
2 years	Making off without payment
2 years	Distributing documents that promote racial hatred
2 years	Polluting a river
3 years	Causing a violent nuisance in a public place
4 years	Carrying an offensive weapon in public
6 months	Shoplifting something worth £20
6 years	Violently stealing £200 from a stranger in the street
7 years	Possessing heroin
7 years	Threat to kill
7 years	Making sexual advances to young children
8 years	Harassing someone by constantly phoning them and sending them text messages
8 years	Deliberately starting a fire that results in death
9 years	Collection of terrorist information
10 years	Fraud
14 years	Aiding suicide
14 years	Causing death through dangerous driving
14 years	Blackmail
14 years	Knowingly selling stolen goods
19 years	Forcible rape of a stranger
20 years	Planned commercial robbery
Whole life	Murder

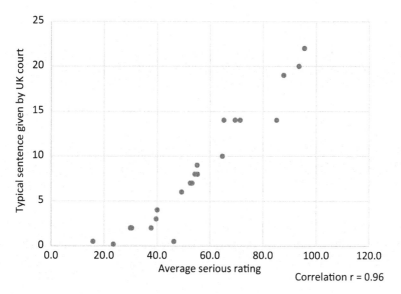

Correlation r = 0.96

Figure 5.4 Relationship of average seriousness rating to typical sentence

CONCLUSIONS

The processes involved in developing and analysing a questionnaire survey have been described. Using the example of views about the seriousness of crimes the various stages in developing a questionnaire have been discussed. The value of a pilot study was described to check various aspects of the questionnaire. This included a careful consideration of the distribution of the responses. The need to establish the reliability and validity of any questionnaire has been emphasised. In the project described this was done both by comparing boys' views with girls' views and the overall ratings of seriousness with the typical sentences the law gives for each crime. Contrary to expectations, there were no large differences between these boys and girls in their overall ratings of seriousness. This, however, provided support for the reliability of the instrument. The correlation with the legal assessment of seriousness through sentencing supported its validity.

OTHER STUDIES THAT COULD USE THIS RESEARCH DESIGN

The possibilities for survey research are endless, but some studies that expand the considerations of crime seriousness are noted:

1. The *experience of being a victim of crime*, or even a person fearing they may be a victim, is an important area for study. A recent extensive exploration by Janssen, Oberwittler, and Koeber (2020) indicates what is possible.

2. Janssen et al. (2020) also illustrate the value of *surveying topics at different points in time*. This allows the exploration of trends, which can relate directly ongoing circumstances, turning the study into a sort of field experiment.

3. An important area of research is *children's experiences of bullying*. Kowalski and Limber (2013) provide a useful example of the sort of survey that can be carried out, demonstrating links of the experience of bullying to other issues, notably physical health and school achievement. A more recent study by Kobayashi and Farrington (2020) looks at bullying cross-nationally in relation to measures of personality.

4. Another related area of research are *views about the conditions under which the serious crime or rape occurs*. There are many myths about this that have become a topic of study in its own right, with standard questionnaires used to explore which myths various groups believe (see McMahon & Farmer, 2011, who use such a questionnaire).

QUESTIONS FOR DISCUSSION

1. What issues influence the judgements of how serious a crime is?

2. In what circumstances are girls' views of crime seriousness likely to be different from that of boys?

3. When might people's judgements of crime seriousness vary from the legal sentencing?

4. Which groups can you think of that might disagree on how serious crimes are? Why might they disagree?

5. Are there any aspects of personality that might relate to judgements of crime seriousness?

NOTES

1 See https://en.wikipedia.org/wiki/Repertory_grid.
2 See https://en.wikipedia.org/wiki/Cognitive_flexibility.
3 Based on Byers (1999).

FURTHER READING

One of the definitive books on questionnaire design, first published in 1966 but updated and reprinted many times since, is:

Oppenheim, A.N. (2000). *Questionnaire design: Interviewing and attitude measurement.* New York, NY: Continuum.

A recent up-to-date overview of survey research is the mammoth handbook:

Vannette, D.L., & Krosnick, J.A. (Eds.) (2018). *The Palgrave handbook of survey research.* London: Palgrave Macmillan. https://doi.org/10.1007/978-3-319-54395-6.

This is too expensive for most students, but should be in any good university library.

REFERENCES

Byers, B. (1999). Teaching about judgments of crime seriousness in research methods. Journal of Criminal Justice Education, 10(2), 339–348. doi: 10.1080/10511259900084651.

Canter, D. (2016). Revealing the conceptual systems of places. In R. Gifford (Ed.), *Research methods for environmental psychology* (pp. 137–159). Chichester, UK: Wiley & Sons.

Einat, T., & Herzog, S. (2011). Understanding the relationship between perceptions of crime seriousness and recommended punishment: An exploratory comparison of adults and adolescents. Criminal Justice Studies, 24(1), 3–21. doi: 10.1080/1478601X.2011.544183.

Hammond, K.R. (1948). Measuring attitudes by error-choice: An indirect method. *Journal of Abnormal and Social Psychology*, 43(1), 38–48. https://doi.org/10.1037/h0059576

Janssen, H.J., Oberwittler, D., & Koeber, G (2020). Victimization and its consequences for well-being: A between- and within-person analysis. *Journal of Quantitative Criminology*. https://doi.org/10.1007/s10940-019-09445-6.

Kobayashi, E., & Farrington, D.P. (2020). Why do Japanese bully more than Americans? Influence of external locus of control and student attitudes toward bullying. *Educational Sciences: Theory and Practice*, 20, 5–19.

Kowalski, R.M., & Limber, S.P. (2013). Psychological, physical, and academic correlates of cyberbullying and traditional bullying. *Journal of Adolescent Health*, 53(Suppl. 1), S13–S20. http://dx.doi.org/10.1016/j.jadohealth.

McMahon, S., & Farmer, L.G. (2011). An updated measure for assessing subtle rape myths. *Social Work Research*, 35(2), 71–81. https://doi.org/10.1093/swr/35.2.71.

Miethe, T.D. (1984). Types of consensus in public evaluations of crime: An illustration of strategies for measuring consensus. Journal of Criminal Law & Criminology, 79(2), 459–473.

Miliaikeala, S.J., Heen, M.A., Lieberman, J.D., Terance, D., & Miethe, T.D. (2014). A comparison of different online sampling approaches for generating national samples. Retrieved from www.unlv.edu/sites/default/files/page_files/27/ComparisonDifferentOnlineSampling.pdf.

O'Connell, M., & Whelan, A. (1996). Taking wrongs seriously: Public perceptions of crime seriousness. British Journal of Criminology, 36(2), 299–318. https://doi.org/10.1093/oxfordjournals.bjc.a014087.

Paulhus, D.L., & Reid, D.B. (1991). Enhancement and denial in socially desirable responding. *Journal of Personality and Social Psychology*, 60, 307–317.

Robson, C., & McCartan, K. (2017). Real world research (4th ed.). Chichester, UK: Wiley.

Rossi, P.H., Berk, R.A., & Campbell, A. (1997). Just punishments: Guideline sentences and normative consensus. Journal of Quantitative Criminology, 13, 267–290. https://doi.org/10.1007/BF02221093.

Sinden, P.G. (1981). Offender gender and perceptions of crime seriousness. *Sociological Spectrum*, 1(1), 39–52. doi: 10.1080/02732173.1981.9981617.

Sommer, R. (1976). The end of imprisonment. Oxford: Oxford University Press.

Taber, K.S. (2018). The use of Cronbach's alpha when developing and reporting research instruments in science education. *Research in Science Education*, 48, 1273–1296. https://doi.org/10.1007/s11165-016-9602-2.

Appendix: The Questionnaire Used in the Example Study[3]

This is an anonymous survey of the views people have on how serious different sorts of crimes are.

It just requires you to indicate for each of the crimes listed below how serious you think that crime is.

Put a number between 1 and 100.

1 for not at all serious

100 for extremely serious indeed.

It is your honest opinion that is required. There are no right or wrong answers. It is up to you what you take seriousness to mean.

Put a number between 1 and 10 in the column to the right to indicate how serious you consider each crime to be	
Aiding suicide 1	
Blackmail 2	
Carrying an offensive weapon in public 3	
Causing death through dangerous driving 4	
Causing a violent nuisance in a public place 5	
Collection of terrorist information 6	
Deliberately starting of a fire that results in death 7	
Distributing documents that promote racial hatred 8	
Rape of a stranger 9	
Fraud leading to stealing over £10,000 10	
Harassing someone by constantly phoning them and sending them text messages 11	
Knowingly selling stolen goods 12	
Making off without payment 13	
Making sexual advances to young children 14	
Murder 15	
Planned commercial robbery 16	
Possessing heroin 17	
Practising medicine without a licence 18	
Shoplifting something worth £20 19	
Soliciting men as a sex worker 20	
Threat to kill 21	
Throwing away litter 22	
Violently stealing £200 from a stranger in the street 23	
Polluting a river 24	

It would be very helpful if you would now answer the following questions:

Are you male/female/other?

What is your age?

The seductions of crime

Synopsis

The title of this chapter is taken from the fascinating book by Jack Katz (1988) in which he explores the emotional aspects of breaking the law. His argument is that crimes are supported by the feelings that are created by carrying them out. One process that gives some dynamism to considerations about emotions is to think of them as part of an unfolding narrative, such as the sadness of a tragedy or the joys of a romance. This idea is developed to consider the implicit or explicit roles that people play when being a criminal.

As a further illustration of the questionnaire survey method, the study proposed in this chapter consists of administering and analysing a simplified version of the narrative role questionnaire (NRQ) (Youngs & Canter, 2012). This was developed for use with criminals as a way of exploring their personal narratives: being a victim, being a hero, being a professional, and acting out revenge.

Access to convicted people to collect this data is difficult, so an example is given of surveying people available through social media, asking them to consider minor illegal activity and misdemeanours.

Some Key Concepts

- personal narratives

- narrative roles questionnaire (NRQ)

- online surveys

- smallest space analysis (SSA).

Background

Most psychological and sociological theories of the causes of criminality focus on the factors beyond the perpetrator's control: their biology, upbringing, social circumstances, or culture. This view of offenders as biosocial organisms is at variance with the legal perspective, which emphasises free will and intentionality. The law regards criminals as actively making decisions, unless there is some very clear reason that they could not, for example because of severe mental illness.

The study proposed in this chapter introduces a narrative approach to criminality. This casts criminals in the leading roles of their own drama. It emphasises the agency of the offender, the positions they take on, leading to or as part of their offending. The narrative approach draws psychology closer to the law, as I've argued in some detail (Canter, 2010). It takes as a starting point that people are explicitly or implicitly acting out their own life stories. These narratives may be a way of making sense of their actions after the event, as some studies suggest. Or they may shape what they do and how they do it. It is difficult to carry out research to distinguish between these possibilities because inevitably studies are conducted after a crime has been committed. Nonetheless, it is fruitful to explore the sorts of roles offenders see themselves as having played when committing crime. Access to offenders for this research is challenging, although not impossible (see, for example, the recent compendium of articles on 'narrative criminology' in Fleetwood, Presser, Sandberg, & Ugelvik, 2019). Therefore, a study is proposed that explores the experiences of people, who have not been convicted of a crime, when carrying out illegal acts and misdemeanours.

The idea of people making sense of their lives through storylines of their unfolding experiences was articulated by Jaques in Shakespeare's *As You Like It*, with the well-known quote: "All the world's a stage, and all the men and women merely players: they have their exits and their entrances; and one man in his time plays many parts." This emphasises the roles people play and the positions they take in different situations. That idea became a dominant part of Goffman's (1959) seminal analysis of social processes, first elaborated in his book *The Presentation of Self in Everyday Life*. His drawing of links between theatrical performance and daily behaviour became known as 'dramaturgical analysis'. The idea that we are all involved in some form of self-presentation, as are actors on a stage, has been extremely influential in sociology and social psychology. It helps in understanding how people see themselves as well as how they want others to see them. This has been the starting point for considering the roles criminals play, the active positions they put themselves in when carrying out crimes, and the narrative forms those roles are part of.

It is important to emphasise that reference to roles, positions, narratives, and storylines, does not imply any sort of falsification or mere 'play-acting' (although it may in some cases, of course). Rather, it is to propose that our experiences are shaped and our actions are influenced by the unfolding narrative we implicitly, or explicitly, regard ourselves as being part of.

Narrative Theory in Criminology

An important aspect of **personal narratives** is that they integrate views of the self. They are not merely a means of sharing an interpretation of experience. As Sclater (2003, p. 317) puts it: "Persons think, feel, act and make moral choices according to narrative structures". Ward (2012, p. 254) describes a narrative role as "a set of beliefs about the self"; he sees these beliefs revolving around "dynamic themes", based upon people's awareness of their emotions, thoughts, and actions. I (Canter 1994) was one of the first to draw attention to the significance of the stories offenders tell themselves and to point to the link between these stories and the actions and the characteristics of offenders, calling these stories "inner narratives" (p. 121). These narratives are shaped by the protagonist's view of his/her self in interaction with the immediate, as well as the broad, social surroundings and culture.

Underlying themes

A number of studies of literary work have proposed that there are only a limited number of dominant narrative themes within any culture. Frye (1957) makes the case that there are four storylines that characterise Western literature, which he calls tragedy, comedy/romance, irony, and adventure. Frye was at pains to insist that he was discussing fictional literature, arguing that lived lives are more complex than structured, imagined fiction. However, it is interesting to note that those exploring how people interact with the world have also been ready to claim some underlying themes, which, as we shall see, resonate with Frye's dominant narratives.

McAdams (2001) draws from a series of studies the proposal that an individual's underlying interaction with others revolves around the two main concepts of agency and communion. This is not so different from the much earlier proposal by Leary (1957), of dominance/submission and love/hate being key characteristics of how people relate to others. Schutz (1992) proposed control and openness/inclusion as central dimensions of his model of social aspects of personality. S (striving for superiority) and O (strivings for intimacy) are the crucial aspects of Herman's (1996) model of personality.

Relating these major themes to the criminological context, Youngs and Canter (2011) used the labels *potency* and *intimacy*. They argued that narrative roles could be identified by drawing on these two facets. They argued the combinations of these facets relate in interesting ways to Frye's dominant storylines. Positive and negative aspects of each facet when combined, yield four narrative roles, summarised in Table 6.1. The roles might have different connotations in the life of an offender, so as part of the adaptation process, Canter and Youngs (2009) changed Frye's comedy/romance theme to 'quest'.

McAdams's (2001) proposal that the narratives of people with high intimacy, who feature love and friendship as a dominant part of their approach to the world, requires some reconsideration for the criminal context. In relation to offences we have proposed that intimacy relates to the role of the victim in the offender's criminal narrative. Do offences involve direct consideration of how the victim may suffer? From this perspective criminal intimacy may be thought of as being brutal or hurtful to others. The proposal is that the concept of intimacy be redefined for crimes as an awareness of the victim and the level of interaction between the victim and offender (Youngs & Canter, 2011).

The potency theme can be redefined as offenders' mastery of the victim and the crime-related circumstances. The imposing of control over the situation and the victim, rather than pursuing success, and showing achievement, which are the core concepts of the agency theme among non-criminal adults.

One of the values of this narrative model of criminality is that it incorporates various psychological processes. For example, the justifications they offer for their deviance can be seen as an integral part of their narrative roles. It is also interesting to note the justifications that support each offence narrative role. Offenders with low levels of potency would have a tendency to deny their responsibility and/or attribute responsibility to others.

Table 6.1 Summarising the way in which the relationship between potency and intimacy combine to generate the four narrative roles (and Frye's fundamental storylines)

Potency / intimacy	High	Low
High	Revenger (quest)	Victim (irony)
Low	Professional (adventure)	Hero (tragedy)

However, offenders with high levels of potency would own the responsibility of their actions with a different interpretation of the meaning of their actions and distort the consequences. People who think of themselves as powerful would not be expected to consider the consequence for their victims unless they were also high in intimacy. Offenders who are low in intimacy would tend to minimise the impact of their actions on the victim through suggesting that the victim was not the real target and/or that the victim deserved it (Youngs & Canter, 2012).

Furthermore, roles incorporate affective components. Adventures are associated with excitement and feelings of significance. Being a tragic victim involves sadness and despair. A professional would be predicted to be emotionally calm. These emotional aspects serve to illustrate how the narrative framework embraces a number of different psychological components, making it a rich basis for research.

THE NARRATIVE ROLES QUESTIONNAIRE

Although an approach that asks offenders to give an account of their lives and their crimes has proven fruitful in revealing their personal narratives (Canter & Youngs, 2012), and as mentioned, a new area of narrative criminology is emerging (Fleetwood et al., 2019), the life-story procedure turns out to be rather time-consuming and does not necessarily give enough emphasis to particular crimes. As indicated earlier, a fruitful way of investigating offence narratives of offenders is to study the roles they recognise as being relevant to their offence actions. These roles draw attention to particular episodes. They emphasise event-related narrative themes that help to make sense of the crimes (Youngs & Canter, 2012).

The need for a standard measure

One of the challenges in the application of the narrative roles to criminal activity is to create standard measures that can be used in future studies and various settings (e.g. prisons, rehabilitation programme, etc.) so that the results can be replicable. Therefore, to develop this approach into an effective survey instrument, narrative roles were derived from open-ended interviews with offenders in discussions about their experiences of committing crimes. This gave rise to a 33-item **narrative roles questionnaire (NRQ)** (Youngs & Canter, 2012). Multivariate analysis of responses to this questionnaire revealed four offence roles, which were labelled: professional, victim, hero, and revenger.

The items representing each narrative role included "the offender's interpretation of the event and his or her actions within that event; the offender's self-awareness or identity in the interpersonal crime event and the emotional and other experiential qualities of the event for the offender" (Youngs & Canter, 2012, p. 6). Taken together these four roles provide a profile of the experience offenders describe. This provides the basis for the proposed study.

The items being drawn from the offenders' statements, in their own words, the questionnaire captures their interpretations of the event and the justifications of the crime. They encapsulate their identity and emotional state at the time of the crime as they remember them.

The quantitative measures of offence narratives do not require an articulate and coherent storytelling. This can be difficult to achieve by most offenders considering their education levels and psychosocial background. Also, the issue of social desirability can be minimised by asking direct, non-threatening, non-judgmental questions to assess their offence roles. This puts fewer demands on the respondent than open-ended qualitative storytelling, which can activate the justification/neutralisation techniques in offenders' stories (discussed in Study 8).

Analysis of responses to the questionnaire allowed Youngs and Canter (2012) to strengthen their model by combining the facets of potency and intimacy; a framework that has been repeated in subsequent studies (e.g. Spruin, Canter, Youngs, & Coulston, 2014).

Summary of narrative roles

As further background to the narrative roles model, here are more details of how each aspect of the implicit narrative is articulated.

Professional role (adventure)

The actions of the professional role are high in potency and low in intimacy. They are focused on achieving control over the environment in order to acquire emotional satisfaction and solid rewards. This role is mostly "provided by burglars and robbers" (Youngs & Canter, 2012, p. 243). The victim is irrelevant to the offender's actions. As a professional, responsibility is accepted for the actions taken. The experiences are essentially reported as pleasurable because of the fulfilment of the main goal (e.g. monetary gains). There is a distinction within offenders who act out the role of professional. Some see the crime as an adventure and focus on the aspects of it as being fun and interesting, while others focus on being in control.

This role maps on to Frye's *adventure narrative*. It captures the excitement of achieving a series of objectives. In such plots those who suffer the consequences of the actor are of little significance. It is the power (potency) of the protagonists that is demonstrated through their actions.

Victim role (irony)

The offender with Frye's *irony narrative* is low in potency and high in intimacy. This is the victim role. The offenders taking this role feels confused and helpless and has no control over the situation. The actions are against their will and consent. They are drawn into the offence by external parties who are significant to them. They cannot make sense of things, they feel that there are no rules. They think they are involved in the crime because of their powerlessness and confusion, which makes them the "main victim of the event" rather than the offender (Canter & Youngs, 2009, p. 129). The responsibility of their actions is attributed to others.

Revenger role (quest)

Frye's *quest narrative* is associated with the revenger role, being high both in intimacy and potency. Offenders believe that they have been treated unfairly, deprived, and wronged. They feel there is nothing else to do but to take revenge and make the people who wronged them pay for it. They seek vengeance for what has been done to them or to significant others. The offence is a justified quest to redress the wrong that has been done.

Hero role (tragedy)

In the criminal context it is proposed that Frye's *tragedy narrative* is one in which the fates are in control. Although the individual can be regarded as a hero, because he is the protagonist in his own story, he is focused on his own experiences, and not interested in others. It is the event that is important not its outcome. He believes that his actions and their consequences are part of a doomed mission. Consequently, perhaps counterintuitively, this is low both in potency and intimacy.

STUDY OF EXPERIENCES OF OFFENDING

Access to convicted people to collect this data is difficult and probably impossible for many students. But again, Katz (1988) led the way. He used his students for most of his data collection, getting them to consider minor illegal activity and misdemeanours. Something similar is proposed here. The possibility of utilising the Internet to collect anonymous responses is illustrated, thereby opening up consideration of how social media may be harnessed for social science research, with its strengths and pitfalls. In the age of COVID-19 the use of **online surveys** will inevitably become even more prevalent than they were before. Therefore, understanding their strengths and pitfalls is increasingly important.

Ethical issues

Exploring the sense people make of their experience while committing a crime is a sensitive matter. Ethical committees will want to be sure that neither you nor the respondents will suffer from participating in the study. Further, in order to get clear and honest responses it is crucial that those answering the questions are totally confident that everything is securely confidential and preferably anonymous. Usually, when collecting such information in prisons responses would either be collected in face-to-face interviews, so the prisoner knows the researcher will take the response away, or if questionnaires are given out, then a sealed envelope is also provided. These are put directly in a box and sealed with no identifying information on the envelopes. The collected data are further anonymised with only identification numbers assigned to each participant with no indication of the participant's identity. This ensures that the prison staff cannot see the responses. As with all voluntary participation, those taking part are informed that their participation is voluntary and unpaid and that they are free to withdraw at any time and without giving a reason. Of course, in a questionnaire survey like the one proposed here, not completing the questionnaire creates complications in the analysis. Those participants would just be excluded from the data.

Procedure

As an example, for the proposed study I made use of the Internet. This did mean that some of the ethical issues that would be crucial when getting data directly from criminals in face-to-face contact had to be made clear in other ways. I was at pains in the initial contact message and on the questionnaire itself to state that anonymity and confidentially was guaranteed and no personal information was collected. However, when I tried this initially, I discovered that the online survey system I used automatically recorded the unique IP address of the respondents, which compromised any claim of total anonymity. I therefore made sure that this aspect was disabled so this information was not recorded.

Other aspects were implicit. It is clear that if people are asked to participate in an online survey that their participation is voluntary. They can also drop out of the survey at any time without anyone knowing who they are or having any opportunity to question them about that. Using a number of different Internet sources for respondents also makes identifying who they are or where they are impossible to identify.

The use of the Internet as a way of accessing respondents

As I have a Twitter account with around 3,000 followers, I thought it would be intriguing to see whether this could be used to generate responses. I therefore posted a series of tweets.

On the specified website I had already uploaded (with the help of an erstwhile PhD student of mine, Miroslava Yaneva) a 12-item questionnaire, shown in Figure 6.1, This is a distilled version of the original 33-item NRQ (Youngs & Canter, 2012). This shorter questionnaire was constructed by selecting three questions for each of the four narrative roles, allowing specific analyses, as in Table 6.2. The question numbers relate to the points in Figure 6.2. The survey as it appeared online is presented in the appendix at the end of the chapter.

Challenges with online surveys

There are some potential problems using online surveys. It is difficult to control, or be sure of, who is completing the questionnaire. The conditions under which people answer the questions and how seriously they take the task of answering is difficult to monitor or to ascertain. Obtaining an appropriate number of responses is also a challenge unless an established panel is available, with the possibility that people are paid, in some way, to respond. When a researcher has someone in front of them being encouraged to participate in a project there is more possibility of enthusing them to take part and to answer questions.

It is possible to invite a specific group of people to respond online, for example if a database of police officers' emails was available, or psychology students. It would never be certain if they were the ones answering, though, as it would be if they were sitting in front of you in a lecture theatre.

Figure 6.1 Tweets inviting people to participate in the study

Table 6.2 Items relating to each role derived from the NRQ

Role	Question	Question no.
Victim	I was helpless	1
	I was a victim	2
	I just wanted to get it over with	3
Revenger	I was getting my own back	4
	I was trying to get revenge	5
	It was right	6
Hero	It was interesting	7
	It was a mission	8
	I felt like a hero	9
Professional	I was like a professional	10
	I was doing a job	11
	It was routine	12

Source: Adapted from Youngs and Canter (2012).

In the tweets I sent out you will see my attempt to encourage people to participate. I repeated the tweets three times to get more responses. The Twitter data shows there were diminishing returns in doing this. The first tweet got ten retweets and ten 'likes', the second only two retweets and four 'likes', the third only two retweets and one 'like'. This is against the backdrop of around 3,000 'followers'. In my experience unsolicited postal surveys get about a 10% response rate, but the indications are that my Twitter approach was far less successful than that. However, the use of social media and online survey systems to obtain data is doubtless growing. With a more committed and organised system than my attempt here there is doubtless great potential in using these opportunities.

Many of the potential problems with online surveys are also present when a questionnaire is given out to people in face-to-face contacts, such as a class of students, or when people are stopped in the street. But the inherent anonymity of Internet contacts can make the process more problematic. On the other hand, the possible secrecy of social media participants also has some advantages. If the information being sought is of a sensitive nature, or something that people may not wish to share in public, then the anonymity of revealing this on the Internet may make people more likely to participate than if they were called upon to admit that information to someone who is physically present.

There are also assessments that can be made of online surveys that are more difficult if a questionnaire is handed out to a group of people. The most direct and obviously useful measurement is the length of time it takes a person to complete the pro forma. A comparison of the time it took any individual to answer the questions can be compared with the average for all respondents. This survey is very short and the average time to complete it is around three minutes. Therefore, a completion in under one minute seems very unrealistic. That suggests the person just rushed through without reading the questions or thinking about the answers. Extremely long response times, for example five hours or a day, are also suspicious, especially for a short, uncomplicated, tick-box questionnaire such as the present one. Consequently, it is prudent to exclude those that are completed very quickly or very slowly indeed.

Another advantage of an online survey is that it is possible to ensure every question is answered. Of course, people can drop out whenever they wish, but their contribution is automatically ignored. They cannot, though, accidentally miss a question. The software insists they give an answer. They have to answer every question in order to exit the survey. One other potential problem is that the same person could answer the questions over and over again. The computer system can assign each access a random number and not allow responses if that access emerges again. This is more difficult to stop if questionnaires are handed out and collected in again. A person could obtain a bundle of them and complete them all.[1]

Although this was not included in this brief survey, there is another way to ensure that participants are focused on the statements and do not just give random responses. It is called an attention filter question, which asks participants to choose a specific answer, for example, the statement would be: "This is an attention filter question, please choose 'Always'". If they do not choose 'Always' their participation is automatically terminated. If they do, they are allowed to continue with the survey. These are not necessary in short surveys with a few statements though. They are more productive in lengthy surveys of many pages where participants may get bored and choose random responses just to get it over with.

Including some questions that are negative in relation to the others is another way of checking that people are actually reading them carefully. For example, you could include the question "I did not feel like a hero", or "I was just an amateur" as well as the positive versions, then checking that the answers to the positive and negative questions were strongly negatively correlated.

There is a further way of ensuring the answers are appropriate and are not just random, or thoughtless. That is whether the results make any sense. This is really an aspect of the reliability and validity of the questionnaire discussed in Study 5. As mentioned, the present questionnaire was constructed of three questions for each of the four roles derived from an earlier literature. Do the results support this model? If they do not it could be due to a weakness of the model, ambiguities in the questionnaire, or that people have not answered it seriously. If some other interesting result emerges that makes psychological sense, then it does indicate that people are answering carefully and the questionnaire is capturing something interesting. In this case it is the hypothesised model that is open to question, not the questionnaire or the respondents.

Results of example study

A total of 13 women and 9 men responded to my Twitter invitation. Their ages ranged from 18 to 67, with a mean of 34 years. That is a useful spread of various adults. This was a very small sample, but serves to illustrate the approach with results that do make sense.

The time it took them to complete the survey ranged from 47 seconds to 6 minutes and 44 seconds, with the modal time being about two and a half minutes. That is a notable range and may suggest that the extremes should be looked at rather carefully, but as a pilot exploration of the way a study like this may be done, no times seem extremely different from the average.

Activities described

A surprisingly wide range of illegal activities were described by the anonymous respondents, for example:

- I was involved in buying and selling drugs.
- When I was little, I threw a rock at my brother that concussed him.
- I fought someone and knocked his teeth out.
- I stole money from my best friend.
- I hit someone repeatedly who hurt my son.
- I stole a silly toy from a shop when I was a child.
- I conned my way into getting phones that I sold on.

Interestingly, they divide neatly into violent actions – crimes against the person, and forms of theft. This allows some interesting comparisons.

Multivariate analysis

As with any new instrument, the first stage is to see how well it is working. In this case that means considering the underlying model from which the data was derived. This is operationalised in Table 6.2, which lists the way each of the sets of three questions should relate to each other to reflect each of the four roles and be distinguished from the other roles. A powerful way of testing this is to use a statistical procedure that has been in use for over half a century.

The idea behind this procedure is relatively straightforward: if two questions mean something similar then they are likely to be answered in a similar way across a number of respondents. In other words, the two questions will correlate with each other. Therefore, a direct test of the model summarised in Table 6.2 would be that the questions for each role would correlate highly with each other, and less highly with those related to other roles.

In the present case, for example, the statements "it was right" and "I was getting my own back" are both hypothesised to be aspects of the *revenger* role. In this sample they correlate 0.61. In contrast, the statement "I was like a professional" has a negative correlation of -0.18 with "it was right", indicating that answering 1 being "very much" is likely to have an answer to the other of "not at all". It is therefore possible to consider the correlation of every one of the 12 questions with every one of the others. That requires examining 66 different correlations and attempting to find the pattern within them.

Unless there is a very strong and obvious pattern within the matrix of every correlation with every other, it is extremely difficult to make sense of so many individual relationships. Statisticians have developed very many ways of helping to reveal the patterns within a set of correlations. These are sometimes known as complexity reduction procedures, or when they use spatial representations of relationships, they may be called data 'visualisations'. Because they are working with a large number of variables, they are a branch of multivariate statistics. One of these procedures that I have used widely for many different sets of data was developed over half a century ago, but still has great power and is now easy to run on many domestic computers. Its great advantage is that it can be understood without the need to make sense of the underlying matrix algebra. It was developed by Guttman and Lingoes (Guttman, 1968; Lingoes & Guttman 1967), and is known as **smallest space analysis (SSA)**. A more detailed account of SSA and the software available for producing these results is given in Appendix B at the end of this book.

The procedure represents the correlations as distances in space. The higher the correlation between two variables the closer they will be in the resulting spatial configuration. For the present example it is not really necessary to understand more than that. There is, though, one very fruitful consequence of the visual representation of correlations between questions. A test of a model, as illustrated in Table 6.2, would be the expectation that questions that related to the same role would form a distinct region of the space. They would relate to each other and be at some distance from questions relating to other roles.

A further note of explanation is probably necessary here. This is the idea that items that have similar meaning will form identifiable regions in the spatial representation of the relationships between all items. These are known as 'regional hypotheses'. This is different to saying the items will form 'clusters'. Regionality implies a recognition of what the items represent and how they help to identify an area of conceptually similar issues. Regions have borders; therefore, items close to a border are more likely to have some similarity with items near the other side of that border. There is not expected to inevitably be a totally distinct set of groupings, as is assumed in clusters, where an item is within or outside the cluster.

Figure 6.2 shows the SSA results (in just two dimensions) for the responses from the 22 people to the 12 questions.

The dashed lines in Figure 6.2 are drawn to indicate boundaries between different regions. They present an interpretation of the configuration. In the present case they show a test of the hypothesised regions. They demonstrate that it is possible to identify the four regions hypothesised as derived from the earlier study by Youngs and Canter (2012). This is encouraging support for the model, although it is only based on 22 respondents and is a reduction of the original 33 questions to 12 selected from the original published SSA.

The caution that is needed when drawing results from such a small sample is important to clarify, especially when this is an anonymous selection of unknown respondents. When the sample is so small, any one individual's response can have a material impact on the overall results. Consequently, any ambiguities in the questions, or lack of careful consideration by those answering, or even an unusual experience that is being described, can all add 'noise' to the data. This has to be taken into account when interpreting the results. It is another reason why interpreting the results as regions of the space makes sense. Regions imply that each question represents a variety of possible questions, or interpretations of a question. They are regarded as a sample of possible questions in that area. Just as taking some soil samples would be used to indicate the nature of the soil in an area although only a few samples were taken, not the whole area.

Interestingly, the SSA configuration reveals more than support for the original model. Always taking account of this being a small sample, Figure 6.2 also provides some further insight into how these roles relate to each other. The horizontal axis, ranging from feeling being a victim on the left to being a hero on the right, ranges from negative to positive emotions. It is even possible to interpret the items at the middle of this axis, "I was doing a job" and "it was routine" as having neutral emotional implications.

Another aspect of the configuration, which shows how helpful this visualisation of relationships can be, is that the items to the right of the line drawn from bottom left to top right are spread out. This implies

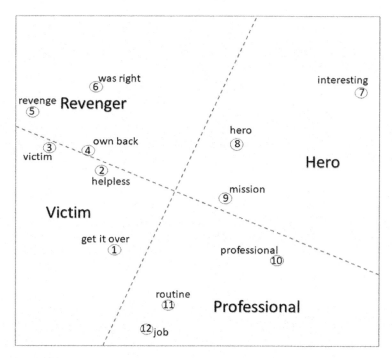

Figure 6.2 SSA results from 22 respondents

Note: The numbers refer to the statements in Table 6.2. Brief summaries of those statements are given as labels next to each question

that there are lots of subtle variations in those regions. This can be seen by the range of questions in the professional region of the original Youngs and Canter (2012) SSA. Questions such as "felt powerful" and "knew what I was doing" imply different aspects to other items in the region, such as "it was exciting" or "it was an adventure".

By contrast, the items to the left of Figure 6.2 are rather close together, especially those on the border of the line running from left to right. The three questions, "was a victim", "getting my own back" and "was helpless" could be interpreted as being on either side of that line. This makes sense in suggesting that being a victim and seeking revenge are closely related. In the present case people are remembering something that happened some time ago. It is therefore very possible that the narratives of being a victim and then seeking revenge run into each other. This is supported by looking directly at the scores from the person whose actions were "hit someone repeatedly who hurt my son". That person gave a score of 4 for "getting my own back" and 3 for "I was a victim" and for "I was helpless". The respondent even helpfully added a comment indicating they felt their actions were appropriate because they were defending someone who could not defend themselves (an interesting illustration, by the way, of a justification for violence that is discussed in Study 8).

Role profiles

Having demonstrated the validity of this short questionnaire, by showing that the hypothesised components have been revealed, the next step is to consider the actual levels of each role across the crimes. To do this the responses to the three questions identified for each role are added together. From the earlier consideration of the details apparent in the SSA, I am aware that sticking close to the model

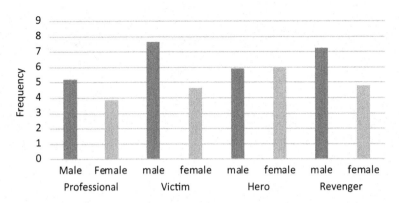

Figure 6.3 Comparison of male and female role profiles

in Table 6.2 does hide some subtleties, but as an illustration of the way forward this is reasonable. From the current sample, it is interesting to compare the role profiles of men and women and violent actions compared with those relating to property crimes.

Figure 6.3 shows the average scores on each of the four profiles for men and for women. These averages were calculated by adding the responses for each of the three questions then dividing by the number of people responding in each category. Because there are 5-point scales, added across three items, the lowest value possible is 3 and the maximum is 15. It has to be emphasised again that the sample here is very small and only used for illustration. It would also be necessary to carry out some inferential statistics to determine if the results were above chance level. However, the profile shown in Figure 6.3 is intriguing and would be of note if replicated with a larger sample.

With the exception of the hero role, men tend to have higher average scores than the women. Interestingly they are particularly likely to see themselves as victims involved in revenge. It would be necessary to look closely at the crimes involved in order to determine the basis of this. A simple point, as would be expected, is that men are more likely to commit violent crimes. The great majority of crimes committed by women relate to thefts of one sort or another.

The suggestion that violent crimes are more likely to involve victim and revenger roles is supported by the averages illustrated in Figure 6.4. This figure also indicates that the professional role is more likely to be associated with property crime than violent crime.

These findings do accord with earlier studies with larger samples of convicted criminals, notably Canter and Ioannou (2004) who found that violent offenders described the experience of their crimes as less pleasurable than those who committed property crimes. There does therefore seem to be an interesting and important way of making sense of the experience of committing a crime, at least in retrospect, when thinking of the narrative role enacted.

There are a number of practical implications for these findings. For example, as Youngs and Canter (2009) and Read and Powell (2011) have proposed, the way in which an interview may be carried out could appropriately be different for people living different offender narratives. The inferred offender/suspect characteristics from the narrative roles contribute to forming the initial contact, determining the approach and the strategies that are going to be used during the interview.

The speculation is that people who think of themselves as professionals would be more open to a considered, well-organised interview that treated them as being in control. By contrast suspects who regard themselves as victims may be willing to admit their crimes if dealt with in a conciliatory manner. The rich hypotheses derived from this perspective have yet to be tested.

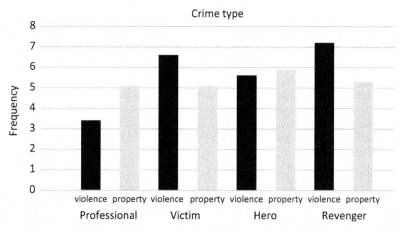

Figure 6.4 Comparison of property and victim role profiles

Another interesting direction for research is to consider how interpreting the role-related aspects of the actions during a crime might indicate the characteristics of the criminal. This is the idea of using the narrative framework for helping to develop the inferences that can link criminal actions to offender characteristics – which I have summarised as the A→C equation (Canter, 2011), or more exotically the 'profiling equation'. This, for example, would lead to the hypothesis that the professional role would be associated with rather different criminal actions to the victim role. The details of these hypotheses do require development and obtaining data would be quite challenging. But the illustrative study in the present chapter indicates one possible way of achieving this.

Further practical applications come from considering what it is that leads a person to desist from crime. Maruna (2001), among others, has emphasised that helping people to stop their criminal activity relates to them building a different narrative that no longer supports offending. I was struck by this possibility when I unexpectedly got a letter from a man in South Africa who was in prison for violent crimes. He wrote that he had read my book *Criminal Shadows* and had realised that he had always thought of himself as a victim. By revising his idea of himself he managed to control his violence.

Another study using this narrative perspective, which follows a similar model of major themes discussed here and points to practical implications, is the consideration of suicide as revealed in suicide notes (Grayson, Tzani-Pepelasi, Pylarinou, Ioannou, & Artinopoulou, 2020). For example, what is described as an 'altruistic professional' identity relating to suicide suggests the need to help people with suicidal ideation, or failed attempts, to see the significance of that view as less altruistic and more hurtful to others.

CONCLUSIONS

Starting with the emotions experienced during a crime as highlight by Katz (1988), it has been argued that a narrative perspective gives a more dynamic focus on the unfolding life stories that offenders (like all of us) live. One particular episode in that life story, when committing a crime, has been the basis for proposing a rather unusual study. That of asking people who are not identified as criminal, or convicted offenders, to think of an illegal act they have carried out and to complete a shortened form of the NRQ to describe their experiences of doing that, as they remember it. A sample solicited through the Internet, invited through my Twitter account, with an online questionnaire using an established online survey system (Qualtrics) also demonstrated the potential for this sort of study.

OTHER STUDIES THAT COULD USE THIS RESEARCH DESIGN

The use of online surveys has proven valuable in this example even though only a few people responded. With a more extensive search for participants, or the use of an available panel it is likely many more responses would have been forthcoming. Online surveys have become very popular in many areas of social and psychological research and will undoubtedly become the dominant form of survey research in the post-COVID-19 era. They are relatively easy to set up, but are fraught with potential problems. Careful consideration needs to be given to recruiting respondents and the management of the survey. Just sending out a questionnaire to an emailing list without thinking through the implications is essentially lazy and likely to be unproductive.

The brief version of the NRQ has also proven interesting enough to people not selected for their criminal history to obtain enlightening responses. This could therefore be used in relation to many other aspects of anti-social activity. For example, people who bully or have been bullied, those involved in gangs, or specific groups such as recreational drug users could all be a focus of research using this instrument.

The range of illegal activity that people were willing to admit to in this quick, short study, also suggests that there is a source of information on criminality that is not widely explored. Most studies have a captive audience, often literally in prison. Those who may never have been convicted of a crime, but who have carried out illegal activity are an important source of information. Are those who have been convicted very different from those who get away with crimes without ever being detected? Current data sets make it difficult to know.

QUESTIONS FOR DISCUSSION

1. What are the advantages and disadvantages of using social media as a source of survey responses? What differences might there be between different social media, for example between Twitter and Facebook and Snapchat?

2. What roles other than those considered in this chapter may be relevant to carrying out illegal activity?

3. What needs to be considered when asking people to describe their experiences when doing something illegal?

4. How else could you find out what people experience when they do something illegal?

5. Can you think of any situations in which you could explore offenders' experiences while actually committing a crime?

NOTE

1   This may seem unlikely, but I do know of fraudulent researchers who have done just this.

FURTHER READING

Canter, D. (Ed.). (1985). *Facet theory: Approaches to social research.* New York, NY: Springer Verlag.
Canter, D., Kaouri, C., & Ioannou, M. (2003). The facet structure of criminal narratives. In S. Levy & D. Elizur (Eds.), *Facet theory: Towards a cumulative social science* (pp. 27–38). Ljubljana, Slovenia: Faculty of Arts, Center for Educational Development.

McAdams, D. (2001). The psychology of life stories. *Review of General Psychology*, 5(2), 100–122.
Presser, L. (2009). The narratives of offenders. *Theoretical Criminology*, 13, 177–200.

References

Canter, D. (1994). *Criminal shadows*. London: HarperCollins.
Canter, D. (2010). Criminals' personal narrative. In J.M. Brown & E.A. Campbell (Eds.), The Cambridge handbook of forensic psychology (pp. 791–794). Cambridge, UK: Cambridge University Press.
Canter, D. (2011). Resolving the offender 'profiling equations' and the emergence of an investigative psychology. *Current Directions in Psychological Science*, 20(1), 5–10. https://doi.org/10.1177/0963721410396825.
Canter, D., & Ioannou, M. (2004). Criminals' emotional experiences during crimes. *International Journal of Forensic Psychology*, 1(2), 71–81.
Canter, D., & Youngs, D. (2009). *Investigative psychology: Offender profiling and the analysis of criminal action*. Chichester, UK: John Wiley & Sons.
Canter, D., & Youngs, D. (2012). Sexual and violent offender victim role assignment: A general model of offending style. *Journal of Forensic Psychiatry and Psychology*, 23(3), 297–326. doi:10.1080/14789949.2012.69012.
Fleetwood, J., Presser, L., Sandberg, S., & Ugelvik, T. (Eds.) (2019). *The Emerald handbook of narrative criminology*. Bingley, UK: Emerald Publishing.
Frye, N. (1957). *Anatomy of criticism: Four essays*. Princeton, NJ: Princeton University Press.
Goffman, E. (1959). *The presentation of self in everyday life*. New York, NY: Doubleday.
Grayson, S., Tzani-Pepelasi, C., Pylarinou, N.P., Ioannou, M., & Artinopoulou, V. (2020). Examining the narrative roles in suicide notes. *Journal of Investigative Psychology and Offender Profiling*, 17(2), 142–159. https://doi.org/10.1002/jip.1545
Guttman, L. (1968). A general nonmetric technique for finding the smallest coordinate space for a configuration of points. *Psychometrika*, 33, 469–506. https://doi.org/10.1007/BF02290164.
Herman, H.J.M. (1996). Voicing the self: From information processing to dialogical interchange. *Psychological Bulletin*, 119, 31–50.
Katz, J. (1988). *Seductions of crime: Moral and sensual attractions in doing evil*. New York, NY: Basic Books.
Leary, T. (1957). *Interpersonal diagnosis of personality*. New York, NY: Ronald Press.
Lingoes, J.C., & Guttman, L. (1967). Nonmetric factor analysis: A rank reducing alternative to linear factor analysis. *Multivariate Behavioral Research*, 2(4), 485–505. doi: 10.1207/s15327906mbr0204_6.
McAdams, D. (2001). The psychology of life stories. *Review of General Psychology*, 5(2), 100–122.
Maruna, S. (2001). *Making good: How ex-convicts reform and rebuild their lives*. Washington, DC: American Psychological Association.
Read, J.R., & Powell, M.B. (2011). Investigative interviewing of child sex offender suspects: Strategies to assist the application of a narrative framework. Journal of Investigative Psychology and Offender Profiling, 8(2), 163–177. https://doi.org/10.1002/jip.135.
Schutz, W. (1992). Beyond FIRO-B – 3 new theory-derived measures – element B: behaviour, element F: feelings, element S: self. *Psychological Reports*, 70, 915–937.
Sclater, S.D. (2003). What is the subject? *Narrative Inquiry*, 13(2), 1–14.
Spruin, E., Canter, D., Youngs, D., & Coulston, B., (2014). Criminal narratives of mentally disordered offenders: An exploratory study. *Journal of Forensic Psychology Practice*, 14(5), 438–455. doi: 10.1080/15228932.2014.965987.
Ward, T. (2012). Commentary: Narrative identity and forensic psychology – a commentary on Youngs and Canter. *Legal and Criminological Psychology*, 17(2), 250–261.
Youngs, D., & Canter, D. (2009). An emerging research agenda for investigative interviewing: hypotheses from the narrative action system. *Journal of Investigative Psychology and Offender Profiling*, 6(2), 91–99. .https://doi.org/10.1002/jip.105.
Youngs, D., & Canter, D. (2011). Narrative roles in criminal action: An integrative framework for differentiating offenders. *Legal and Criminological Psychology*, 17, 233–249.
Youngs, D., & Canter, D. (2012). Offenders' crime narratives as revealed by the narrative roles questionnaire. *International Journal of Offender Therapy and Comparative Criminology*, 57(3), 289–231.

Appendix: The Survey as it Appeared Online

This questionnaire asks about your experiences of doing something, wrong. It may have been illegal or just something that many people would find unacceptable. It could have been stealing something from a shop, hitting out at somebody, or any of the range other misdemeanours that we all do from time to time.

We want to know how you felt when doing that. This survey is completely anonymous and only one researcher will see the results. No individuals will be mentioned in any summary accounts. So please be honest and make sure you deal with every statement below.

Please very briefly describe what you did that you remember well. This is anonymous and there is not enough detail for identification so please tell us.

Now, for each statement below please indicate how much that related to your experience of carrying out that action, by clicking on the appropriate button from "not at all" to "very much".

1. I was like a professional

Not at all	Just a little	Some	A lot	Very much
○	○	○	○	○

2. It was right

Not at all	Just a little	Some	A lot	Very much
○	○	○	○	○

3. It was interesting

Not at all	Just a little	Some	A lot	Very much
○	○	○	○	○

4. It was routine

Not at all	Just a little	Some	A lot	Very much
○	○	○	○	○

5. I was doing a job

Not at all	Just a little	Some	A lot	Very much
○	○	○	○	○

6. I was getting my own back

Not at all	Just a little	Some	A lot	Very much
○	○	○	○	○

7. It was a mission

Not at all	Just a little	Some	A lot	Very much
○	○	○	○	○

8. I was helpless

Not at all	Just a little	Some	A lot	Very much
○	○	○	○	○

9. I was a victim

Not at all	Just a little	Some	A lot	Very much
○	○	○	○	○

10. I just wanted to get it over with

Not at all	Just a little	Some	A lot	Very much
○	○	○	○	○

11. I was trying to get revenge

Not at all	Just a little	Some	A lot	Very much
○	○	○	○	○

12. I felt like a hero

Not at all	Just a little	Some	A lot	Very much
○	○	○	○	○

Please let us have any comments on this.

Are you:

Male	Female	Other
○	○	○

What is your age?

Section 3
Case studies

FRAUD

STUDY 7
How fraudsters persuade

SYNOPSIS

A lot can be learned about the psychology of persuasion from examining Internet-based fraud. This is so rampant that many examples can be found in many email inboxes. Detailed consideration of exactly how this fraud is constructed provides a good example of case study methodology. The study reveals the components of any communication that increases its plausibility. One aspect of this, which is often undervalued, is how the fraudulent communication is embedded in a recognisable narrative. The structure that characterises meaningful narratives is therefore also of value in studying cybercrimes.

SOME KEY CONCEPTS

- individuating information
- components of persuasion
- plausible narratives
- qualitative versus quantitative research
- content analysis
- unitisation
- inter-rater reliability.

BACKGROUND

Internet-based fraud is now the largest form of financial crime in any modern economy. The amount of money that is illegally obtained by fraudsters using contact with their victims over the Internet is absolutely astonishing. The overall amount of money lost in any year runs into many billions of pounds. In the United Kingdom, over 100,000 people have been scammed, including over 40% of small businesses. The cleverness of Internet-based fraudsters is such that I myself had nearly £20,000 fraudulently taken from my bank accounts due to my being persuaded to give online access to them. Fortunately, I got all the money back, but the experience did make me fascinated with how these criminals managed to get past my usual caution.

Many individuals lose hundreds or thousands of pounds, but some lose millions. This can be devastating, especially when people lose their life savings or their business no longer has the funds to survive. Some victims are known to have committed suicide because of the shame they felt for succumbing to the scam, or because they could no longer see how they could survive. The people who swindle vast amounts of money from the National Health Service (NHS) or other public institutions limit the funds those organisations have to pay for the services they offer. The scams consequently impact everyone who relies on those services.

The varieties of types of fraud are legion. Just about any legitimate activity can be harnessed by criminals to obtain money illegally. The following list details ten frequently occurring types of fraud in the United States:[1]

1. *Online auctions.* Misrepresented or undelivered goods.

2. *General merchandise.* Misrepresented or undelivered goods.

3. *Work-at-home schemes.* Fraudulent opportunities that allow individuals to earn thousands of dollars a month in work-at-home ventures. The consumer sends money for start-up materials, but the materials are not adequate.

4. *'Nigerian' money offers.* Deceptive promises of large sums of money, if consumers agreed to pay the transfer fee.

5. *Lotteries.* Asking winners to pay before claiming their non-existent prize.

6. *Advance-fee loans.* Request a fee from consumers in exchange of promised personal loans.

7. *Phishing.* Emails pretending to represent a credible source, ask consumers for their personal information (e.g. credit card number).

8. *Prizes/sweepstakes.* Request a payment from consumers in order for them to claim their non-existent prize.

9. *Internet access services.* Misrepresentation of the cost of Internet access and other services, which are often not provided.

10. *Investments.* False promises of gains on investments.

The proportion, types, and frequencies of fraud are changing all the time as criminals develop new ways of cheating people. As would be quite predictable, the COVID-19 pandemic has already spawned many fraudulent activities taking advantage of people's anxiety and gullibility.

The great majority of frauds are perpetrated over the Internet, either through websites or email, although a growing number are coming through text messages and social media. There can be little doubt that the increasing uptake of Internet communication has increased the opportunity for scams. Why rob a bank when you can steal much more money from the comfort of your own home in a different country to where the victim is?

The reasons for the power of the Internet as a vehicle for fraud are not difficult to see.

1. Many Internet users do not understand how the Internet works. They think of it as like a book. They do not understand the computer code that is behind every aspect of a web page or email.

2. A lot of people work on the assumption that someone who deals with them in an organised and apparently professional way, although by electronic communication, is as trustworthy as they would be if they met them in person.

3. The distance from the source of communication over emails and other electronic media provides an anonymity that allows fraudsters to present themselves in any way they want. Men can pretend to be women. People in Lagos can pretend to be in London. The possibilities for deception are virtually endless.

4. The scammers can automatically target, thousands, probably even millions, of people at the same time. They only need a minuscule proportion of those people to respond for their crime to generate large sums of money.

The essence of these scams is to convince people that what is on offer is genuine. That the message and messenger can be trusted. This is about persuading the victim that they should believe what they are told and that the trust ensures the money they spend is appropriate. How this is achieved can teach us a lot about the arts of persuasion and the psychological processes involved.

PERSUASION

There are plenty of studies on the psychology of persuasion that can be drawn on to establish whether or how fraudsters utilise these psychological processes. A widely cited approach based on studies of salesmen and fundraisers has been proposed by Cialdini (1993), although it has been built on by many others (e.g. Oyibo, Orji, & Vassileva, 2017; Whitty, 2013). The six aspects that influence how effective persuasion is from Cialdini's (1993) framework are:

1. *Authority.* The source of the message has high credibility. He (typically a man but not always) indicates, directly or indirectly, that he knows what he is talking about and has access to specialist sources that give him authority.

2. *Scarcity.* The claim that what is on offer has limited availability. This is used to indicate both that the offer has value because others are taking advantage of it, as well as requiring the victim to act quickly without due diligence.

3. *Liking and similarity.* If the source of the information is believed to be similar to the person receiving the message this enhances the likelihood of accepting that message. When, in addition, the person making the offer indicates they like the recipient, for example by complimenting them, this can overcome any reticence, fear, or even threat that the offer may pose.

4. *Reciprocation.* Most people will tend to respond to a person who does something for them. For example, in an early study by Kunz and Woolcott (1976) 28% of people who received Christmas cards from complete strangers replied to those cards. Reciprocation is, after all, the basis of many social interactions. Doing something for a person, even if the person did not request it, can set in motion a responding action.

5. *Consistency.* People like to be reliable in what they do. Once they've made a commitment to a course of action there are personal and social pressures to maintain that action. Even a small step in a particular direction will encourage a person to carry on consistently. A persuasive technique that emerges from this is to get people to commit to a relatively minor action, then to encourage them to proceed with

something a little more significant. This can accumulate over time to enable fraudsters to obtain large sums of money.

6. *Social validation.* Do others support the actions being proposed? If the message implies that there are general norms that encourage actions their value is more likely to be accepted. Most people want to be seen to be part of a social group, behaving like others do. Consequently, if the message includes information about what others do then it is more likely to be acted on.

These six processes can be used as a framework for considering fraudulent messages. They provide a content analysis structure as a starting point for examining actual messages.

Embedded Narratives

There is another interesting aspect of communications when they come out of the blue, from people you've had no previous contact with. How do they establish their credentials and lead those few victims who fall for their proposals to believe them? They have to establish a context within which their persuasive techniques can work. They do this by providing a narrative, an account of what and where they are that can create a plausible story.[2] A story is more likely to seem plausible when it draws on general expectations of what a story will consist of. One of the most influential accounts of the constituents of a convincing story is derived from the fascinating work of Labov (1972), who was an American sociolinguist. He identified six components that exist in most stories. But although his exploration was to discover what stories consist of, his work can be taken to indicate the components that make a story plausible. Although he dealt with oral traditions, written accounts that have a vernacular quality to them also lend themselves to his analysis. The components Labov (1972) identified are:

1. *Abstract.* This introduces the story and its context, giving some hint of its theme.

2. *Orientation.* The actors involved, where and when, are indicated to provide clues to the context in which the story takes place.

3. *Complication.* Here the events in the narrative are recounted. They typically involve some complications, often a reaction to events that make the sequence of events necessary. There may be various strands to these.

4. *Evaluation.* The significance of the account is emphasised in order to state or imply the reasons for telling the story.

5. *Resolution.* After the evaluation the central message is indicated, often with the description of the consequences or outcome of the events.

6. *Coda.* This indicates that the story has an end by bringing the listener back to the here and now, possibly summarising the moral or message of the account.

Not all stories have all components. The coda, in particular, is not always needed. Embedding the techniques of persuasion in a narrative helps to support many of the aspects of the fraudster's message. For example, by indicating who the storyteller is, within a viable context within the orientation aspect, serves to strengthen his authority. A typical story also has some complicating features that make it more interesting and adds to its plausibility.

Another aspect of storytelling is that the six components usually follow the sequence listed here. Modern novelists and film-makers do break up this sequence to engage their audiences more, but this is done in subtle way so that although the temporal sequence may not be maintained the roles of the six aspects still occur in the same sequence. As the French New Wave film director Jean Luc-Goddard put it: "A story should have a beginning, a middle and an end, but not necessarily in that order." There are a number of studies that show that narratives are easier to understand (Johnson & Bransford, 1972) and remember (Carroll & Korukina, 1999) when presented in a logical order. Canter et al. (2003) also demonstrated that stories are more likely to be believed if the six components were presented in the order indicated by Labov.

More recent studies, elegantly summarised by Street, Bischof, Vadillo, and Kingstone (2015), have addressed the common finding that people are not very good at detecting whether a communication is true or false. These studies are most often laboratory-based in which the experimental conditions are very constrained. In daily life, outside of psychologists' contorted explorations, people are often very trusting (Bond & DePaulo, 2008. This is perhaps not surprising because society would not function unless people told the truth most of the time, as demonstrated by DePaulo et al. (2003).

Part of the reason why many attempts at fraud are not successful is that they lack what Street calls, with a rather unnecessarily invented term, **"individuating information"** (Street et al., 2015). He means the particular aspects, relating directly to that message, that may give an indication that it is true or not. Such things as the amount of verifiable detail. Many researchers have shown this is important in judging whether something is genuine or not. Nahari, Vrij, and Fisher (2013) for example, demonstrate that liars are more likely to offer details that are not verifiable. The verifiable details are typically specific to the message and thus 'individuating'. Fraudsters are implicitly (or possible consciously) aware of the need to indicate specific features in their messages that will make them believable. The **components of persuasion** and narrative structure, described above, provide a framework for considering how they provide this 'individuating information'.

Fraudsters also have to guard against the general context of what their audience is likely to believe. As Street et al. (2015) point out, many studies have demonstrated that there is a tendency in daily life, for quite appropriate reasons, to assume you are being told the truth. There are contexts in which the opposite tendency is present. For instance, there is evidence that salespeople are often not believed (DePaulo & DePaulo, 1989); that officers disbelieve suspects (Meissner & Kassin, 2002), but only when judging statements related to their job (Masip & Herrero, 2017); or that people trained to be more suspicious in general can lead them to be biased to disbelieve (Masip, Alonso, Garrdio, & Herrero, 2009).

Fraudsters have to find ways of buying into the truth-believing tendency or overcoming the assumption that an approach is fraudulent. Again, I would suggest they do this by embedding their persuasive techniques in **plausible narratives**. The most direct example of this is when a fraudster pretends to be someone else. There are often attempts from fraudsters on the Internet to present themselves as coming from reputable organisations such as Internet providers sending emails, or creating websites that look just like genuine organisations. This type of fakery has become legion on social media. The fact that the Twitter handle for the president of the United States is @realDonaldTrump shows the need to overcome the possibility of false tweets from those pretending to be the president.

I get emails every day that present as if they are messages from my Internet provider, or some utility organisation or bank, asking me to log on to a website to upgrade, pay an outstanding bill, avoid having my account closed, or any number of other reasons. If I were to log in and give my security details, the criminal would then have access to my email system and possibly even my banking details. However, there are relatively straightforward checks that can be carried out to establish if it is a genuine email, as well as what Street et al. (2015) call 'individuating information', such as my being aware that I do not owe the company any money, that no upgrade is possible, and that it would not come by that route anyway.

Where the people carrying out the scam are not pretending to be a well-known person or organisation, they have to establish their credibility in other ways. This is where the embedding of their account in a plausible story is crucial. The skill with which they do that will have an impact on how successful they are. We can consequently learn a lot about persuasion and the art of storytelling by studying scams.

One further reason why fraudulent communications using the Internet are so useful as an educational tool, is that they almost certainly benefit from what might be thought of as evolutionary development. There can be little doubt that the people who carry out scams over the Internet send out hundreds, probably thousands, of messages. A small proportion of them will be successful in duping one or more people in giving the fraudsters money. Those messages that 'work' in this way will be used again and the principle on which they are based will be considered. This will mean that some messages survive this process and others are not used again. Therefore, the deceitful messages that are widely available are likely to reflect particularly powerful aspects of persuasion. They are the 'fittest' ones and therefore have 'survived'.

One further introductory point is worth emphasising. The psychological literature on detecting deceit (reviewed extensively by Vrij, 2015) is almost entirely based on the experimental paradigm that is used in the laboratory experiment example of Study 2 in this book. In those studies, carefully selected examples of both truthful and deceptive accounts are prepared. Participants in the experiments are then asked to determine whether the account is a lie or not. In some studies people are encouraged to lie under different conditions. How easy it is to detect their lies is then explored. It is extremely rare in these studies for the deceptive activity to occur in natural situations, although research in that direction is emerging (Eapen, Baron, Street, & Richardson, 2010; ten Brinke & Porter, 2012), discussed in more detail in Study 2. The emphasis is on cues to deceit and how people may use them. The present study complements that area of research by examining actual fraudulent communications in order to determine the strategies and tactics the criminals use.

A STUDY OF EMAIL SCAMS

Objectives

The purpose of the study is to examine actual fraudulent messages in order to reveal what it is about them that supports their plausibility. It is hypothesised that the aspects of persuasion drawn from Cialdini (1993) and the narrative structure proposed by Labov (1972) will be found in these scams. This will facilitate a further understanding of how techniques of persuasion that utilise explicit or implicit plausible narratives are more likely to be effective.

The study also has the practical value of drawing your attention to how to detect fraudulent messages (so that you won't be duped as I was!).

Method

This study draws on actual examples of fraudulent messages. In effect, it is therefore a series of case studies unpacking how these messages are organised and their content structured. This is an aspect of what if often known as **'qualitative' research**. This focuses on the actual content of material rather than assigning numbers to measurements in what is contrasted as **'quantitative' research**.

As we shall see, numbers can be assigned to the content categories generated by looking at their frequency across a number of examples. More sophisticated statistical analyses can also be carried out based on the co-occurrence of categories across cases, as illustrated in many of studies of criminal and deviant activity (e.g. Canter & Fritzon, 1998; Canter & Kirby, 1995; Grayson, Tzani-Pepelasi, Pylarinou, Ioannou, & Artinopoulou, 2020). At the heart of all these analyses is the assigning of components of the material to different categories, as will be illustrated once we consider some possibilities for examples to use.

Examples to use

The Internet is awash with fraudulent messages. Almost certainly you and your associates will have received some. Just search online for 'examples of Internet/online scams'. They come in many different forms, but for this project you need to get actual examples as directly as possible, with all their details.

Figure 7.1 Phishing scam pretending to be a message from BT

Figure 7.1 and the following three examples illustrate some of the scam messages I've recently received. For research purposes a reasonable number of scams need to be collected. About 20 to 30 will provide a useful selection, but of course if many more are amassed they will reveal more detailed patterns.

For simplicity and to make the research manageable I suggest you focus on one type of scam. Say, blackmail scams, or advance-fee fraud scams. There are more details of how these scams work in Appendix 7A at the end of this chapter.[3]

Advance-fee 'begging scam'

Hello,

May the peace of the Lord be with you in Jesus name.

I am Prophet Esodus, the voice of God speaking from the wideness. I have been instructed by God to deliver a prophetic message to you in other to destroy and to stop the planes of Satan concerning your life.

You have to contact me immediately so that I can speak to him that sent me on your behalf.

Do not take this message as a joke because is about life and death, I will tell you what you will do in other to see that you are safe from the spiritual arrows that your enemies programmed against you.

Before getting back to me, I want you to read from the BIBLE IN THE BOOK OF/ Jeremiah 29:11 and Zechariah 4:6. Am a meaagenger of God, the voice from the wideness.

Obey the voice of him that sent me and it will be well with you and your people in.

https://biblehub.com/acts/26-17.htm.

Prophet Esodus.

Advance-fee (Nigerian or 419) scam

My name is Najla Mohammed Al Awar, Secretary General of United Arab Emirates and Managing Director for the United Arab Emirates (Dubai) World Expo 2020 Committee.

I am writing you to stand as my partner to receive my share of gratification from foreign companies whom I helped during the bidding exercise towards the Dubai World Expo 2020 Committee.

As a married Arab women serving as a minister, there is a limit to my personal income and investment level. For this reason, I cannot receive such a huge sum back to my country, so an agreement was reached with the foreign companies to direct the gratifications to an open beneficiary account with a financial institution where it will be possible for me to instruct further transfer of the fund to a third party account for investment purpose which is the reason i contacted you to receive the fund as my partner for investment in your country.

The amount is valued at $47,000,000.00 United States dollars with a financial institution waiting my instruction for further transfer to a destination account as soon as I have your information indicating interest to receive and invest the fund.

If you can handle the fund in a good investment, get back to me for more details on this email: najlaalawar7@gmail.com

Sincerely,

Najla Mohammed Al Awar

Blackmail scam

Hi dvcanter check you. You may not know me and you are probably wondering why you're getting this email?

Well, I setup a malware on the 18+ vids (adult porn) site and guess what, you visited this website to experience fun (you know what I mean). When you were watching video clips, your browser initiated working as a Remote control Desktop having a keylogger which gave me access to your display as well as web camera. Just after that, my software program obtained all of your contacts from your Messenger, FB, and e-mailaccount. Next I created a video. First part shows the video you were watching (you've got a fine taste haha …), and next part displays the recording of your webcam, & its u.

There are not one but two alternatives. Why dont we explore each of these choices in details:

1st solution is to skip this message. As a consequence, I most certainly will send out your video to each of your your personal contacts and thus you can easily imagine concerning the shame you will get. Furthermore in case you are in a relationship, just how it will affect?

Latter choice should be to pay me $2000. We will regard it as a donation. In this case, I will without delay delete your video footage. You can go on with your life like this never took place and you would never hear back again from me.

You will make the payment by Bitcoin (if you do not know this, search for 'how to buy bitcoin' in Google).

BTC Address to send to: 1675gW4bpjVYs74MNhNoNY5zcpGg6DwPAP

[CASE SENSITIVE copy & paste it]

In case you are wondering about going to the law enforcement officials, good, this message can not be traced back to me. I have covered my moves. I am not looking to ask you for money a whole lot, I simply want to be paid for. I have a specific pixel in this message, and right now I know that you have read through this mail. You now have one day in order to pay. If I don't get the BitCoins, I will certainly send your video to all of your contacts including family members, colleagues, and so forth. Nonetheless, if I receive the payment, I will erase the recording immidiately. This is the nonnegotiable offer, so don't waste my personal time and yours by responding to this mail. If you want to have evidence, reply with Yeah! then I definitely will send out your video recording to your 12 contacts.

Process

There are many different ways that the raw material of the fraudulent messages can be prepared for analysis. They all consist of breaking each message down into its component parts. This is the essence of what is known as **'content analysis'**. An extensive review of approaches to this form of qualitative research is given by Bazeley (2013). A briefer overview is given by Masson (2002), but there is now a plethora of such guidebooks for doing qualitative research, especially on the list of qualitative methodology books published by Sage.

One perspective on qualitative research is that it is more honest to the phenomena being studied than social science approaches that impose a numerical framework. It is argued that qualitative exploration draw directly on the raw materials being studied without feeding them through the filter of an inevitably predetermined measurement instrument (see, for example, Silverman, 2017, and other publications listed in the further reading and references at the end of this chapter). A well-established elaboration of the view that qualitative research should approach its subject matter without preconceptions is 'grounded theory' (Straus & Corbin, 1998). This approach to qualitative research provides detailed guidelines on how to allow the data 'to speak for itself'. It makes the assumption that a researcher can tackle a set of material in an objective way that allows the dominant themes inherent in the raw data to be revealed without them being imposed by the researcher. A detailed, careful, and self-aware process is necessary to achieve this. Aspects of grounded theory could be of value when exploring scams for the first time, as indicated later in the chapter, but the approach developed in the present study takes theories of persuasion and narrative structure as a starting point.

Approaches to content analysis

It is useful to think of two dimensions to content analysing material. One is the examination of how the material is organised, such as its length, complexity, or aspects of its structure. The other is to focus on the content. The detail of what is said. This can vary from dealing in detail with the actual vocabulary – the words used – to the larger scale of what is covered in what is written. To do any analysis you have to decide of the size of the units you are going to work with: words, clauses, themes, topics.

Unitisation

The rather ungainly term **'unitisation'** refers to the breaking down of the original material into units for analysis. This can occur at many levels of detail:

1. *Words.* The actual words used can be catalogued and systematically analysed to build up an account of the vocabulary of the fraudsters. This, for example, could be used to explore how often the word 'trust' was used, or words relating to emotions. Present-day digital word-processing software makes it relatively easy to search for key words in a piece of text and to count their occurrence. However, an important aspect of any language is the way in which meanings are enshrined in words in many different ways. For instance, in English many words can be nouns or verbs, implying different meanings for different uses, as in the well-known book title *Eats Shoots and Leaves*. Plural and singular forms of the same word can confuse simple word searches, as can present and past tense of irregular verbs such as 'sit' and 'sat'. Even the word 'mouse' can mean an animal or a computer pointing device!

    Tausczik and Pennebaker (2010) have used the capabilities of modern computers working with digitised text to develop the Linguistic Inquiry and Word Count (LIWC) software system. This includes dictionaries that enable words to be categorised and the prevalence of different categories to be calculated. They have shown that such calculations are able to reveal attentional focus, emotionality, social relationships, thinking styles, as well as reliable differences between individuals. I have not been able to find the utilisation of LIWC for fraudulent communications. That remains in interesting possibility for future research.

2. *Phrases* can be identified at a larger scale than just words. These could be significant forms of words, or even in the present examples logos, or sign-off notes such as 'Managing Director, Customer Care'. An online check would establish if these are the same as the genuine ones. They usually are. Such a check could, for instance, provide a basis for collecting information on what aspects of an organisation are selected to provide authority in relation to the implicit narrative (as might be the case in the BT scam illustrated in Figure 7.1).

3. *Themes* are the level at which, I propose, the role of persuasive techniques and narrative structure can be most readily determined. This consists of drawing out the essential components of the meaning of what is being claimed. Instead of working only with how the text is written, the essence of what is being communicated is drawn out.

    If you have a framework of what could/should be included in the email then you could also record what is missing. For example, in the phishing scams the actual name of the recipient or a genuine, personal reference code for the recipient would be omitted (although sometimes a fake one is put in the hope the recipient will not check whether it is theirs). Checking the actual email address the email is sent from will also reveal that it is not from the official organisation that it seems to come from.

    This can be illustrated with reference to the apparent message from BT in Figure 7.1. The sentence "you don't need to do anything to pay it" can be seen to carry a number of themes. There is a direct reference to the recipient "you". The indication that no action is necessary, and a mention of payment.

    There is a well-established area of social science research, usually referred to as 'discourse analysis' (reviewed in Study 8, drawing on Edwards, 1997). There are many approaches to carrying out this form of analysis, but their essence is to explore 'the work' that a written or spoken utterance is doing. This can include the underlying purpose of the utterance, for example to convince the recipient of the authority of its author, or to indicate a lack of interest in a topic, or to demonstrate a shared interest. An intriguing illustration is the use of 'anyway', especially in speech. This rarely carries its overt meaning, but rather indicates that the topic of conversation is to be changed as in "Anyway, as I was saying before" (Park, 2010).

In the present study the framework of persuasion and narrative is proposed, but many of the other aspects of discourse could be explored. Although, or course, many of these will overlap with the model presented here. It is worth mentioning, though, that many approaches to discourse analysis overlap with the broader semiotic analysis that has been spearheaded particularly by French thinkers such as Jacques Derrida. In that form of examination of material, the meaning of various symbols is explored and the layers of those meanings. An intriguing demonstration of this is the consideration of the Apple computer logo that is the outline of an apple with a piece taken from it. This can be connected to the Apple of Knowledge in the biblical Garden of Eden, which when bitten removed humanity's innocence, as well as many other nuanced associations. I know of no discourse or semiotic analysis of fraudulent communications; eccentric though this is, it is an area ripe for research.

4. *Features*. This is the categorisation of messages at a general level. For example, the advance-fee frauds can be organised in terms of the type of narrative they are built around. In explorations of these types of fraud I've come across stories of widowed wives of African generals who squirrelled away large sums of money, bank employees who've had access to accounts whose originators have long since died without heirs, and religious orders that were left piles of money that they cannot get access to except through some overseas contact. They may inform the recipient that a large sum of money has been won in an international lottery but it can only be accessed by transferring the money overseas.

Categorising the type of story that is being pedalled is an important first stage in understanding how the narrative is structured. The details that may make a story credible are likely to be different, say, if pretending to come from a religious order rather than the wife of a deceased general.

There are many other broader features of the material that can be assessed. These could even drift into some sort of quantitative assessment such as asking respondents to assess how plausible the message is, for instance on a scale from 1 to 10. The overall emotional tone, urgency, detail, and many other aspects could be evaluated as a basis for further exploration.

Thematic analysis

There are a number of stages in preparing material to carry out effective analysis of it. These include:

- identifying the type of fraud being studied;
- differentiating the subtypes within that general type; and then,
- breaking each communication down into coherent, meaningful units.

At all of these stages the decisions need to be made as objectively as possible. This means that any category derived can be clearly agreed and reproduced by another researcher using the same specified criteria as you. The most common way of demonstrating that your categorisation scheme is objective is to get one or more other people to go through all, or a proportion, of your material, working only from your written definitions of your categories, to see if they arrive at the same assignments as you.

Inter-rater reliability

The process of checking how successfully one or more other people make the same assignments as you is known as checking **inter-rater reliability**. For each of the themes identified you provide an example and a description of what that theme covers. This list of descriptions is the content 'dictionary'. You then get one or more colleagues to use your dictionary, independently, on a representative or random sample of material, or all of it, assigning the utterances to your categories. Comparison of the results from the different judges opens up the possibility of discussing the reasons for disagreements. This can then enable you to refine your definitions, adding more or combining some, so that a reasonably high level of agreement can be achieved.

At the simplest level this can be just an indication of the proportion of assignments to categories on which the raters agree. A more sophisticated measure for the agreement between two raters is Cohen's kappa (more details of this in Appendix 7B at the end of this chapter).

If you have three or more raters there are a variety of ways of estimating the inter-rater reliability depending on the details of how their categorisations are carried out. They include:

*   *Fleiss's kappa*, which is really a development of *Cohen's kappa*.

*   *Kendall's tau*, for when you have ranked data, for example putting frauds in order of plausibility.

*   *Krippendorff's alpha*, for when you have many people doing the rating and a number of different forms of rating.

There are many worked examples available on the Internet to illustrate how to use these measures.

Stages in carrying out thematic analysis of Internet scams

1. The first stage is to decide which fraudulent communications you want to focus on. Do you just deal with advance fee frauds, or phishing scams, or a mixture? Your decision will be influenced by what you have available to study. Have you been able to locate enough advance-fee frauds, for example, to be able to derive results confidently across the sample? Or are you interested in comparing the parallels in structure and content of different sorts of fraud? How easy is it going to be for you to carry out content analysis (or discourse analysis) on the material you can accumulate?

2. Having decided the material you are going to be dealing with it will probably be necessary to further divide it into subtypes. For advance-fee frauds this would be the identification of the different storylines that are being put forward (e.g. bank employee, widow of a general, business man, lottery representative, etc.). The blackmail scams may be divided into the types of activity the victim is being blackmailed about. The phishing scams could be divided into the different organisations that the email is supposed to have come from.

3. Now the real work begins. The communication needs to be broken down into component utterances. This requires careful reading through the material and developing a 'content dictionary', which consists of a set of summary terms that describe each category of material that you have identified.

    If you are using a 'grounded theory' approach you would read through the material many times in order to establish what appear to you to be the dominant themes that are emerging. If you are testing the narrative and persuasion hypotheses outlined above then you can define themes in relation to the components of those models. (The points listed earlier in the chapter regarding Cialdini's (1993) framework and Labov's (1972) components therefore act as content dictionaries for this study.)

Recording the results

Once you have created a reliable content dictionary and examined the material available to you there are then many ways of summarising the results so that that you can see whether the original hypotheses were supported. Or if it is a more exploratory study, following the 'grounded theory' approach you can produce a summary table and narrative account of what you have discovered.

At the most elementary level of the comparison of case study examples a straightforward table can be most instructive. Table 7.1 illustrates this for Cialdini's (1993) model of persuasion for an example

Table 7.1 Examples of each of the persuasion components found in four advance-fee fraud narratives

	Bank employee	Businessman	Terminally ill individual	Lottery representative
Authority	"I am senior assessor for the International Bank of Africa."	"I am Mr Richard Eze, chairman of the National Energy Committee under the Ministry of Lands, Mines and Energy in Liberia."	"Until recently I was in Iraq as we belonged to the ruling class."	"I am Josephine van Daal, lottery co-ordinator, and I am pleased to be in a position to process your $400,000 USD winnings claim."
Social validation	"In confidence this matter has been considered with an attorney who is able to generate the legal documents we need to proceed in order to support any claims."	"A similar transaction was successfully carried out on a previous over-inflated contract with great benefit to both parties."	"I have researched the idea and found that it is not uncommon for such transactions to occur."	"You are one of several winners in this year's promotional draw who must now claim their winnings."
Scarcity	"I will not contact any other person with this offer if I hear back from you."	"… as this is the last major contract undertaken before my company is sold on …"	"I have only a few months to live and therefore this opportunity only presents itself for a short time."	"… and all winnings must be claimed no later than June 8th 2004."
Liking	"Accept my warm regards as I await your response."	"… someone who is intelligent such as yourself."	"… as I believe you are an honest and caring person."	"Congratulations once more from our members of staff and thank you for being part of our promotional programme."
Reciprocation	"You are not expected to travel down to London because we intend transferring the funds to our oversea affiliate office for easy access and to save you the stress of coming down to London. Your presence will only be required at the offshore payment centre in Philippines."	"The finance is affordable and will be provided only if we can be guaranteed of fair play, equity, transparent, and good partnership."	"I honestly pray that in return for my trust in you that this money when transferred will be sure for the said purpose."	"We hope that once we have released your winnings you will use some of it to take part in our next year USD100 million international lottery."
Consistency	"Once you have completed and sent the application, me and my colleague will continue our part by exacting pressure on the bank for the release of the funds."	"I am available to entertain any questions concerning the clarity of this transaction and to help see it through to the end."	"Once you have agreed to this transaction and taken the necessary steps I will instruct my lawyer to release the funds to you, as promised."	"Please note we have provided you a reference number to quote that enables us to deal with your queries personally and prevent any unnecessary delays and complications."

Note: I am grateful to Clifford Robert John for preparing this table.

Table 7.2 Examples of the narrative components found in four advance-fee fraud narratives

	Bank employee	Businessman	Terminally ill individual	Lottery representative
Abstract	"With due respect and humility, I write to you this proposal."	"I am contacting you regarding a business proposal/joint venture."	"This mail might come to you as a surprise but please consider it a divine wish and accept it with a deep sense of humility."	"We are pleased to inform you of the result of the Lottery Winners International Programmes held on the 13th of July 2004."
Orientation	"I am the manager of bill and exchange at the Foreign Remittance Department of Bond Bank of Benin."	"I run an international business promotion and consultancy firm and I got your contact through the Internet in my quest for a foreign investment for one of my clients."	"I am Mrs Mudisat Brown, a widow to the late Coffling Brown and have recently been diagnosed with oesophageal cancer and from all indication my condition is really deteriorating"	"Your email address attached to winning ticket number 20511465897 drew lucky numbers 8-66-97-22-46-88, you are therefore entitled to a pay out of USS 500,000.00."
Complicating actions	"We discovered an abandoned sum of $18.5 million US dollars in an account that belongs to Mr Burke Sean a US citizen and foreign customer who died in tragic plane crash."	"During construction of this project, I was able to make some money, which I kept in an escrow account from where contractors were paid. To my amazement late last year I discovered that this money has reached an astonishing USD$5.2 million."	"My late husband was very wealthy and after his death, I inherited all his business and wealth. The doctor has advised me that I may not live for more than six months, so now I decided to part with this wealth."	"Note that all winning must be claimed by the participant not later than 13th August 2004."
Evaluation	"Our banking policies state we cannot release it unless someone applies for it as next of kin but sadly we learned they all died with him in the plane crash."	"I can not claim this money in my name as I have declared it a contractor's money while depositing it."	"During the period of our marriage we couldn't produce any child and therefore have no person to leave the wealth to."	"After this date all unclaimed funds will be retained and included in the following year's stake."
Resolution	"If such money remains unclaimed after six years, the money will automatically be transferred into the bank treasury as unclaimed funds."	"As a government worker the civil service code of conduct does not allow me to own or operate a domiciliary account with such a huge amount on it due to the credit ceiling on savings."	"I decided to divide this wealth to contribute to the development of the church in Africa and have selected you to help distribute the funds to the less privileged."	"To file for your claim, please contact our fiducial agent, quoting your reference number and batch numbers in all correspondence."
Coda	"I have decided to make this business proposal to you to transact this deal with you and to act as the next of kin to the deceased for safety and subsequent disbursement."	"All I want you to do is to assist me in clearing this amount from the bank while standing as one of the foreign contractors who have executed projects but has not been paid and on whose behalf I have made the deposit."	"That fund is in a security company and upon my instruction, my attorney will file an application for the transfer of the money in your last name. You can then distribute it among charity organisations."	"Congratulations once more from our members of staff and don't forget to make your claim soon. Thank you for being part of our promotional programme."

Note: I am grateful to Clifford Robert John for preparing this table.

of four different fraud narratives. Table 7.2 illustrates the presence of Labov's (1972) components of narrative for four different types of fraud.

Tables 7.1 and 7.2 demonstrate that examples of all the hypothesised components can be found in the four examples of advance-fee fraud emails analysed. That in itself is an interesting discovery. It seems unlikely that the people generating these emails have studied theories of narrative and persuasion (although not impossible). Rather, it would appear that they naturally draw on these components, presumably without being aware that is what they are doing. Perhaps that is no surprise because, after all, the components were derived from the study of naturally occurring forms of persuasion and storytelling. What these fraudsters teach us, though, is that for the components of the persuasive techniques to be plausible they have to be embedded in a coherent narrative.

Further analysis is possible beyond these basic illustrations. A detailed consideration of how the elements of persuasion are integrated into the narratives could usefully include detailed consideration of the forms of discourse employed. For example, Areni's (2003) account of the elaboration likelihood model, which explores details of structural and grammatical variables in the processes of persuasion, would be a useful development.

The elaboration likelihood model, originally espoused by Petty and Cacioppo (1984). despite its rather arcane label, emphasises how seriously listeners will pay attention to the communication. In other words, how likely it is that they will attempt to explore, or elaborate, the details of the communication. This is based on a rather similar distinction to that made by Street et al. (2015). Recipients of the message either focus on the internal details (Street's 'individuating') or on the general context. These different forms of elaboration, it is claimed, can be influenced by the details of how the message is presented.

A number of studies have explored what details make a message more plausible by carrying out the detailed linguistic analysis developed by Pennebaker and his colleagues (Newman, Pennebaker, Berry, & Richards, 2003). This includes the LIWC software development already mentioned (Pennebaker, Francis, & Booth, 2001). This counts the frequency of words in various categories considered to be of psychological significance, such as emotion, cognition, abstract, social, and temporal processes. The use of different personal pronouns ('I', 'we', 'you', etc.) as well as the forms the verbs can take, are all detailed aspects of the vocabulary used, which may help to indicate aspects of communications that influence their persuasive power.

Bar charts of frequencies and inferential statistical tests comparing different narratives would make this a more detailed study. If in addition people were asked to rate how plausible each message was, this assessment could be related to the frequencies of the various aspects and components of those messages. These relationships would indicate what it is that gives the power to those messages. A further development would be to create messages using the effective components and testing their impact in further studies.

CONCLUSIONS

The purpose of this chapter has been to demonstrate the possibilities for exploring the details of fraudsters' communication. The material for such research is widely available through personal contacts and across the Internet. The processes involved provide an interesting introduction to qualitative research and the many ways in which content analysis can be carried out. The study also opens up the areas both of the psychology of persuasion and of the structure of narratives. Many more sophisticated analyses can be carried out on the initial results indicated here, especially once the determined categories are turned into quantitative measures, either by simple counts or the creation of structures, as illustrated in Study 6.

OTHER STUDIES THAT COULD USE THIS RESEARCH DESIGN

Any recorded utterances, whether initially spoken or written, can be subjected to the same study. Of particular relevance to anti-social behaviour are the communications that terrorist organisations issue to try and recruit people to join them. An important warning, though, should be mentioned: the security services, appropriately, often monitor those visiting terrorist websites, so due caution and full ethical approval is therefore needed before collecting examples of terrorist communications. However, once available the many such websites from right-wing, jihadi, or other extremist organisations would make a rich set of material for the sorts of case study illustrated here.

Yet another possibility is the consideration of the interaction between paedophiles and law enforcement decoys posing as children. Corey (2010) was able to get access to the chat logs of convicted offenders and carried out an interesting content analysis of them.

Many legitimate organisations also promote views on crime and various forms of anti-social behaviour. How are their narratives constructed? What do they do to give authority to their claims?

QUESTIONS FOR DISCUSSION

1. What aspects of the recipients of messages may make them vulnerable to being defrauded?[4] How would you study this (see, for example, Lichtenberg, Stickney, & Paulson, 2013)?

2. Who do you think sends these scams? How would you find out?

3. Consider how the aspects of persuasion mentioned might be applied to non-criminal situations.

4. Do general aspects of deceit draw on similar processes (cf. Study 2)?

5. What are the major weaknesses of qualitative research?

6. What are the main strengths of content analysis?

NOTES

1   From the National Consumers League Fraud Center, see www.nclnet.org/fraud_org_content.
2   When I was defrauded, my emails had been interfered with. I initially thought this was a technical hitch, so when I got a phone call saying the email problem was a scam and needed fixing to prevent money being stolen, they had set up the narrative for me to believe in.
3   See also www.419eater.com/html/letters.htm for many more examples of advance-fee frauds.
4   I was very busy, and rather stressed, when I was contacted by fraudsters. I just wanted to get my computer sorted out so did not give enough attention to the many warning aspects of the contact. The vulnerability of people to fraud has not been widely studied.

FURTHER READING

Sage has a whole list of books on qualitative research available at:

https://uk.sagepub.com/en-gb/eur/disciplines/L20.

There are also a number of journals that focus on qualitative research available at:

https://qualpage.com/2016/09/20/qualitative-research-journals.

The Wikipedia entry is interesting, although is only one of many perspectives:

https://en.wikipedia.org/wiki/Qualitative_research.

Very detailed accounts of exactly how to work with the data are available in:

Bazeley, P. (2013). *Qualitative data analysis: Practical strategies.* London: Sage.

The following 572-page compendium is available online with lots of videos from the author:

Silverman, D. (2017). *Doing qualitative research* (5th ed.). London: Sage. Retrieved from https://study.sagepub.com/ dqr5.

The 'fundamentalist' approach can be explored in:

Straus, A., & Corbin, J. (1998). *Basics of qualitative research: Techniques and procedures for developing grounded theory* (2nd ed.). London: Sage.

The following are also useful:

Feeley, T.H., & deTurck, M.A. (1995). Global cue usage in behavioral lie detection. *Communication Quarterly, 43,* 420–430.

Pennebaker, J.W., Mehl, M.R., & Niederhoffer, K.G. (2003). Psychological aspects of natural language use: Our words, our selves. *Annual Review of Psychology, 54,* 547–577.

Petty, R.E., & Cacioppo, J.T. (1986). *Communication and persuasion: Central and peripheral routes to attitude change.* New York, NY: Springer-Verlag.

REFERENCES

Areni, C.S. (2003). The effects of structural and grammatical variables on persuasion: An elaboration likelihood model perspective. *Psychology & Marketing, 20*(4), 349–375.

Bazeley, P. (2013). *Qualitative data analysis: Practical strategies.* London: Sage.

Bond, C.F. Jr., & DePaulo, B.M. (2008). Individual differences in judging deception: Accuracy and bias. Psychological Bulletin, 134(4), 477–492. https://doi.org/10.1037/0033-2909.134.4.477.

Canter, D., & Fritzon, K. (1998). Differentiating arsonists: A model of firesetting actions and characteristics. *Legal and Criminal Psychology, 3,* 73–96.

Canter, D., Grieve, N., & Benneworth, K. (2003). Narrative plausibility: The impact of sequence and anchoring. Behavioral Sciences & the Law, 21(2), 251–267. https://doi.org/10.1002/bsl.528.

Canter, D., & Kirby, S. (1995). *Prior convictions of child molesters, Journal of Science and Justice,* 35(1), 73–78.

Carroll, M., & Korukina, S. (1999). The effect of text coherence and modality on metamemory judgements. Memory, 7(3), 309–322. doi: 10.1080/096582199387940.

Cialdini, R.B. (1993). *Influence: Science and practice.* New York, NY: HarperCollins.

Corey, D. (2010). *Sexual seduction of children in cyberspace: A content analysis of Internet deviance and pedophilic criminality* (PhD thesis, Capella University. Minneapolis, MN). Retrieved from http://search.proquest.com/openview/7ea8c0 8b6cd7217b993fd1b64918440f/1?pq-origsite=gscholar&cbl=18750&diss=y.

DePaulo, B.M., Lindsay, J.J., Malone, B.E., Muhlenbruck, L., Charlton, K., & Cooper, H. (2003). Cues to deception. *Psychological Bulletin, 129,* 74–118.

DePaulo, P.J., & DePaulo, B.M. (1989). Can deception by salespersons and customers be detected through nonverbal behavioral cues? *Journal of Applied Social Psychology,* 19(18), 1552–1577. https://doi.org/10.1111/ j.1559-1816.1989.tb01463.x.

Eapen, N.M., Baron, S., Street, C.N.H., & Richardson, D.C. (2010). The bodily movements of liars. In Proceedings of the 32nd *annual meeting of the Cognitive Science Society* (pp. 2548–2554). Portland, OR: Cognitive Science Society.

Edwards, D. (1997). *Discourse and cognition.* London: Sage.

Grayson, S., Tzani-Pepelasi, C., Pylarinou, N.P., Ioannou, M., & Artinopoulou, V. (2020). Examining the narrative roles in suicide notes. *Journal of Investigative Psychology and Offender Profiling,* 17(2), 142–159. https://doi.org/ 10.1002/jip.1545.

TEN STUDIES

Johnson, M.K., Bransford, J.D., Nyberg, S.E., & Cleary, J.J. (1972). Comprehension factors in interpreting memory for abstract and concrete sentences. Journal of Verbal Learning and Verbal Behavior, 11(4), 451–454.

Kunz, P.R., & Woolcott, M. (1976). Season's greetings: From my status to yours. Social Science Research, 5(3), 269–278. https://doi.org/10.1016/0049-089X(76)90003-X.

Labov, W. (1972). Language in the inner city. Philadelphia: University of Pennsylvania Press.

Lichtenberg. P.A., Stickney, L., & Paulson, D. (2013). Is psychological vulnerability related to the experience of fraud in older adults? Clinical Gerontologist, 36(2), 132–146. doi: 10.1080/07317115.2012.749323.

Masip, J., Alonso, H., Garrido, E., & Herrero, C. (2009). Training to detect what? The biasing effects of training on veracity judgments. Applied Cognitive Psychology, 23(9), 1282–1296. https://doi.org/10.1002/acp.1535.

Masip, J., & Herrero, C. (2017). Examining police officers' response bias in judging veracity. Psicothema, 29(4), 490–495. doi: 10.7334/psicothema2016.357.

Masson, J. (2002). Qualitative researching (2nd ed.). London: Sage.

Meissner, C.A., & Kassin, S.M. (2002). "He's guilty!": Investigator bias in judgments of truth and deception. Law and Human Behavior, 26, 469–480.

Nahari, G., Vrij, A., & Fisher, R.P. (2013). The verifiability approach: Countermeasures facilitate its ability to discriminate between truths and lies. Applied Cognitive Psychology, 28(1), 122–128. https://doi.org/10.1002/acp.2974.

Newman, M.L., Pennebaker, J.W., Berry, D.S., & Richards, J.M. (2003). Lying words: Predicting deception from linguistic styles. Personality and Social Psychology Bulletin, 29(5), 665–675.

Oyibo, K., Orji, R., & Vassileva, J. (2017). Investigation of the influence of personality traits on Cialdini's persuasive strategies. In R. Orji, M. Reisinger, M. Busch, A. Dijkstra, M. Kaptein, & E. Mattheiss (Eds.), Proceedings of the Personalization in Persuasive Technology Workshop, Persuasive Technology 2017. Amsterdam, the Netherlands: CEUR. Retrieved from http://ceur-ws.org.

Park, I. (2010). Marking an impasse: The use of anyway as a sequence-closing device Journal of Pragmatics, 42(120), 3283–3299. doi:10.1016/j.pragma.2010.06.002.

Pennebaker, J.W., Francis, M.E., & Booth, R.J. (2001). Linguistic Inquiry and Word Count (LIWC 2001): A computer-based text analysis program. Mahwah, NJ: Lawrence Erlbaum.

Petty, R.E., & Cacioppo, J.T. (1984). The effects of involvement on responses to argument quantity and quality: Central and peripheral routes to persuasion. Journal of Personality and Social Psychology, 46, 69–81.

Straus, A., & Corbin, J. (1998). Basics of qualitative research: Techniques and procedures for developing grounded theory (2nd ed.). London: Sage.

Street, C., Bischof, W., Vadillo, M., & Kingstone, A. (2015). Inferring others' hidden thoughts: Smart guesses in a low diagnostic world. Journal of Behavioral Decision Making, 29(5), 539–549.

Tausczik, Y., & Pennebaker, J. (2010). The psychological meaning of words: LIWC and computerized text analysis methods. Journal of Language and Social Psychology, 29(1), 24–54.

ten Brinke, L., & Porter, S. (2012). Cry me a river: Identifying the behavioral consequences of extremely high-stakes interpersonal deception. Law and Human Behavior, 36, 469–477.

Vrij, A. (2015). A cognitive approach to lie detection. In P.A. Granhag, A. Vrij, & B. Verschuere (Eds.), Detecting deception: Current challenges and cognitive approaches (pp. 205–229). Chichester, UK: Wiley.

Whitty, M.T. (2013). The scammers persuasive techniques model: Development of a stage model to explain the online dating romance scam. British Journal of Criminology, 53(4), 665–684. https://doi.org/10.1093/bjc/azt009.

Appendix 7A Brief Explanations of the Scams Illustrated and how they Work

Note that all these scams do have the email address of the recipient, but only very rarely is that used within the actual email sent. This is probably because these scams are generated automatically in vast numbers working from a stolen, or illegally purchased email list.

Phishing Scams

The term phishing refers to the obtaining of crucial details about access to email accounts or a website, rather like stealing the key to a safe so that the contents can be stolen. These work by encouraging the recipient to click on an apparently ordinary link. This may introduce a virus into the recipient's computer that allows the criminal to search for crucial details. Or it may go to what seems like a genuine website where the victim is encouraged to fill in the login and password details, which the criminal can then use.

Blackmail Scams

These claim to have information about the recipient that would be embarrassing if made public. The generic quality of the email, referring for example in the illustration in this chapter to social media I do not use and activities that I do not carry out, but would find particularly embarrassing if I did. The technical claims in that email are also beyond the bounds of current computing.

Advance-Fee Fraud

If the recipient accepts the offer of untold wealth then s/he is asked for a small amount of money, to pay a bribe, set up a bank account, or for some other apparently innocuous purpose. That is the 'advance fee'. Subsequently the victim is encouraged to pay further amounts. When the criminals are successful, they can obtain many thousands of pounds from a victim. There is evidence that some of the victims have been murdered when they tried to tackle the fraudsters directly. It is also known as '419 fraud' because that is the Nigerian law that makes it clearly illegal. It was also called 'Nigerian fraud' because a lot of the earlier examples had their origins there.

Among other sources of information there are details of advance-fee fraud at www.scamwatch.gov.au/types-of-scams/unexpected-money/nigerian-scams.

Appendix 7B　Cohen's Kappa

$\kappa = 1 - \dfrac{1-P_o}{1-P_e}$, where P_o is the relative observed agreement and

P_e is the probability of chance agreement.

A good illustration of how to calculate this is available at www.statisticshowto.datasciencecentral.com/cohens-kappa-statistic.

STUDY 8
Justifications for criminality

Synopsis

There are many accounts of their lives given by criminals. These may be in the form of autobiographies or posts on the Internet. There are also details widely available of responses criminals have made in police interviews, or actual confessions. The proposed project therefore focuses on case studies of these personal accounts. It proposes that the justifications for criminality, especially violence, draw on some central narratives in a culture. These may be revenge, the need to keep 'face', to protect a greater good, or even an accident of circumstances. Intriguingly, these are the sorts of reasons that politicians give for going to war. Perhaps this is not surprising because they draw on the same culturally embedded narratives that criminals have available.

Some Key Concepts

- cognitive distortions
- minimisation
- neutralisation
- discourse analysis
- conversational analysis
- criminal thinking styles.

BACKGROUND

If asked, many criminals will try to justify their criminality. Even if they admit their guilt and indicate some sort of remorse, they will still have an explanation of why they broke the law that often provides some sort of exoneration for their misdeeds. At the very least their accounts will seek some mitigation for the seriousness of their crimes. These provide psychological excuses for continuing criminality. It is therefore valuable to understand what they are and how they are maintained in order to help explain criminality and to provide appropriate interventions.

Explanations of criminality usually draw on factors that are essentially external to the person. They may be aspects of society and culture, upbringing, and family life. Even those of a more psychological nature such as personality or learned behaviour are, in essence, conceived of as aspects of criminals over which they have no control. Physiological, neurological, and hormonal explanations similarly put the blame on criminality outside of the control of the individual.

These explanations are starkly different from the ways in which legal processes consider breaking the law. For the courts it is the decision by a person that is paramount. It has to be clear that they knew and intended what they did and that they knew it was wrong (legally summarised as *mens rea*). Here the cause of the crime is firmly part of the offender's awareness and control. Indeed, if there is any possibility that the offender did not have control or intention, for example because of mental illness or brain damage, then they would normally not be found guilty of committing a crime.

One approach to bridging the gap between the psychological explanation and the legal requirement is to explore what criminals think are, or offer as, the reasons for their crimes. Understanding these thought processes reveals what it is that sustains criminal activity. These 'justifications' that provide excuses for offending are considered by psychologists as '**cognitive distortions**' and 'maladaptive beliefs'. Framing the reasons offenders give for their crimes as 'distortions' of their ways of thinking is an interesting example of making an implicit value judgement about their explanations, but masking this as what seems like a technical term. It is understandable that the reasons offenders give may be regarded as mistaken or distorted because they are, in effect, justifying something that is socially and legally unacceptable. A glaring example of this is when a paedophile claims that a child 'seduced' him or the sexual contact was 'consensual' (as discussed by Maruna & Butler, 2013). Such a claim ignores both the illegality of the action and that a child cannot fully understand what they are being coerced to do.

However, it is apparent that most people will, from time to time, justify anti-social or illegal activity. The concept of 'white lies' implies that it is acceptable not to tell the truth in order to save someone from distress. There is even a concept in law that a minor crime may be acceptable to prevent a more serious crime. At a broader level cognitive bias is common to most people. Even, or perhaps especially, police investigators may be vulnerable to such distortions of thinking (Roach, 2019). Indeed, Daniel Kahneman was awarded the Nobel Prize in Economics for his work showing how prevalent biases are in human decision making, reviewed in his popular book (Kahneman, 2011). Many criminals may draw on similar explanations for what they have done. But when the logic of what they are claiming is open to challenge then it is probably reasonable to regard their cognitions as distorted.

Studies of these thought processes by offenders have been considered for many different types of offence (Dennis & Sheldon, 2007; Walters, 2002; Ward, 2000; Ward, Hudson, & Marshall, 1995). These are particularly interesting for violent offending because it is reasonable to assume that there is rarely any strong justification for such actions. There are also many examples available of accounts by convicted criminals of their actions with implicit or explicit justifications for them (Chester, 2016).

One interesting study that looked directly at justifications (and gave me the idea for this project) is the examination that Emma Barrett carried out (cited in detail in Canter & Youngs, 2009, p. 326). She identified the actions that were described in gangsters' autobiographies. From an analysis of the explanations of these events she was able to distinguish four themes to the justifications for the violence:

- retribution for earlier misdeeds;

- defence against potential attack;

- dealing with disrespect, or breaking of accepted norms;

- accidental (victim unlucky to be in the wrong place at the wrong time).

There are a number of explorations of the psychological bases for offenders' cognitive distortions. Ward (2000), for example, reviews how people justify their aggressive and violent behaviour, arguing that they have implicit theories of how the world works and what processes shape human actions. It is these that underlie the distortions in their thinking. A straightforward example of this would be the claim: "If I allow anyone to insult me and get away with it without suffering a physical comeback, I will become more vulnerable." This theory rules out other ways than violence of dealing with insult. Consequently, understanding that provided a basis for intervention.

Maladaptive beliefs have also been related to 'hostile attribution bias'. This is the habit of thought that typically interprets the actions of others as being inherently hostile (Pornari & Wood, 2010). Another commonly identified rationalisation for crimes, especially violent offences is **'minimisation'** (Auburn, 2010); that is, claiming that the consequences of the actions are very limited, or overexaggerated. The rapist who claimed he had not hurt his victim but 'only had sex' with her would be an example of this.

These 'techniques of **neutralisation'** form the basis of a concept known as 'neutralisation theory', which was posited by sociologists Gresham Sykes and David Matza (1957). The theory holds that criminals are able to neutralise values that would otherwise prohibit them from carrying out certain acts by using one or up to five methods of justification: 'denial of responsibility', 'denial of injury', 'denial of the victim', 'condemnation of the condemners', and 'appealing to higher loyalties'.

As with so much crime psychology research, there is a fundamental challenge to using accounts offenders may give that excuse their crimes. These may be defensive responses after the event, not necessarily the psychological processes that gave rise to their actions. Or, as Auburn (2010) argues, they may be more fruitfully considered as social practices; socially acceptable rhetorical devices that are drawn on in particular situations.

The extensive literature on these processes makes clear that it is a fascinating, theoretically rich area of study, with practical implications for working with offenders in the courts and in various attempts at rehabilitating them.

A Study of Justifications for Violence

Although there are standard questionnaires that explore cognitive biases, notably Walters's (2002) Psychological Inventory of Criminal Thinking Styles (PICTS), the proposed study is a qualitative one that considers detailed examples provided by case studies (Davis & Klopper, 2003). The purpose is to determine what criminals offer as explicit or implicit justifications, or excuses, for their criminal activity. These are then to be examined to see if the justifications reveal cognitive distortions, minimisation, or other forms of bias that help to reveal the psychological processes that maintain the criminality. This is explored through the lens of discourse and conversation analysis as a way of introducing this rich area of qualitative research, which Davis and Klopper (2003) argue has particular value in criminological research.

Material

The proposal is to work directly with first-person accounts by criminals of their offence actions. It is important to have these as close to their own unprocessed words as possible. So many distortions can creep in if another person is retelling what the offender has said. The Internet has very many interviews or statements from convicted offenders. There are also many true-crime autobiographies that give – often in graphic, gory detail – descriptions and explanations of incidents in their lives.

It is probably best to focus on a particular type of crime, such as sexual offences, other violent offences, paedophilia, property offences such as robbery, or fraud. A comparison of the justifications given for different types of offences would also be fruitful.

Although people who are convicted of crimes and imprisoned are remarkably difficult to get access to for research purposes, once they are out of prison it is easier to speak to them. The various organisations that help people once they are out of prison, such as the social justice charity the National Association for the Care and Resettlement of Offenders (NACRO),[1] do encourage research with ex-prisoners, provided that they and the participants can see the benefits of taking part. The probation services also support appropriate research. It therefore may be possible to carry out interviews with offenders if these and other similar organisations are approached in the right way. Ethical issues will always be paramount (as discussed in Part one), but equally important are the logistics involved, that the interviews do not disturb participants, and that the research can be seen to be of real benefit.

Process

A very interesting and useful website is www.famous-trials.com, which contains many full transcripts of trials, mostly of murders. These therefore have verbatim texts of what the people on trial have said. They provide a rich source for examining how defendants give an account of their actions. There are many other such resources available on the Internet. A particularly intriguing set of testimonies now accessible are the witness statements from the 1881 well-known Gun-Fight at the OK Corral.[2]

It has to be kept in mind, though, that the defendants are responding to questions put to them in open court, or are being interviewed by police officers in regard to serious crimes. This is a social interaction that will influence what is said and how it is expressed. Some degree of justification and drawing on acceptable rhetoric is therefore to be expected (Boonzaier & De la Rey, 2004), but nonetheless they do reveal the forms of justification that offenders will utilise.

Limitations in this material has to be mentioned, though. Although transcripts claim to be precise verbatim accounts of exactly what was said, it is rare for them to be totally accurate. They also do not contain details of all the rhythms, gestures, and emphases that would be available in an audio recording, or even better, a video recording. It is therefore not possible to carry out some of the detailed conversational analysis that would be of great value. More general aspects of the way the criminals present themselves and what they, usually implicitly, are trying to achieve has to be the focus of the analysis.

One fruitful example from this website is 'People's Exhibit 54 in the Trial of Dan White'. This is a lengthy confession by Daniel White. It provides a fascinatingly telling example of how a person, who admitted to shooting two people and gave himself up, used his confession to implicitly create mitigation circumstances to build his defence. The police interview with Dan White was carried out in November 1978, a couple of hours after he had killed San Francisco Mayor George Moscone and Supervisor Harvey Milk. The crucial issue for White is whether he can imply that his actions were impulsive rather than premeditated. This difference would have considerable impact on any likely sentence he got.

There are consequently many aspects of the confession that are interesting to examine. A selection from the transcript is given in the appendix at the end of this chapter. The full account is considerably longer. The non-verbal aspects of what is said are not clear in the transcript, nor are other important aspects such as the prosody, pauses, repetitions, and so on discussed in Study 2. It is not possible to tell if voices are raised, if White cries, or has a subdued voice, all of which can contribute to the impressions he gives of his emotional state. Furthermore, although the interviewer makes clear from the start that they want

White to say what happened "in a narrative form" rather than answering questions, the flow of that account is part of a conversation with the police officers. Their objectives in the interview are therefore part of the dialogue that unfolds. In essence, the police are seeking details that would indicate a deliberate conscious plan to kill, while White is building a case for mitigation because of a troubling conversation when he was in an agitated state.

The questions from the police are especially revealing when they do not follow directly from what White has said. As we shall see, their purpose relates to building a case in court with regard to premeditation and intention. In essence White creates the impression of reacting impulsively when in an agitated state, but the police are trying to establish if this could be regarded as a planned, callous killing.

Discourse and conversation analysis

When tackling existing accounts as a starting point for understanding the latent aspects of any events there are a number of broad approaches, which have been reviewed in Studies 6 and 7. The present study therefore focuses on discourse and conversation analysis. However, it is useful to be aware of the general framework that psychologists have provided when considering the forms of justification that offenders offer for their criminality, especially violent behaviour (e.g. Gudjonsson & Sigurdsson, 2010). These are often discussed as 'cognitive distortions' (Ward et al., 1995) or **criminal 'thinking styles'** (Walters, 2002).

A somewhat different approach is to recognise that any communication is part of a social interaction and therefore is seeking to achieve some objectives. It is 'doing work'. What explicit and implicit messages is the communication intended to convey? Over many years there have been detailed studies of the underlying processes involved in many different forms of communication. These studies operate within an aspect of what is known as **discourse analysis** (Edwards, 1997), which is a very broad area of social science research ranging into linguistics and even anthropology, education, and political science. Wiggins and Potter (2017) and his colleagues have taken a particular approach to this, which has contributed considerably to social psychology.

From a social psychological perspective, the 'work' that is done in what people say is best understood as recognising that it is part of an interaction between people. As such it is sometimes presented as part of **conversation analysis**. The utterances are considered in terms of what they contribute to the social interchange when two or more people are communicating with each other. A police interview, in particular, is best considered as a form of conversation. Therefore, there are aspects of conversation analysis that complement discourse analysis, as we shall see in the example discussed here.

An intriguing example of this, of relevance to considering what suspects say in interviews, is the very detailed study by Edwards (2006) of how both police interviewers and suspects use the verb form 'would' (technically known as a 'modal verb' because it modifies the meaning of other verbs) in their questions and answers. Edwards demonstrates that what might sound like a simple comment from a suspect, "I would never do that", in fact draws on deep claims. It is a way of proposing the nature of the person he is – his 'dispositional tendency'. This in turn refers to general principles of what are accepted ways of behaving. It implies that the action he is accused of is socially unacceptable and therefore not one in which he would engage.

The police interviewer may use a similar form of words to challenge the suspect's claim. He may ask the suspect, "Why would she say that?" Here again the question draws on a proposal that the victim is not the sort of person to make a false claim. That also assumes that doing so would be breaking social norms.

These very brief examples, drawn from a 25-page article, provide only a small illustration of the detail to which conversation analysts can go when studying naturally occurring utterances. They also serve to show how general principles may be derived from a few carefully chosen examples. There is no suggestion, when identifying these principles, that these are the only way in which particular words may be used.

Indeed, Edwards (2006) specifically points out that there are many other ways in which the verb form 'would' is used. However, demonstrating how a particular aspect of conversation can be identified in a few cases, provides insights of relevance to other similar cases.

This is very different from the form of argument that is central to experimental studies and surveys. In that context there is a suggestion of generality of the results. This comes from the nature of the sampling process and the controls introduced to ensure the results are not influenced or biased by 'uncontrolled' variables. This suggestion is certainly open to challenge. Such challenges are reflected in what is currently called a 'replicability crisis' in psychology, especially social psychology (as discussed by Świątkowski & Dompnier, 2017). This is the common finding that major results from well-known studies have either never been repeated or been found impossible to repeat. Studies of individual cases that provide illustrations of processes, which can be found in other examples, do not suffer from the same claims of generalisation as more experimentally organised research.

Narrative analysis

A further approach, already described in some detail in Studies 6 and 7, is to consider the account given by an offender as an unfolding story. Within this framework the components of the story are identified, the key episodes, and how one event leads into another. The ways in which the accounts draw upon dominant narratives within the storyteller's culture is of interest. Such connection to culturally dominant stories helps to reveal the way their construction encourages a belief in their plausibility. With regard to murder and other violent crime the credibility of the account in court is likely to be derived from beliefs about what are typical or convincing narratives. Bex (2016) draws on the idea of 'anchored narratives' in judicial proceedings as a way of drawing attention to the power of assumptions about what makes evidential narratives plausible.

Example analysis

Although these various approaches to offenders' accounts of their crimes may seem rather different, and certainly encapsulate different ways of thinking about the nature of social science research, in practice they overlap considerably, as will become apparent from examining the confession that White gave in response to police questions. Let us look closely at the first major, uninterrupted section.

> Ah well, it's just that I've been under an awful lot of pressure lately, financial pressure, because of my job situation, family pressure, because of ah … not being able to have the time with my family. It's just that I wanted to serve the people of San Francisco well an I did that. Then when the pressures got too great, I decided to leave. After I left, my family and friends offered their support and said whatever it would take to allow me to go back in to office – well they would be willing to make that effort. So since I felt the responsibility for the people that elected me I went to Mayor Moscone and told him that my situation had changed because of the support of family and friends and I'd like to be, retain my seat, to be appointed to my seat. Initially he told me that he felt that I was an elected representative of District 8, that I was doing an outstanding job, people of District 8 were lucky to have me, and that if it came to a legal ruling that he would appoint me, reappoint me, because of the type of person I was. So with that in mind I tried to set my personal affairs in order, preparing to take my seat. And then it came out that Supervisor Milk and some others were working against me to get my seat back on the board. I learned of this [when] I was in the City Attorney's office, when Supervisor Milk called, stating that he, he was of that mind. He didn't speak to me, he spoke to the City Attorney but I was in the office and I heard the conversation and that he was going to try to prevent me from taking my seat again. I went back to the Mayor and he told me that he had had some comments made to him that he felt that some of the people in District 8 didn't want me to, to serve, and I told him that these were people that had opposed me in my election, had traumatized my family by taking me, taking, pressing charges against me at the District Attorney's office twice on false charges. They put a lot of pressure on me and my family.[3]

How a person begins an account sets the scene in many different ways. Do not forget that the police officer Frank Falzon used an interviewing technique that gave White the opportunity to give an account in his own words. This is rather different from the confrontational approach that is common in police fiction. Falcon said: "I would prefer, I'll let you do it in a narrative form as to what happened this morning if you can lead up to the events of the shooting and then backtrack as to why these events took place." The instruction is to provide a narrative account of what led up to the shooting. There was also the point that the reasons for the events were something that would be considered later. However, the opening response from White is: "A well, it's just that I've been under an awful lot of pressure lately, financial pressure, because of my job situation, family pressure." This is not an account of the actions leading up to the shootings as might have been expected. This is not an account of the actions leading up to the shootings in response to the instructions from Falzon. It is an initial explanation of why the shooting happened. White is positioning himself as someone under pressure, already here seeking to imply mitigation, as someone who may not be fully in control of his reactions, not premeditation. An attempt to place the responsibility for the killing on his circumstances, rather than his active decision.

This may be regarded as a form of cognitive reinterpretation of the event, neutralising his culpability by implying diminished responsibility for his actions. This could be seen as a cognitive distortion by placing the responsibility for the killing on his circumstances. Fortunately, very few people who experience those sorts of stresses take a gun to a meeting with the mayor and then shoot him. Or, a conversation analyst could see this as a way of managing the possibility of any accusation that the killings were premeditated.

The next aspect of this opening statement also can be seen as developing an account of the sort of person he is: "family pressure because of ah ... not being able to have the time with my family". Here he is presenting himself as a family man, someone who suffers from not being able to spend time with his family. There are a number of implicit suggestions in this that also contribute to the picture he is building of himself as an upstanding citizen. He is creating an identity for himself in which the killings are an unlikely part of his personal narrative.

The next comment elaborates this further: "It's just that I wanted to serve the people of San Francisco well an I did that." His commitment to the community is emphasised. This does not follow quite so logically from his wanting to have time with his family, emphasising that he is keen to layout his credentials as a good citizen and family man, although there is an inherent contradiction here. His conscientious service would seem to keep him away from his family.

These opening couple of sentences therefore can be seen as building a case for him as a good person, but one who was under considerable stress. They are a basis for his legal defence (which was actually used in the court case), directly related to his character and the situation, rather than giving an account and being requested to say, "what happened this morning if you can lead up to the events of the shooting". The fact that he chooses to depart from the constraints of the question is further evidence of the comments being a product of the nature of this particular interaction in which the central issue is whether he can provide evidence relevant to building a case for mitigation.

The next component of the confession does provide the stages of a storyline: "I decided to leave ... my family and friends offered their support ... my situation had changed." This offers a conventional account of a person dealing with pressure (although exactly what that was is not made clear), being helped to deal with it, and thus turning his life round, determined to start again. This is presented as him wishing to provide a service, "I felt the responsibility for the people that elected me", further developing his account of himself as just wanting to make a contribution to his community.

The narrative gets more confusing after that, although White uses some opportunities to claim that he had done a good job in his previous position. He states the mayor initially said, "I was doing an outstanding job". Such a comment in context hints at the possibility that the mayor was fickle, probably not to be trusted, and thereby possibly creating the circumstances of the confrontation with him. There are further claims that repeat the mayor's view of him as being worthy of regaining the previous position to which he was elected. A view White implicitly endorses. He is building a view of his identity as he sees it. This places him in the position of a victim. An individual who has been stressed by the actions of others, who has not been shown appropriate respect for his former effectiveness: "had traumatized my family by taking me, taking, pressing charges against me at the District Attorney's office twice on false charges". Other interpretations of his circumstances, such as why he suffered such earlier stress and financial difficulties are not provided by him. He thus avoids providing potentially troubling information about his job performance, competence, and trustworthiness (although he does later firmly deny the allegations made against him). The possibility that the views others have of him might prevent him taking up his seat again is never considered. Instead some hostile attribution is perceived, which colours his thinking about what is going on. This can also be seen as part of the building of the case for mitigation, avoiding any information that may have indicated his intention to kill.

It is therefore possible to see even in this brief section from his confession the way it illustrates many aspects of justifications for violence. It provides an unfolding narrative that contains within it his view of himself as a victim whose reputation is inappropriately besmirched. He uses this initial account of the lead-up to the shooting as a way of defining the identity he wishes to portray and the role of others in creating the circumstances that so angered him. At the heart of this is the underlying consideration of whether he had set out that day with the clear intention to kill two people, or whether he can lay the groundwork for some form of diminished responsibility that would undermine a conviction for first-degree murder.

Further aspects of the interview show how the interviewers seek to challenge this claim that extenuating circumstances lead to impulsive unplanned killing:

> Question: Dan can you tell Inspector Erdelatz and myself, what was your plan this morning? What did you have in mind?

> Answer: I didn't have any, any devised plan or anything, it's, I was leaving the house to talk, to see the Mayor and I went downstairs, to, to make a phone call and I had my gun down there.

The question is a direct attempt to elicit some indication that there was premeditation – a plan – for the killing. But the fulsome answer indicates that White is very aware of this. He elaborates by referring to a 'devised' plan and adding 'or anything', ruling out the possibility that he knew he was going to kill. He even comments, almost in passing, that he kept his gun by the phone, implying it was therefore a natural process to pick it up out of habit. He even says: "This is the gun I had when I was a policeman. It's in my room an ah … I don't know, I just put it on. I, I don't know why I put it on, it's just …" The comment serves to emphasise that there was no plan behind taking the gun with him. He 'just put it on' as you would a shirt. The next question from the interviewer does take the conversation in another direction, possibly because the interviewer is anxious to know whether the gun is available to White now: "Where is this gun now, Dan?"

Summary of example analysis

The appendix at the end of the chapter gives more of the transcript, allowing further exploration of the interaction between White and his interviewers. This reveals how White develops his account further to demonstrate that he just became extremely agitated, not knowing what he was doing. His unfolding confession builds a picture of himself, plagued with others falsely accusing him and undermining his stalwart contributions to the community. He is using his confession as a preparation for his defence.

This achieved some degree of success. In a controversial judgement he was convicted of manslaughter, not murder, and served five years of the seven-year sentence. However, his view of himself as a victim, suffering from what has technically been called 'hostile attribution bias', eventually had its tragic consequences. Not long after he got out of prison, he killed himself. White's confession served many purposes, but inadvertently revealed the psychological processes that gave rise to him becoming a murderer.

Comparative case studies

This illustration has been for just one case and even that has only been briefly explored. There is considerably more information available both in the online transcript and subsequent trial, as well as discussions of the trial and the sentence White was given. Such material is very often available for cases that had a lot of interest from the public. It is therefore possible to consider approaches taken to justifications, mitigation, and other aspects of confessions of guilt in many other cases. This allows for a comparison of the psychological processes involved in confessions and will reveal the variety of psychological issues involved. For example, what forms of denial do offenders offer? How does this relate to their background and the circumstances of the crime? Within some subgroups of offenders are there particular forms of justification? How do the accounts criminals give of their actions relate to the situations in which they are giving those accounts?

Summary of stages when conducting the study

The qualitative analysis of an individual case never follows exactly the same process for every example. However, the following broad stages can be identified:

1. Identify relevant material and consider its strengths and weaknesses.

2. By reviewing the relevant literature, create a framework for considering the central themes likely to be present in the material.

3. By continuous examination of the material identify the dominant processes as they relate to conceptualisations in previous publications. It is crucial, though, to provide as much detail of the context and examples from the material you are working with to support any claims you make about the underlying processes.

4. Previous studies help to provide guidance on the issues to look for in the material. But when working with the details of naturally occurring specific cases, you will always be generating ways of thinking about this material. Those creations are part of the contributions you are making to knowledge.

5. Producing a summary of your findings that highlights the general principles you are proposing is a very important part of your final report. It is this that will be used by other researchers to develop their own perspectives in other contexts.

OTHER STUDIES THAT COULD USE THIS RESEARCH DESIGN

There are many studies of the police interview process (e.g. Webber, 2020, chap. 9 is a useful review) and many interesting developments based on psychological research (Alison, Alison, Noone, Elntib, & Christiansen, 2013). Such studies are usually conducted to develop ways of improving the effectiveness of police interviews. They examine the way police officers prepare for an interview and their objectives for the interview. The general trend in these studies is to emphasise the benefits of building rapport with the interviewees rather than challenging them or trying to coerce them into making a confession. For this reason, in the United Kingdom at least, there is a reluctance to use the term 'interrogation' for a police interview because of its association with using pressure to get the response the police officer wants.

Treating any account of a police interview as a case study of the processes involved, and the underlying psychological mechanisms, would open a rather different approach to those usually employed. It would assist in developing new ways of thinking about what goes on in police interviews with witnesses, victims, and suspects. This would be rather different from the dominant approaches that exist at the moment.

Court proceedings are another arena where case studies to reveal fundamental processes can be very revealing. Many aspects of what goes on in courts are carefully recorded and generally available for research. They do have a format and constraints derived from legal requirements, such as not asking 'leading questions' that imply an answer, as illustrated by the well-known example, "When did you stop beating your wife?" which assumes the respondent did beat his wife at some point. The examination and cross-examination of someone in the witness box therefore is a rich area for study. Although, as with all studies of naturally occurring situations, the influence of a particular context has to be carefully kept in mind.

The studies of court room interactions are mainly focused on ways of making them more effective. Their use with children and adults who have various forms of vulnerabilities, such as learning disabilities, are a particular aspect of research (Morrison, Forrester-Jones, Bradshaw, & Murphy, 2019). The detailed consideration of the implicit or explicit narratives that shape the plausibility of courtroom evidence is a fascinating area for research (see, for example, the early work of Jackson, 1988).

Beyond the many interesting examples of justifications and plausible narratives within legal situations there are many other opportunities to study these processes. One of the most interesting is the accounts that politicians give for acts of violence, as in wars or the definition of who are enemies. The similarities of what politicians claim with the justifications and attempts at mitigation that criminals offer have never been carefully studied. There would seem to be a limited number of explanations/excuses that leaders from different countries draw upon when making statements about violent actions they have authorised. They therefore provide a fascinating and important area for study.

Another detailed set of justifications/explanations for violence are those promulgated by terrorist and other radical groups. These have been subject to many studies, in part to find ways of countering their propaganda (e.g. Shaw & Bandara, 2018). Their accounts are available on many websites. Although, it is best to get official permission to look at this material if you do not want to become a target for the security services. The ways in which terrorist groups create plausible storylines is an important topic for study.

QUESTIONS FOR DISCUSSION

1. How does the form of the questioning of suspects influence the way they defend their actions?

2. What are the major strengths and weaknesses of case studies?

3. What are the differences and similarities between cognitive distortions/biases and justifications?

4. Consider Freudian 'defence mechanisms' such as *rationalisation*, *projection*, and *displacement*. How do they relate to justifications and cognitive biases?

5. How do criminals' accounts of the events leading up to a crime – their personal narratives – help to understand what causes or maintains their criminality?

NOTES

1 See www.nacro.org.uk.
2 If you want to read nineteenth-century accounts from participants in legendary violence, transcripts of witnesses to the Gunfight at the OK Corral on 26 October 1881 are now available at the Arizona Memory Project: https://azmemory.azlibrary.gov/digital/collection/ccolch/search/searchterm/OK/field/materi/mode/all/conn/and/cosuppress.
3 This extract is taken from the transcript available at https://caselaw.findlaw.com/ca-court-of-appeal/1834395.html.
4 This extract is taken from the transcript available at www.famous-trials.com/danwhite/598-whiteconfession.

FURTHER READING

An early major overview of discourse analysis in the context of psychology is:

Edwards, D. (1997). *Discourse and cognition*. London: Sage.

This is not an easy read but does provide an in-depth perspective.

A more recent review is:

Wiggins, S., & Potter, J. (2017). Discursive psychology. In C Willig & W. Stainton Roger (Eds.), *Sage handbook of qualitative research in psychology* (2nd ed., pp. 93–109). London: Sage.

A straightforward way into conversation analysis is:

Liddicoat, A.J. (2011). *An introduction to conversation analysis* (2nd ed.). London: Continuum.

Or this compendium:

Sidnell, J., & Stivers, T. (Eds.) (2012). *The handbook of conversation analysis*. Oxford: Wiley.

REFERENCES

Alison, L.J., Alison, E., Noone, G., Elntib, S., & Christiansen, P. (2013). Why tough tactics fail and rapport gets results: Observing rapport-based interpersonal techniques (ORBIT) to generate useful information from terrorists. *Psychology, Public Policy, and Law*, 19(4), 411–431. https://doi.org/10.1037/a0034564.

Auburn, T. (2010). Cognitive distortions as social practices: An examination of cognitive distortions in sex offender treatment from a discursive psychology perspective. *Psychology, Crime & Law*, 16(1–2), 103–123. doi: 10.1080/10683160802621990.

Bex, F. (2016). Analysing stories using schemes. In H. Prakken & H. Kaptein (Eds.), *Legal evidence and proof: Statistics, stories, logic* (pp. 93–116). London: Routledge. https://doi.org/10.4324/9781315592015.

Boonzaier, F., & De la Rey, C. (2004). Woman abuse: The construction of gender in women and men's narrative of violence. *South African Journal of Psychology*, 34(3), 443–463.

Canter, D., & Youngs, D. (2009). *Investigative psychology*. Chichester, UK: Wiley.

Chester, N. (2016). Criminals explain how they justified their crimes to themselves. *Vice*, 21 April. Retrieved from www.vice.com/en_uk/article/gqmz4m/how-criminals-justify-crimes-psychology-gangsters-uk.

Davis L., & Klopper H. (2003). The value of a qualitative methodology in criminological research, *Acta Criminologica*, 16(1), 72–81.

Dennis D., & Sheldon, K. (2007). The role of cognitive distortions in paedophilic offending: Internet and contact offenders compared. *Psychology, Crime & Law*, 13(5), 469–486. doi: 10.1080/10683160601060564.

Edwards, D. (1997). *Discourse and cognition*. London: Sage.

Edwards, D. (2006). Facts, norms and dispositions: Practical uses of the modal verb would in police interrogations. *Discourse Studies*, 8(4), 475–501. https://doi.org/10.1177/1461445606064830.

Gudjonsson. G.H., & Sigurdsson. J.F. (2010). Motivation for offending and personality. *Legal and Criminological Psychology*, 9(1), 69–81.

Jackson, B.S. (1988). *Law, fact and narrative coherence*. Liverpool, UK: Deborah Charles Publications.

Kahneman, D. (2011). *Thinking fast and slow*. New York, NY: Farrer, Straus & Giroux.

Maruna, S., & Butler, M. (2013). Violent self-narratives and the hostile attributional bias. In D. Youngs (Ed.), *Behavioural analysis of crime: Studies in David Canter's investigative psychology* (pp. 27–48). Aldershot, UK: Ashgate.

Morrison, J., Forrester-Jones, R., Bradshaw, J., & Murphy, G. (2019). Communication and cross-examination in court for children and adults with intellectual disabilities: A systematic review. *International Journal of Evidence and Proof*, 23(4), 366–398. doi:10.1177/1365712719851134.

Pornari, C., & Wood, J.L. (2010). Peer and cyber aggression in secondary school students: The role of moral disengagement, hostile attribution bias, and outcome expectancies. *Aggressive Behavior*, 36(2), 81–94.

Roach J. (2019). The retrospective detective: Cognitive bias and the cold case investigation. In M. Roycroft & J. Roach (Eds.), *Decision making in police enquiries and critical incidents* (pp. 129–149). London: Palgrave Macmillan. https://doi.org/10.1057/978-1-349-95847-4_8.

Shaw, M., & Bandara, P. (2018). Marketing Jihad: The rhetoric of recruitment. *Journal of Marketing Management*, 34(15–16), 1319–1335. doi: 10.1080/0267257X.2018.1520282.

Sherif, M. (1961). Conformity-deviation, norms, and group relations. In I.A. Berg & B.M. Bass (Eds.), Conformity and deviation (pp. 159–198). New York, NY: Harper.

Świątkowski, W., & Dompnier, B. (2017). Replicability crisis in social psychology: Looking at the past to find new pathways for the future. *International Review of Social Psychology*, 30(1), 111–124. doi: http://doi.org/10.5334/irsp.66.

Sykes, G., & Matza, D. (1957). Techniques of neutralization: A theory of delinquency. American Sociological Review, 22(6), 664–670.

Walters, G.D. (2002). The Psychological Inventory of Criminal Thinking Styles (PICTS): A review and meta-analysis. *Aggression and Violent Behavior*, 9(3), 278–291. https://doi.org/10.1177/1073191102009003007.

Ward, T. (2000). Sexual offenders' cognitive distortions as implicit theories. *Aggression and Violent Behavior*, 5(5), 491–507. https://doi.org/10.1016/S1359-1789(98)00036-6.

Ward, T., Hudson, S.M., & Marshall, W.L. (1995). Cognitive distortions and affective deficits in sex offenders: A cognitive deconstructionist interpretation. *Sex Abuse*, 7, 67–83. https://doi.org/10.1007/BF02254874.

Webber, C. (2020). *Psychology and crime* (2nd ed.). London: Sage.

Wiggins, S., & Potter, J. (2017). Discursive psychology. In C. Willig & W. Stainton Roger (Eds.), *Sage handbook of qualitative research in psychology* (2nd ed., pp. 93–109). London: Sage.

APPENDIX: PEOPLE'S EXHIBIT 54 IN THE TRIAL OF DAN WHITE[4]

Today's date is Monday, November 27th, 1978. The time is presently 12:05. We're inside the Homicide Detail, room 454, at the, Hall of Justice. Present is Inspector Edward Erdelatz, Inspector Frank Falzon, and for the record, sir, your full name?

A: Daniel James White.

Q: Now, Dan, before I go any further I have to advise you of the Miranda rights. Number 1 you have the right to remain silent. Number 2 Anything you say can and will be used against you in a court of law. 3. You have the right to talk to a lawyer and have him present with you while you are being questioned. 4. If you cannot afford to hire a lawyer, one will be appointed to represent you before any questioning, if you wish one. Do you understand each of these rights I have explained to you?

A: I do.

Q: And having these rights in mind, do you wish to ah ... tell us about the incident involving Mayor George Moscone and Supervisor Harvey Milk at this time?

A: I do.

Q: Would you, normally in a situation like this ah ... we ask questions, I'm aware of your past history as a police officer and also as a San Francisco fireman. I would prefer, I'll let you do it in a narrative form as to what happened this morning if you can lead up to the events of the shooting and then backtrack as to why these events took place.

A: Well, it's just that I've been under an awful lot of pressure lately, financial pressure, because of my job situation, family pressure because of ah ... not being able to have the time with my family. It's just that I wanted to serve the people of San Francisco well an I did that. Then when the pressures got too great, I decided to leave. After I left, my family and friends offered their support and said whatever it would take to allow me to go back in to office —well they would be willing to make that effort. So since I felt the responsibility for the people that elected me I went to Mayor Moscone and told him that my situation had changed because of the support of family and friends and I'd like to be, retain my seat, to be appointed to my seat. Initially he told me that he felt that I was an elected representative of District 8, that I was doing an outstanding job, people of District 8 were lucky to have me, and that if it came to a legal ruling that he would appoint me, reappoint me, because of the type of person I was. So with that in mind I tried to set my personal affairs in order, preparing to take my seat. And then it came out that Supervisor Milk and some others were working against me to get my seat back on the board. I learned of this [when] I was in the City Attorney's office, when Supervisor Milk called, stating that he, he was of that mind. He didn't speak to me, he spoke to the City Attorney but I was in the office and I heard the conversation and that he was going to try to prevent me from taking my seat again. I went back to the Mayor and he told me that he had had some comments made to him that he felt that some of the people in District 8 didn't want me to, to serve, and I told him that these were people that had opposed me in my election, had traumatized my family by taking me, taking, pressing charges against me at the District Attorney's office twice on false charges. They put a lot of pressure on me and my family.

Q: Can you relate these pressures you've been under, Dan, at this time? Can you explain it to the Inspector Erdelatz and myself?

A: Well, it's just that some of these people have charged me with taking money from big corporations and not recording it but I never did that. I never took money from anybody but the papers print it. Like, my constituents believe it. They, they asked me about it. These people that are irresponsible and bring these charges. Two months later the District Attorney said they're unfounded but no one hears about it, that the charges are false. But my family suffers and I suffer for it, phone calls we get.

Q: These meetings that you were having with the Mayor, were they occurring last week or, or were they going into the weekend, this past weekend?

A: No, I, I hadn't spoke to the Mayor since last Saturday. This would be Saturday a week ago and he told me that I would have to show some support from the people of District 8 if I was going to be reappointed. I could see the game that was being played, they were going to use me as a scapegoat, whether I was a good supervisor or not, was not the point. This was a political opportunity and they were going to degrade me and my family and the job that I had tried to do and, and more or less hang me out to dry. And I saw more and more evidence of this during the week when papers reported that ah … someone else was going to [be] reappointed. I couldn't get through to the Mayor. The Mayor never called me. He told me he was going to call me before he made any decision, he never did that. An it was only on my, my own initiative when I went down today to speak with him. I was troubled, the pressure, my family again, my, my son's out to a babysitter. My wife's got to work, long hours, 50 and 60 hours, never see my family.

Q: Dan, can you tell Inspector Erdelatz and myself, what was your plan this morning? What did you have in mind?

A: I didn't have any, any devised plan or anything, it's, I was leaving the house to talk, to see the Mayor and I went downstairs, to, to make a phone can and I had my gun down there.

Q: Is this your police service revolver, Dan?

A: This is the gun I had when I was a policeman. It's in my room an ah … I don't know, I just put it on. I, I don't know why I put it on, it's just …

Q: Where is this gun now, Dan?

A: I turned it in to Officer ah … Paul Chignell who I turned myself in to at Northern Station. I, I …

Q: You turned yourself in, I wasn't aware of that.

A: I turned myself in at Northern Station to Officer Paul Chignell who, who I could trust and I, I know would do things properly. An then, an then I, I went to the, to the Mayor's office.… A: No, no, it's before I went to the back room and then he could obviously see, see I was obviously distraught and upset and then he said, let's go in the back room and and, and have a drink and I, I'm not even a drinker, you know I don't, once in a while, but I'm not even a drinker. But I just kinda stumbled in the back, went, went, went in the back room and he sat down and he was all, he was talking and nothing was getting through to me. It was just like a roaring in my ears an, and then em … it just came to me, you know, he.

Q: You couldn't hear what he was saying Dan?

A: Just small talk that, you know it just wasn't registering. What I was going to do now, you know, and how this would affect my family you know an, an just, just all the time knowing he's going to go out an, an lie to the press an, an tell 'em, you know, that I, I wasn't a good supervisor and that people didn't want me an then that was it. Then I, I just shot him, that was it, it was over …

STUDY 9
How to rob a bank

SYNOPSIS

Bank robbery often requires more than one person to be involved. Simulating the planning of a robbery is therefore is a very interesting basis for considering the social psychology of criminal activity. This includes exploring how criminal groups are formed and their organisation, which includes the different roles that may be taken before, during, and after the crime. For this study plans of banks are provided (although there are plenty of such plans available on the Internet). Each small group of researchers is required to go through the motions of deciding which bank to rob and then work out how they would rob that particular place. While doing this they are encouraged to monitor their own activities and the different roles they would undertake. The basis for these different roles in the experiences and skills of the participants is explored. Out of this experience consideration can be given to different ways in which criminals can interact. The implications this can have for their responses when they get caught are also considered. The differences between groups, teams, and networks are discussed as well as the meaning of 'organised crime'. The significance of criminality as a social process is highlighted.

SOME KEY CONCEPTS

- leadership
- group structure
- destructive organisational psychology
- offending styles
- linkage analysis
- social network analysis (SNA).

BACKGROUND

There is an important sense in which all crime involves social interaction. Even burglary of a deserted
house has an implicit victim. A drug addict's self-harm may be the focus, but there will still need to be
some transaction with another person to get the drugs. Yet it is surprising how rare it is to find a social
psychological analysis of the interactions between criminals. The vast literature on what used to be called
'group dynamics', the study of interpersonal influences, **leadership**, and other roles in social groups,
has hardly gained a foothold in consideration of criminal activity. The book I co-edited (Canter & Alison,
2000), The Social Psychology of Crime, is still the only one I can locate that has this focus. Psychologists' focus
on the individual criminal tend to ignore the social and organisational aspects of criminality. Not one of
the recent textbooks I have on my desk has the terms 'organised crime' in its index. Sadly, they leave this
extremely important aspect of criminality to brilliant journalists like Glenny (2009), or sociologists and
political scientists like Allum and Gilmour (2019). This is even more surprising because there is a long
and rich history of the psychology of groups as any textbook on social psychology will reveal
(e.g. Franzoi, 2005), and also of organisations (e.g. Cooper, Johnson, & Holdsworth, 2012)

It is useful to distinguish different variations of interpersonal **group structures** that are relevant to
understanding criminals' interactions with each other.

- *Groups.* More than three people who are together for one reason or another may be regarded as
  group. Two is usually thought of as a 'dyad'. When a group becomes a 'crowd' is a matter of debate.
  The important point is that the term 'group' does not imply any close relationship or organisation,
  although it usually suggests some sort of interdependence. Just people who happen to be together in
  one way or another.

  There are nonetheless legal consequences in many jurisdictions for just being together when a crime
  is committed. For example, you could be considered an 'accessory to the crime' by not reporting it.
  By assisting the criminal activity after the crime was committed can be seen as 'obstructing justice'.
  A more contentious aspect of criminal law is the concept of 'joint enterprise'. In the United Kingdom
  this has been used to convict people who were associated with criminal activity, for example if they
  were part of a group, or merely present at the scene, when one of the group committed a crime,
  although the others were not actively involved. This law goes back 300 years to a time when harsh
  laws were in place to control public order.

- *Teams.* When a group of people work together with some sort of inherent organisation it is helpful to
  call them a 'team'. The proposed study deals with a criminal team. More details of the organisation
  of criminal teams and the relevance of that organisation will be elaborated later. The crucial point,
  though, is that any team member will have a role within the group, although this may vary from time
  to time.

- *Gangs.* If a group of people do things together over a period of time the 'term' gang seems appropriate.
  They usually have some form of shared identity, and will often have more of an organisational
  structure, such as having a leader, than a group. Interestingly, of all the terms describing associations
  of people, 'gang' is the only one that is strongly pejorative. It seems to have its origins in people
  going together, referring to 'any band of persons travelling together'. It was when these persons
  caused a nuisance or their travelling together caused anxiety in others that the term took on criminal
  associations. The term also seems to imply a less well-organised group than a 'team'.

- *Organised crime.* There is a considerable literature on criminals who work together in various ways,
  being made up of various teams and gangs who have some sort of agreed relationship with each
  other. These can be highly organised in the strict managerial, corporation sense. They have leaders and
  subordinates and different roles. But these may not be very stable or strictly hierarchical. Mars (2000),
  drawing on theories from anthropology, proposed some interesting distinctions between the different
  ways in which criminal groups operate. These are related to ideas about criminal cultures. They can,

for example, be a set of individuals working in relative isolation, only coming together for specific tasks when they need to. This contrasts with an ideologically driven criminal organisation, such as a terrorist group, who share a common belief system. The popular idea in fiction of a 'Mr Big' running everything with an iron hand, is relatively rare in reality. Criminal organisations tend to be very fluid often with little in the way of a central management structure. This makes them particularly difficult to eradicate. Once one key figure is removed another can quickly take their place.

- *Networks.* When there is a rather more complex and open set of associations between people their organisation may be referred to as a network. The Internet has made the definition of different combinations of interacting criminals much more complicated. When hundreds or even thousands of criminals are using hidden, secret aspects of the Internet (often called the 'Dark Web') to keep in touch with each other, the idea that they form some sort of distinct entity or lots of different ones loosely connected together is difficult to determine. Considerations of how networks can be examined is the focus of Study 10, in which an exercise I developed for studying group processes that I called the 'communication game' is described. I have run it very successfully in many different countries with many different groups. The outcome is remarkably consistent, thereby revealing that organisational structures carry significance for the effectiveness of groups as well as the emotional reactions of participants.

DESTRUCTIVE ORGANISATIONAL PSYCHOLOGY

Understanding more about how robbery happens, especially the nature of the interactions between offenders and the wider perspective on criminal networks, has a number of practical benefits for law enforcement. It can help in identifying the key players as well as what forms of intervention or prevention may be most effective. This amounts to drawing on the rich area of organisational psychology and the social psychology of group processes to understand how criminal teams and networks operate.

Organisational psychology and related disciplines are usually harnessed to help make organisations and associated groups more effective. When studying criminal social processes, the objectives are the opposite of this. I even coined the term **'destructive organisational psychology'** to characterise the applications of psychology that were aimed at disrupting, reducing, or preventing the success of criminal organisations (Canter, 2000). For example, identifying individuals on the periphery of networks who will be more open to police influence.

ROBBERY AS A TOPIC FOR STUDY

Robbery is usually defined legally as theft accompanied by violence or the threat of violence. Pointing a gun at a bank clerk and demanding money is the classical legal idea of what a robbery is. Stealing something from a person's handbag when they're not looking is defined as theft, not robbery. Telling them you'll hurt them unless they give you their money is robbery. It is this threat that often requires more than one offender. When the target is an organisation with a number of people working there and there is a need for access to valuables, whether it is money or safely stored objects such as jewellery, then it is difficult for this to be carried out by one person acting alone. That is why this offers the possibility for exploring the social psychology of groups in the context of criminal activity.

Dramas about robberies of banks, and other places storing much of value, are often based on actual events such as the 'Great Train Robbery' of 1963, or the more recent 'Hatton Garden Heist' of 2015. But even those that are pure fiction, such as the much loved films *The Italian Job, Ocean's Eleven, Heat, Reservoir Dogs,* and many, many others (put 'bank robbery films' into Google and you'll get over 2 million hits!), the key plot devices invariably revolve around the relationships between the group involved. Who is in charge? Who plans it all? Who acts in an heroic way? Who lets the side down?

THE DIFFICULTY OF STUDYING ROBBERY TEAMS AND NETWORKS

The study of group activity is problematic even if the group can be brought into a laboratory and observed in action (as in Study 10). Recording what goes on can be difficult with more than one person speaking or acting at a time. The recording of interactions between people add a further layer of complexity. Who initiates the interaction? Who is the recipient? What is the nature of the interaction?

These challenges have not stopped social psychologists carrying out many studies of group processes, including some famous (perhaps even notorious) experiments such as Sherif's and Asch's experiments, which demonstrated the power of conformity to influence what people do (see Mori & Arai, 2010). But those studies have been criticised for being embedded in middle-class US culture. They are also questioned for the fact that expectations are set up in the rather artificial situation the experimenters created. It is therefore claimed that the respondents behaved as they expected the experimenter wanted them to. For the present considerations a weakness of many of these studies is that they treated the group as a single entity. Only the overall actions of the participants are reported. Little detail is given of the interactions between participants within a group.

Studies of groups, their management, and organisation cover a wide range of issues. As a general introduction of their relevance to understanding criminal groups some key concepts are considered here. At the heart of any consideration of the psychology of groups is the idea that at any moment in time there will be some sort of structure to the group activity; meaning a variety of different, interrelated roles. The most basic aspect of this is the notion of a hierarchy. One person is likely to be leading and others following. But even this idea is not as simple as it may seem. Leadership can take many different forms (Platow, Haslam, & Reicher, 2017). The most obvious form is to give instructions as to who should do what. But there is also leadership in knowledge of what to do and how to do it. These two roles may not be held by the same person at the same time. There is a third and more subtle form of leadership that keeps the group working together. This can be through personal knowledge and relationship to each person, by emotional support, or just keeping a confident, even jokey mood for the group. If one person enshrines these three aspects she or he is often regarded as charismatic.

There are also many styles of leadership. These can range from a very distant, autocratic style, in which leadership is focused on control and giving instructions, to a 'hands-on' style in which the leader leads by actions, being in the thick of whatever is going on. Other variants can include a very laid back 'laissez-faire' style, in which the leader nudges others to do certain things, but is not insistent, or takes a very democratic role ensuring the group suggests or agrees with the things they must do.

An interesting aspect of leadership, and the other roles necessary for a team to be effective, is that they may change during the course of the activities in which the group is engaged. The different sorts of roles may also pass between different people. In a robbery there are five broad stages that can be identified:

- selecting the target (in the proposed example, which bank to rob);

- determining how the target is to be accessed and controlled;

- deciding what to do after the robbery;

- actually carrying out the robbery (although that is not proposed for the present study);

- actions after the robbery (typically this is where the planning breaks down).

Beyond the hierarchical issue of leadership there are other aspects of how people in groups interact with each other. Crucial to this is the way a group forms. Tuckman (1965) is still quoted for his identification of the stages that a group goes through as it settles into a working entity. Part of the power of Tuckman's insights was his encapsulating the stages in the memorable "forming, storming, norming, and performing".

Of interest also is the emergence of groups within groups. These may be tight 'cliques' that interact intensively with each other, or looser subgroups that have some affinity with each other. From these interactions various forms of communication networks can often be identified, which are explored in detail in Study 10.

GAINING ACCESS TO ROBBERS' ACTIVITY

Besides the fictional and documentary accounts of robbers' activities it is extremely difficult to get the details of who does what in a heist. Although it is difficult to obtain information about communications between criminals if you are not a member of the relevant law enforcement organisation, it is not impossible. Porter (Porter & Alison, 2006a, 2006b) managed to get details of 105 robbery groups by combing through the publicly available transcripts of court proceedings of cases brought against these criminals when they were apprehended. This was a tireless, time-consuming task, but did provide remarkably full accounts of the actions of the different individuals involved. Although, of course, what offenders say to the police and in court may not be the entire story, or even really what happened.

Furthermore, as with all such studies of solved crimes there is always the open question of whether those robbers who get away without being caught are different from those who do get caught. There are certainly plenty of well-known unsolved bank robberies, but interestingly about two-thirds of large-scale bank robberies do seem to be solved. This is probably because when large amounts of money and valuables are stolen there is intense police activity leading to finding the culprits (but not always finding everything that was stolen). There are also inherent weaknesses in crimes committed by groups of people that will become apparent when you go through the proposed simulation. In comparison, typically, less than 10% of domestic burglaries are solved.

A STUDY OF HOW TO ROB A BANK

The challenge of discovering who does what and how a group works in any criminal activity is problematic, but some of the issues can be revealed through a simulation. Because this is actual people going through an analogous process to that which criminals would go through it does highlight many of the challenges and other aspects of group dynamics. Of course, there is not the threat or urgency, the real risks involved, and other aspects that make the real-world events different from a friendly, even fun, simulation, but from overseeing these simulations in the past it is clear that the participants learn a lot from them, and it can certainly be the basis of an interesting case study.

Equipment

Four plans of banks are provided in the appendix at the end of this study. They are the sorts of sketches that a person might make having had a look at possible plans. Not all the details are there, so groups will need to work out what is going on in various spaces. You can find many other plans of banks on the Internet if you wish to use different ones. Of course, in this exercise you are not able to check the bank over directly, unless there happens to be a virtual reality example somewhere, so you may decide to use the plans just for initial consideration.

Groups

Put together one or more groups of people. It is interesting to have groups of different sizes. A dyad, for example, may not have enough people to do all that is necessary. A larger group, of say half a dozen, may get in each other's way.

Their instructions are that they are thinking of robbing a bank. The task is to plan the robbery. The way that the decision processes involved in doing this reveal group processes is the essence of this study. Each group will, in effect, act as a case study. Their activities will be scrutinised and compared with those of other groups. The task of the group is straightforward: plan to rob a bank. They should be told to just be themselves in the exercise. They are not meant to 'act' like anyone they may have seen in fiction, or how they imagine a person would act. By being themselves the debrief afterwards can be more instructive, because they can explain the reasons for their contribution directly.

Observer

One person, at least, needs to record what goes on. The recording could be an audio or even video recording, but these take considerable time and effort to transcribe and convert into analysable data. Consequently, although such digital recordings can be useful to check on afterwards, it is recommended that notes are taken of who talks to whom and brief summaries of what is said. In particular it is useful to distinguish between:

* suggestions;

* decisions;

* supportive comments;

* distracting irrelevance.

Recording the activity

There are many different ways of recording interactions between people. This can be extremely detailed, with time measurements of each pause and noting every 'um' and 'err'. Although that sort of detail usually requires an audio recording (Toerien, 2014). Or it can be very broadly based summary of the main events. I suggest that somewhere between these two can be productive. A code for each person should be determined, then who says what to whom noted. as succinctly as possible. Such a transcript could look like the example in Table 9.1.

Analysis of bank robbery

There are two aspects of the interactions that are especially worthy of note: what role each utterance indicates, and the emerging structure of the group.

Table 9.1 Example of part of a transcript for one group planning a bank robbery

Who between	Comment	Time from start
B to whole group	Look bank 3 has a fire escape and a main entrance that is easy to get into.	35 secs
C to B	That's a good point. I could go in through the front entrance.	42 secs
D to C	Yeah and we can wait at the fire escape for you to let us in.	56 secs
B to D	But we'll need someone to watch at the front in case C is spotted outside.	1 min. 2 secs
E to B	I'll do that. Stand at the front to keep others out.	1 min. 10 secs
D to C	Would you have a gun or what?	1 min. 15 secs
C to D	Yes. Just run in and shout, "Stick 'em up!"	1 min. 19 secs
B to C	But there'll be too many people to control all of them.	1 min. 23 secs
E to B	Yeah, needs at least two people to go in with guns.	1 min. 27 secs

The roles that people take

In the brief extract in Table 9.1 it would seem that B took something of a leadership role. She took the lead on a number of decisions and the others tended to refer to her in seeking possibilities. C, by contrast, was more of a go-getter keen to lead the action. D was more considerate of the possibilities and E hooked on to D's comments.

In one of the few studies based on interviews with members of ram-raiding gangs to explore their different roles, Donald and Wilson (2000) proposed that a team requires a distinct set of roles. They suggest that these roles are as follows:

- *Leader/planner*. This person manages the activity, typically selecting who will be in the group, making the key decisions about the target, and how the crime will be carried out as well as the distribution of the loot (as when B in Table 9.1 takes the lead in pointing to crucial features).

  These people usually have convictions for dishonesty, sometimes with violence.

  In a larger-scale study Porter and Alison (2006b) were able to identify gradations of leadership roles in robbery groups. They demonstrated that different people may take decisions, carry out actions, or give orders, but generally people recognised as leaders in the group tended to do all three. This is somewhat at variation with the fictional idea of a clever mastermind who does not get his hands dirty or risk detection.

- *'Heavy'*. This member of the team often stands guard, there to threaten anyone who may attempt to interfere with the ongoing action. They may help with gaining access to the valuables. These individuals generally have previous convictions for violent offences (as E in Table 9.1 indicates she is ready to do).

- *Driver*. This person waits with a vehicle ready to make a quick escape. As would be expected they usually have convictions for stealing vehicles, as well as other driving-related offences.

- *Apprentice* or *extra*. This person is sometimes present to provide some sort of general backup to the raid. They may be petty criminals with minor previous convictions, perhaps youngsters hoping to become a more integrated member of the criminal community. Or they may be direct assistants to the leader, in effect, being trained to take that role in the future.

The existence of these roles relates well to an earlier study by Shover (1973) who studied a broad cross section of burglary groups. This is not surprising. A straightforward organisational analysis of the tasks of a group intending to rob a bank leads to the recognition of the need for the skills of organisation, physical threat, and ready escape. All of these could be available to one or two people but a team of three, or even better four, is more likely to cover the roles needed.

Different offending styles

One possible explanation of the patterns of interaction are differences in the ways in which the offences are carried out. These can be a product of the propensities of individuals in the group as well as the norms that emerge. In their study of group robbery, Porter and Alison (2006a) drew on aspects of personality theory to demonstrate the existence of four styles of interpersonal interaction: dominance, submission, co-operation, and hostility. They showed that robbery groups tended to behave according to one of these four styles. For example, acts of hostility by any one member of a group were unlikely to elicit co-operative actions towards the victims by another. They suggest that the behavioural consistency across a group may be due to the influence of one key individual, thus drawing attention to an important aspect of leadership in these criminal groups.

Complex organised crimes

An interesting recent development of the explorations of how criminal groups operate is the study by Synnott, Canter, Youngs, and Ioannou (2016) of the activities involved in the rather unusually named 'tiger kidnapping'. This is where criminals abduct a significant person or object, then require a crime to be committed before the person is released. If the focus is a bank then money is required to be stolen from the bank by some other person than the person being held hostage.

As far as can be established, the perpetrators of these crimes are rarely caught. This seems to be in part because of the detailed planning and strong structure of the teams who carry out these crimes. There is some evidence that some of those involved in committing the offence have their origins in paramilitary groups, especially in Ireland. The process was apparently developed during the time of insurgency, when paramilitary groups used the tactic to get people to deliver bombs. The move across to robbing banks was a relatively small step.

Therefore, when considering the roles that people play in the simulation, it is of value to explore their backgrounds and experiences. Do these relate to their activities in the role play?

Examining group structure

A second aspect of the analysis is to examine the structure of the group interactions. This overlaps with roles, as we shall see, but it requires a rather different form of analysis. The key process is recording who speaks to whom. The frequency of these interactions can be put into a data matrix, as shown in Table 9.2.

The diagonal along the middle of the table is, effectively, the participants talking to themselves. Presumably there will not be many entries there. Note that the top triangle of the table is not the mirror image of the bottom triangle. This is because the table records who the interaction occurs between. It is therefore very possible for A to contact B more often than B contacts A. The values in the A to B cell would therefore be different from the values in the B to A cell.

Analysis of interaction matrix

Some values have been put into the cells of Table 9.2 as an illustration that allows consideration of various features to be drawn from it:

- *Giving and receiving*. In the sample values one person stands out. D only makes a comment to six others but receives 17 comments. You would need to look at the details of these comments to determine what is going on, but it looks as if D is rather different from the rest in terms of her interaction with the others. Closer examination indicates that nearly half of her messages are from B.

  By contrast, E only gets an interaction from seven others but initiates contact with twice that many. Is this someone trying to be part of the discussion but not being engaged with by others?

- *Emergent structure*. This analysis can be taken a step further using simple **linkage analysis**. The stages in this are demonstrated in Figure 9.1. First identify the most common interactions, as already mentioned this is B sending messages to D. This can be readily represented as shown in Figure 9.1.

Table 9.2 Example of an interaction matrix for recording who interacts with whom

From \ To	A	B	C	D	E	Total
A		5	7	2	3	17
B	3		2	8	4	17
C	5	3		2	0	10
D	2	1	3		0	6
E	2	4	3	5		14
Total	12	13	15	17	7	64

First identify the most common interactions, as already mentioned this is B sending messages to D. This can be readily represented as:

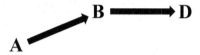

When we consider contacts to B it can be seen that the most frequent are from A. This can therefore be represented as:

C has the most frequent contacts to A, but A also has frequent contacts to C:

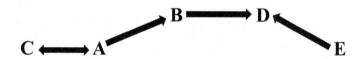

In so far as E has any contacts, they are mainly with D:

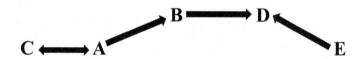

This, intriguingly, puts B in the centre of the network with F as a crucial link to E.

Figure 9.1 Stages in simple linkage analysis

Figure 9.1 could be enhanced by putting all the other connections in and by having the length of the lines as the inverse of the frequency of contact, so that the shorter the line the more frequent are the contacts. The frequencies could also be adjusted as a proportion of the total number of interactions to give a more nuanced illustration of what is going on. That would allow a clearer picture to emerge about the roles that people are playing in the communication process.

Referring back to the total numbers of interactions given and received, it can be seen that B and D are significant in the network. Quite possibly one is the leader and the other is the assistant. Referring back to roles identified from the content could therefore help to give more idea about the way the group was working.

Slowing communication down

As mentioned, recording all this is challenging. One way of making this more feasible is illustrated in some detail in Study 10 where I describe the 'communication game'. For this the participants are only allowed to communicate by sending messages to each other. In the age of Internet communications and social media this is not as artificial as it may once have seemed. The messages can then be more readily examined for their content and the patterns of communication can be very easily recorded.

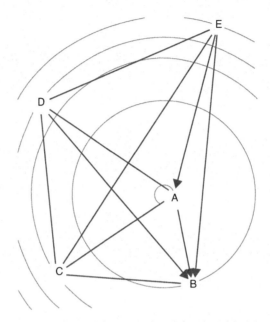

Figure 9.2 Social network analysis derived from simulated data in Table 9.2

Network analysis

The simple linkage analysis illustrated above is, of course, very crude. Putting all interactions in to a diagram is demanding. There is also the problem of organising the diagram so that the network pattern is clear. This becomes even more challenging when the number of people in the network grows. The arithmetic is relatively simple: two people can only have 2 one-way interactions – from A to B and B to A; three people can have 6 one-way interactions; four people can have 12; and as you can see in Table 9.2, five people can have 20 interactions.

The formula is straightforward; for N participants the number of one-way interactions is:

$N^2 - N$.

The complications increase rapidly. There therefore have been a number of computer programs developed to do the calculations and produced the clearest diagrams. These are generally known as **social network analysis (SNA)** tools. Many of them are freely available. I found *Social Network Visualizer: SocNetV*, freely available from www.socnetv.org, especially easy to use. It produced Figure 9.2 from the example matrix in Table 9.2.

This now puts A at the centre of the configuration most closely linked to B, with E the furthest away. This suggests that A is more significant in the network than may have been indicated with a simple linkage analysis. But the importance of the relationship between A and B is still very apparent.

The link between A and B does point to the further levels of analysis that are possible when studying networks. Tightly integrated groups may be regarded as cliques. They are more likely to identify with each other and be less open to infiltration. There are also various measures that can be applied to individuals in a group to determine how central they are to the network, or if they contribute a crucial link between different subgroups.

Illustrations of the way different types of criminal activity give rise to different sorts of networks are given in Canter (2004). Drug cartels are compared with football hooligan gangs and burglary groups. There the different measures of networks and their components are discussed. It reveals that different structures emerge to support the activities of the groups. Football hooligans, for instance, are much less structured in their organisation than those distributing drugs.

Change over time

One important aspect of leadership and other group processes is that they are dynamic. The activity and objectives of a group varies at different stages on its pathway to its goals. In our example, the selection of the bank to target has different features to deciding what to do with the loot afterwards. It is therefore possible, even likely, that leadership and other roles are taken by different people at different stages. For example, choosing a target may draw on knowledge of banks and how they work. By contrast, getting rid of any money stolen will require contacts that can launder the money so that its criminal origins are not apparent.

A very interesting illustration of these changing aspects of group structure is given by Mullins (2009), who used SNA to plot the interactions between those involved in the 9/11 terrorist attack on the United States, as shown in Figure 9.3.

Mullins (2009) gives an in-depth account of the development of the 9/11 terrorist network in spring 2000. Key members of the network are represented as nodes. The ties connecting them signify different

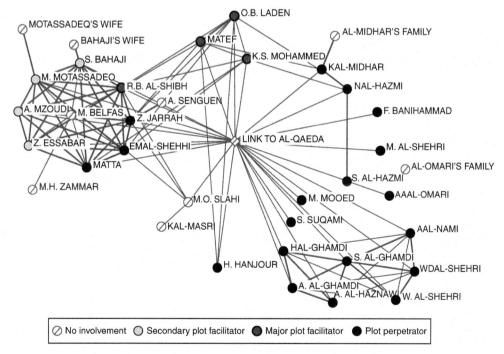

Figure 9.3 Spring 2000 network of associations for people involved in the 9/11 attacks

Source: Mullins (2009).

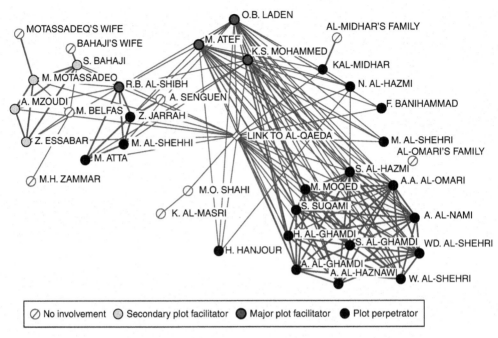

Figure 9.4 Summer 2000: the group that carried out the attack has now become much more distinct

Source: Mullins (2009).

kinds of relationships between members, with thicker ties representing stronger psychological and emotional bonds. As individuals became more committed to violent actions they separated off from most of their associations so that six months later a tight clique had formed of those who went in to carry out the atrocity. They are the team in the bottom right-hand corner of Figure 9.4.

Comparison of teams

In the proposed study it is possible you will have a number of different teams. Can your analysis detect different leadership styles and different ways in which the teams operated? Could different sorts of interaction structures be identified? What impact did these differences have on the outcome of the teams' decision making? Did these differences relate to how long the teams took to finish the exercise or to achieve various stages in the decision making?

Summary of study process

1. Create groups of four or five people, and one person who will observe them.

2. They are given a set of plans of banks.

3. They are instructed to select one of the banks and plan how to rob it.

4. Their discussion is recorded by the observer.

5. The style of planned actions is noted.

6. The summary of the recording is analysed to reveal the roles that different members of the group took.

7. The structure of the interactions is calculated either using simple linkage analysis and/or SNA software.

8. Consideration is given to the leadership roles and styles (e.g. autocratic/democratic) of individuals and the nature of that influence.

OTHER STUDIES THAT COULD USE THIS RESEARCH DESIGN

- Study 10 provides details of a simulation that provides the opportunity to explore, and experience, in more detail many of the issues discussed in the present chapter. It has been carried out with many groups, both students and professionals, in a number of countries.

- A set of studies exploring the social dynamics in bank heist movies would be a fruitful area for future research. Do different countries and/or different directors deal differently with the interactions between the main villains?

- There are also many 'reality television' series in which individuals are put in teams, or even communities, to solve problems. Observations of how these operate could be the basis for research. Although, as with fictional accounts, how these are edited to make exciting television needs to be kept in mind.

- To make the role-play simulation more detailed it would be possible to have people play the part of the bank staff, such as a cashier and bank manager, or even other customers. Then people could go through the motions of the robbery after they've planned what they will do. This of course makes recording the actions more complicated, but allows a more detailed examination of how the group would work in a simulation of an actual event. This would also open up questions about the resources the robbers would need. For instance, where would they obtain a firearm if that was how they intended to control the staff? Louise Porter, who has run many of these studies, mentioned that it is interesting to instruct in one of two approaches: telling participants that they can use anything, or telling them they can use what they like as long as they have access to those resources in real life (i.e. if they don't have access to a gun they cannot say they will use one). In this type of scenario, it would also be possible to debrief everyone. This could include discussions of how actions could have been improved as well as how realistic the simulation was thought to have been. Noting the social processes in this debriefing discussion would be an interesting comparison with what happened in the actual role play.

- As indicated earlier, a few stalwart researchers have explored publicly available records to create details of the social interactions between teams, groups, and networks of criminals. Court reports, true-crime books, and documentary films are all useful resources from which an association matrix, or a series of such matrices, can be derived. Porter and Alison (2001), for example, repeated her study of leadership in robbery dealing with gang rapes.

- The ready availability of SNA software means that hours of fun can be had analysing such material and determining the implications of the results for understanding how criminal groups operate.

- It is worth emphasising that the origins of SNA are within the broader social psychology of group processes and are often traced to the remarkable book by J.L. Moreno called *Who Shall Survive?* (1953), which grew out of his experiences in a concentration camp during World War II. His analysis of social processes became known as 'sociometry' and has been applied to many areas of human interaction, perhaps most productively in the study of school children. It also gave rise to group therapy processes, notably psychodrama.

- There are many other forensic areas of group process that can be simulated, notably jury decision making. Presenting a group of people with evidence for and against the claim of innocence and guilt, then observing how they come to a decision is an important area for research (Lieberman & Kraus, 2009).

Questions for Discussion

• What is the attraction of the robbery team/heist genre of film-making? What does that tell us about attitudes towards this type of criminal activity?

• What are the important differences between the simulation and role play proposed here and the actual experience and activities of a gang of robbers?

• Are there different leadership styles that are appropriate for different sorts of group activities?

• A commonly studied aspect of group characteristics is the consideration of a group's *morale*; that is, the mood, or spirit of a group that makes the members want to be part of it and achieve the group's goals. This is particularly important for groups that face challenges and threats, notably in military contexts. How is this relevant to the consideration of criminal groups? What aspects of group processes may relate to their level of morale? You could explore this further in the proposed study by asking each member of the group to indicate on a score of 1 to 10 how effective they thought the group was. They could even anonymously rate the contribution of each member of the group to the group's objectives. You can then compare those ratings with the other results of analyses of the group activities.

Further Reading

It is remarkable how little has been published on the actual social psychology of bank robberies. Although there is a growing literature on many aspects of robbery, these publications tend to be about the characteristics of individual robbers or criminological examination of trends over time and the types of targets chosen.

A more detailed introduction to the topics considered in this chapter can be found in:

Canter, D., & Alison, L. (Eds.) (2000). *The social psychology of crime*. Aldershot, UK: Ashgate.

Louise Porter's overview of social psychological aspects of robbery is one of few such summaries:

Porter, L.E. (2010). Robbery. In J. Brown & L. Campbell (Eds.), *The Cambridge handbook of forensic psychology* (pp. 535–542). Cambridge, UK: Cambridge University Press.

A clear introductory overview of organisational psychology written by Sir Cary Cooper and his colleagues is:

Cooper, C., Johnson, S., & Holdsworth, L. (2012). *Organisational behaviour for dummies*. Chichester, UK: Wiley.

References

Allum, F., & Gilmour, S. (2019). *Handbook of organised crime and politics*. Cheltenham, UK: Edward Elgar.
Canter, D. (2000). Destructive organisational psychology. In D. Canter & L. Alison (Eds.), *The social psychology of crime* (pp. 321–334). Aldershot, UK: Ashgate.
Canter, D. (2004). A partial order scalogram analysis of criminal network structures. *Behaviormetrika, 31*(2), 131–152.
Canter, D., & Alison, L. (Eds.) (2000). *The social psychology of crime*. Aldershot, UK: Ashgate.
Cooper. C., Johnson, S., & Holdsworth, L. (2012). *Organisational behaviour for dummies*. Chichester, UK: Wiley.
Donald, I., & Wilson, A. (2000). Ram raiding: Criminals working in groups. In D. Canter & L. Alison (Eds.), *The social psychology of crime* (pp. 189–246). Aldershot, UK: Ashgate.
Glenny, M. (2009). *McMafia: Seriously organised crime*. London: Vintage Books.
Franzoi, S.L. (2005). *Social psychology*. London: Brown & Benchmark.
Lieberman, J.D., & Krauss, D.A. (2009). *Jury psychology: Social aspects of trial processes*. Farnham, UK: Ashgate.

Mars, G. (2000). Culture and crime. In D. Canter & L. Alison (Eds.), *The social psychology of crime* (pp. 21–50). Aldershot, UK: Ashgate.

Moreno, J.L. (1953). *Who shall survive?* New York, NY: Beacon House.

Mori, K., & Arai, M. (2010). No need to fake it: Reproduction of the Asch experiment without confederates. International Journal of Psychology, 45(5), 390–397. doi: 10.1080/00207591003774485.

Mullins, S.J. (2009). Terrorist networks and small group psychology. In D. Canter (Ed.), *Faces of terrorism: Cross-disciplinary explorations* (pp. 137–150). Chichester, UK: Wiley-Blackwell.

Platow, M.J., Haslam, S.A., & Reicher, S.D. (2017). The social psychology of leadership. In S.G. Harkins, K.D. Williams, & J. Burger (Eds.), *The Oxford handbook of social influence* (pp. 339–357). Oxford: Oxford University Press.

Porter, L.E., & Alison, L.J. (2001). A partially ordered scale of influence in violent group behavior: An example from gang rape. *Small Group Research*, 32(4), 475–497.

Porter, L.E., & Alison, L.J. (2006a). Behavioural coherence in group robbery: A circumplex model of offender and victim interactions. *Aggressive Behavior*, 32(4), 330–342.

Porter, L.E., & Alison, L.J. (2006b). Leadership and hierarchies in criminal groups: Scaling degrees of leader behaviour in group robbery. *Legal and Criminological Psychology*, 11(2), 245–265.

Shover, N. (1973). The social organization of burglary. Social Problems, 20(4), 499–514. https://doi.org/10.2307/799711.

Synnott, J.P., Canter, D., Youngs, D., & Ioannou, M. (2016). Variations in the journey from crime: Examples from tiger kidnapping. *Journal of Investigative Psychology and Offender Profiling*, 13(3), 239–252. https://doi.org/10.1002/jip.1454.

Toerien, M. (2014). Conversations and conversation analysis. In U. Flick (Ed.), *The Sage handbook of qualitative data analysis* (pp. 327–340). London: Sage.

Tuckman, B.W. (1965). Developmental sequence in small groups. *Psychological Bulletin*, 63(6), 384–399. https://doi.org/10.1037/h0022100. Online details at www.mindtools.com/pages/article/newLDR_86.htm.

APPENDIX: SOME PLANS OF BANKS

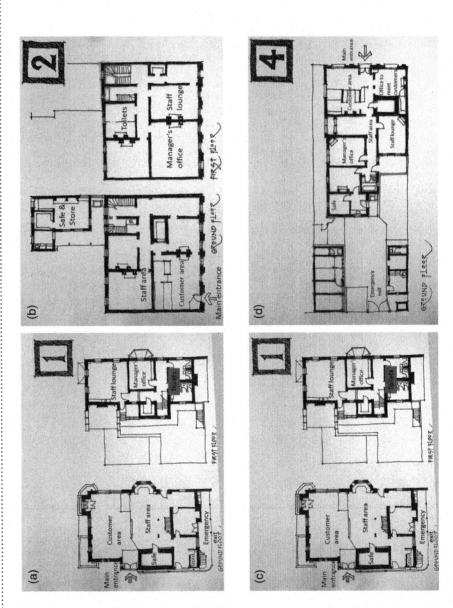

Figure 9.5 Plans of banks

Simulation

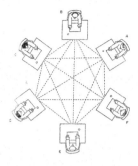

STUDY 10

Exploring investigative and criminal networks: aspects of structure and communication[1]

SYNOPSIS

Although rarely studied, not only is criminal activity inevitably part of a network of contacts, as we considered in Study 9 on bank robbery, but the investigation of crime requires teams and organisations to carry out the work. Consequently, a further understanding of how teams and networks operate, their components and natural strengths and weaknesses, is directly relevant to the study of anti-social behaviour. To explore these issues further, a detailed exercise is described that enables the participants to experience and study communication processes as part of team decision making.

This exercise may be regarded as a form of game playing, or 'simulation'. It provides a rich example of this form of research activity, which is common in business studies and other areas, for training and research. The simulation described has evolved over the years, being carried out with students and professional groups all over the world. It has a number of layers of complexity, revealing many features of group and network processes that are often ignored or misunderstood.

SOME KEY CONCEPTS

- simulations
- network structures
- authoritarian leadership
- democratic leadership
- social identity theory.

1 A full PowerPoint presentation with all of the illustrations and notes for this chapter is available at www.routledge.com/9781138354128.

General Requirements for Production and Direction
of the Study

The project proposed is of a larger scale than others in this book. It requires a small team to manage it. In outline, here is a summary of what is required and the main stages:

1. For each member of each team an envelope needs to be prepared containing (as provided later in this chapter):

   • instructions for each member of each team; and

   • message slips for each member of each team.

2. The general instructions are to be read out to all participants.

3. An assembly of participants is required who are willing to give up a few hours (from 10.00 to 14.00 with a break for lunch works well). The game is played before lunch and the debriefing occurs after.

4. The game is played between teams each consisting of five people. At least one person is needed as a 'coder' and one as a 'messenger'. With a minimum of two teams that is a minimum of a dozen participants. With the five teams described, two coders and two messengers would require at least 27 people. I have run it with even larger groups.

5. Coding sheets are to be provided for the coders in each team.

6. Presentation material illustrating the networks for each team is to be used only in the debriefing, after the game has finished.

7. A location is required to house the game. This requires a minimum of six locations separate from each other. They can be separate rooms or different places in a large hall.

8. A location is required where the participants can be brought together to receive the instructions and later the debriefing.

Background

Summarising the discussion in the previous chapter, the study of criminal teams, groups, and networks is important but rarely studied from a social psychological perspective. There are plenty of general explorations of 'organised crime' (the journalist Misha Glenny (2009) has written an excellent book on international criminal links that was turned into a fictional type of James Bond film). There is also a lot available on terrorist networks (for example published, curiously, in physics outlets; see Fellman & Wright, 2014), drug cartels (e.g. Hesterman, 2013), and corruption (Dupuy & Neset, 2018), as well as the various strategies for dealing with these illegal, fungoid-like growths, which spread through most societies. However, the actual workings of criminal teams and the ways in which the structures of their networks influence how they operate has been less thoroughly explored.

Understanding teams and networks is also highly relevant for all forms of organisations. This includes teams of investigators. Those involved in managing other legal organisations also have a lot to learn from the study and experience provided by the **simulation** study described in this chapter. I usually call this the 'communication game', but that can mean participants do not take it seriously. So although it is meant to be interesting and enjoyable it is an exercise that often enables people to learn something about themselves as well as about the social psychology of teams and networks.

It is of interest to note that I developed this game as part of the training for architects, who do become parts of teams and organisations. An account of this was first published in my book *Psychology for Architects* (Canter, 1975). The teams illustrated in that original version had six members each, but I found this caused the game to take a very long time. The present proposal therefore uses five-person teams.

One of the key points that emerges when considering organisations is that their essence is communication. Without contacting each other they do not exist. This means that the nature of those communications is the heart of their vulnerability. This nature is, in turn, influenced by the pattern of contacts – the **network structure**. This structure can take many forms. Each has its own strengths and weaknesses. A really effective network is one that is flexible enough to change its structure at different stages in its activities. A simple example is that when definite controlled action is necessary, an **authoritarian leadership** style, supported by a strong hierarchical structure with a clear, dominant leader, is best. But when ideas are needed and information is to be gathered, then a much more open interactive structure, a more **democratic leadership** style is of value. Most decisions require both of these management styles. This means that no one communication network structure is good for all stages in organisational activity and decision making.

SOCIAL IDENTITY THEORY

The other fundamental aspect of this exercise is the way it illustrates and helps to explore '**social identity theory**', which has given rise to a major area of social psychology theory and research. This developed from the fascinating 'minimal experiments' carried out by Tajfel (1978). In those studies people were told they were part of groups, in an almost random assignment; for example, on the basis of which painter they preferred. They were then asked to assign rewards to theirs and the other group. The curious finding was that people sought to maximise the difference between their group and the other group rather than give their own group a larger amount. The widespread ideas about 'in-groups' and 'out-groups', from which there is usually in-group favouritism, had its impetus from these experiments.

Developments of the thinking behind these results gave rise to the perspective that people's views of themselves, their identity, has a fundamentally social component. Who we think we are is a collective set of cognitions as well as being personal (thoroughly reviewed by Reicher, Spears, & Haslam, 2010). This comes about by 'self-categorisation' a complementary theory to social identity theory (Postmes, Baray, Haslam, Morton, & Swaab, 2006).

The particular relevance of this far-reaching perspective on social psychological processes for the proposed simulation study is that people self-categorise themselves in relation to the context in which they are acting. Different comparisons of group membership will give rise to different self-categorisations. In the study described here the potential for different group membership is deliberately set up. Participants can think of themselves as part of a designated team, labelled, for example, after a well-known fictional detective, but with the other members of which they can only communicate by sending messages. Or they can identify with the other people who share the same team membership letter. They sit around a table with these people so a different mechanism for social identify can emerges. At a third level they can form a view that they are in a group with all the other participants, possibly distinguishing their identity from those who are managing and organising the exercise.

Besides those who have been designated as members of a team there are other individuals whose self-categorisation is potentially ambiguous: the coders and messengers. They will typically identify with the organisers, but various intriguing processes can interfere with this. For example, following self-categorisation theory, if they do not see a 'fit' between their understanding of what is appropriate for the group (they see themselves as part of) and the actions of some of the members of that group, they will be reluctant to identify with that group. This is notably the case if the leaders act inappropriately (Haslam, Postmes, & Ellemers, 2003; Steffens et al., 2014). These formulations come about through the interactions the groups have (Postmes et al., 2006). The communication between group members develops, and even negotiates, norms. They deal with issues of what the nature of the group is and how it should act. This becomes very clear in the proposed simulation in the amount of effort that goes into clarifying who the group is and how they should act. Giving the group labels/names at the start will also influence this process.

The proposed study therefore reveals many important aspects of how social identities and related self-categorisations emerge through group interactions, with their resultant emotional consequences. However, the proposed simulation takes these processes a stage further by revealing the power of communication network structures and the impact of where an individual is within those structures.

Major Learning Objectives from Participating in the Simulation

The proposed project has a rather broader variety of goals than other studies in this book. In particular, participating in it has direct learning objectives. The experience of participating itself is one of the 'findings' of the project.

This has relevance both for the investigative process and for understanding how criminal networks operate.

For those carrying out Investigations, the following points are worth noting:

- Good data/information is fundamental.

- Inferences require all the information to be brought together.

- There will be different skills in the team to be harnessed.

- Information overload must be managed (the key to this is delegation).

- Various management strategies are needed at different stages in the process.

- People at the end of communication lines need support.

When considering criminal activity

As mentioned, understanding the inherent weaknesses in aspects of how teams and organisations work gives insights into how they can be disrupted. This is captured in the idea of *destructive organisational psychology* (Canter, 2000).

These are the vulnerabilities that are apparent:

- People on the periphery of networks are typically least committed to the organisation and therefore most susceptible to police influence.

- Distorting communications is a powerful way to undermine networks.

- As the network grows it becomes more difficult to manage.

- Some network structures are more prone to confusion than others.

- Never undervalue informal assumptions. Gossip, prejudice, and stereotypes feed group processes.

In terms of personal experience

Although the task of the game is a relatively simple one, participating in it does tend to become very involving. Even the people acting as coders and messengers get caught up in the spirit of it. Some people feel empowered by their role, others can get very frustrated. The participants therefore learn something important about themselves, by virtue of how they handle the situation that they have been assigned. This shapes their identity within the group as well as their understanding of the nature of the group.

- How do they see themselves contributing to the group process? Do they just passively pass on information? Or do they actively try to help? Do they accept their role unthinkingly, or try to work out how to take advantage of it?

- If they get frustrated or annoyed with what others in the group are doing, how do they deal with that? Do they become disruptive or do they try to understand the basis for their concerns?

The game is a good icebreaker for the start of an academic year or a lengthy course. It brings people together and gives them a lot to talk about afterwards. These emotional consequences of participating have to be borne in mind and managed. If you set the simulation up as a highly competitive one, it will raise the stakes and associated feelings. As the organiser of the exercise you may become the target for gossip or animosity. You have to learn to manage it all with good grace and a sense of humour. It is therefore a salutary exercise for the organisers as much as the participants.

The Communication Game

A minimum of a dozen people is needed to run this simulation. That provides two *teams* of five people each and two people to act as *coders* and *messengers*. But a more interesting exercise would be with twice that number so that four teams and four coders and messengers are available. I've run this with many more teams. Details for six teams are given here, so that you have a choice as to which networks to use.

Objective

The objective of the game, as described to the participants, is to solve a problem based on the information given to members of the team. Each member of the team has a specific piece of information. If you want to increase the excitement and commitment of the participants you could say there is a prize for the first team to solve the problem. This can create a lot of energy in the event, which may be too demanding to manage!

Interestingly, you can further ramp up the involvement of people in the exercise by giving each team a recognisable name. This shapes their approach to group identity. I've done that in the details below by giving them the names of fictional detectives. You could give them the names of investigative organisations, such as FBI or Scotland Yard. You usually weaken, but do not remove, the competition by just calling them Team 1, Team 2, etc.

Spatial organisation

A crucial aspect of the simulation is that although there are teams of five people each, with the people in each team labelled A, B, C, D, E, they do not sit together. All the As sit round a table together, all the Bs are together, and so on. There are two key reasons for this. One is to confuse the issue of identity and role between the network a person is part of – their *team* – and the people they are face to face with around a table. This confusion can become crucial in the way the simulation unfolds.

A second reason for having members of the team dispersed, separate from one another, is that *all communication is in writing*, delivered by the *messengers*. This allows the communications to be monitored, by the *coders*, both for later analysis and to check if the rules of the game are being broken. That provides rich insights into the experience of the event, which can be very powerful in the subsequent debriefing.

Team structures

Each team has a different pattern of communication. This is controlled by their need to use *message slips*. These only allow each member of the team to communicate with specified other members, as described in what follows.

By limiting the communication patterns a comparison is possible of the team structures and how they influence their work. Most importantly, these communication patterns also influence the experience of participants. This happens to a marked degree, involving real, serious emotions. What I've found remarkable about this simulation is how real it becomes for the participants and how predicable many of the outcomes are, as I will summarise later.

If you want to explore the consequence of this paper-message communication approach you could create one team that sits together round a table to solve the problem. Comparing the time and result of their activity with that of the other groups is very interesting. But monitoring their discussion is more challenging.

Monitoring communications

For the purposes of feedback to participants, and to allow subsequent analysis, each message sent is first delivered to the coders. I often call them 'censors' to give more excitement to the game. They can first check that the message slip has not been tampered with, notably to enable communication with a member of the team not allowed for that particular network. This is a breaking of the rules that is a very interesting example of the frustrations some team members may feel. The censor can have such messages returned to the sender – with a cryptic message.

The second activity for the monitors is to note who the message is between, using the matrixes below that are provided for each team. This allows an intriguing analysis both of the amount and variety of contacts that each network generates as well as the roles that each person plays in the network.

Third, the monitors can record the interesting and informative messages that are sent. These reveal the roles people are taking. They also indicate the sorts of decision processes that are emerging as well as the frustrations, fake news, gossip, and social support that each team generates.

The results of the monitors' activities are used in the debriefing session at the end of the game.

Note for anyone running the exercise

To keep the mood of the game reasonably light I've sometimes called it the simulation exercise exploring:

Communication

Harmony

And

Other

Skills

Played by:

- 'players';
- 'liaison officers';
- 'messengers'; and
- 'censors'.

The liaison officers are the people who set up the whole exercise and have final jurisdiction over any decisions. They act as what is called in the game the 'CPS',[2] in determining if any team has solved the challenge the exercise requires.

One important aspect of setting up the teams and selecting people for each role is to make public the fact that this is being done randomly. If you don't do that then, given the nature of the simulation,

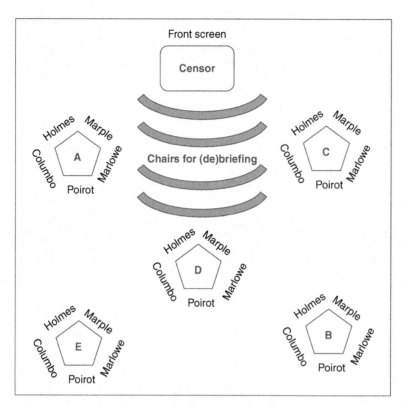

Figure 10.1 A convenient layout for the simulation in a large hall

participants will possibly assume you have deliberately assigned them to roles they consider subordinate or significant. I've usually prepared an envelope for each role and shuffled them in front of everyone, then given them out randomly. People are then led to the position for their labelled role.

In organising the game, then, you need at least six separate tables, one for each of the five team members and one for the monitors/censors (a convenient layout in a large hall is given in Figure 10.1). These tables should be far enough away from each other so that they cannot overhear each other. I've found this to be most effective if they are each in a separate room, say along a corridor, but at the edges of a large hall, with the monitors in the middle, can also work well.

For the present example five networks are specified consisting of five teams. If you are going to use the team names listed below, they should be told they are: Holmes, Marple, Columbo, Marlowe, and Poirot.

Instructions for those participating in the game

The task

A dead body has been found.

Each team is to resolve the central question about the death as quickly as possible to the satisfaction of the CPS.

1. There are teams with names (e.g. here I've given them names of fictional detectives, Holmes etc..) that each have five people designated with letters (i.e. A, B, C, D, E).

2. Each member of the team has a specific piece of information that can contribute to answering the central question, which is given in closed envelopes. These must not be opened until you are seated at your place. It is by sharing this information that the answer can be achieved

3. The letters sit together at one table (i.e. all the As are together, all the Bs, etc.).

4. Consequently, the members of each team can only communicate with people in their team in writing, using special message slips provided for each team member.

5. The message slips indicate for each team member who they are allowed to communicate with. They circle one of the designated recipients to indicate that is the person that the message should be delivered to. For example, person A in the FBI team would send a message to person B in that team by circling the B on their message slip.

6. One member of the team is designated as the person who is allowed to contact the CPS. That person will have special contact forms for that purpose.

7. The messages are collected by roving messengers, who deliver them to the designated recipient. You will need to use the name plate provided at the location in which you are based so that the messengers can locate you.

8. However, the messengers first take the messages to the 'censors' who code them and record anything of interest.

9. The game comes to an end when a correct solution reaches the CPS, or it's time for lunch.

Organisers of this exercise should be aware that it is often very difficult for any team to come up with a solution. If the teams get themselves in a confusing cycle, which will become apparent from the monitoring of communications, then for everyone's sanity it is best to stop the game.

In my experience, it takes a morning for the simulation to reach a conclusion or impasse. It then takes a couple of hours after lunch for a debriefing. The lunch is usually very lively. A party at the end of the day is welcome to ease the tensions.

Information provided to the members of each team

In some runs of this simulation I have given each team member a title, such as forensic herbalist, or senior investigating officer. These labels play no part in solving the task set the teams, but they can be very influential in shaping the way individuals interpret their roles. This can be disruptive, especially if the role is at variance with the position of that person in the communication network. For example, a person who thinks he should be in charge, but who is at the end of a communication chain, could cause great confusion in trying to get the information together. A person at the centre of a network is much more able to do that.

You can avoid the possible confusion of role labels by just using the letters A, B, etc. Role labels are given in the card examples that follow in case you want to use them.

There are actually two 'forensic herbalist' pieces of information that must be given to different teams. Perhaps one piece of information to one team and the rest to all the other teams. The different information is given in Figures 10.3 and 10.4, but of course on the team information there should be no indication that they are different.

Information to be prepared and made available in closed envelopes for participants

The following are the basic materials that need to be reproduced to be made available in packets for each player prior to the exercise being run. You will need a separate copy of each for each team.

In addition, each person should have ten message slips specific to their team position, as indicated when the networks are given. One interesting issue is what does a team member do if she runs out of message slips? This is a useful illustration of how people cope with unforeseen circumstances. I suggest the message slips are relatively small to avoid the possibility of very long message, which puts additional pressures on the coders.

One aspect that I've also noticed is that people rarely take notes of the instructions read out to them initially. This also provides a useful illustration to them of how to prepare for something they may not fully understand at the time.

Do be aware that in the examples given here there are two versions of the location of the body for two different teams, which are indicated by the information held by two different 'forensic herbalists'. Of course, no one should be told about this. This is also to enable people to realise in the debriefing that what might seem like one crime scene in fact is two.

Participants should not be told anything other than the instructions and the material made available to them in closed envelopes. They should be told that they should not open these envelopes until they are seated in their positions. This makes it less likely that people know, initially at least, who the person is with whom they are communicating. This creates a further level of ambiguity in the communication process.

Material that should be on the cards for each member of a team

This is all more manageable if the material here is reduced to a card slightly smaller than the envelopes you have available.

Team member A

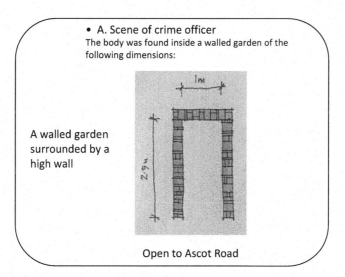

Figure 10.2 A. Scene of crime officer

Note for debriefing. This is a piece of visual information in which the details are crucial for solving the case. But they have to be communicated on message slips or the team needs to be aware that bringing the information to this person could help. However, the title and position in the network of this role can make the individual less aware of the need to find a way of sharing this information and amalgamating it with other information.

Team member B(1)

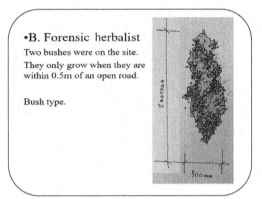

Figure 10.3 B(1). Forensic herbalist

Team member B(2)

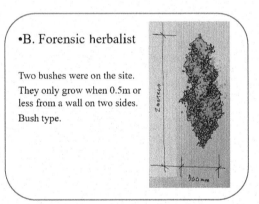

Figure 10.4 B(2). Forensic herbalist

To be clear only one of these forensic herbalist details should be given to a B in any one team.

Note for debriefing. The label 'forensic herbalist' (while being an ironic dig at all the different forensic scientists there are these days) is deliberately unknown to anyone. There is therefore the question among team members of what this role might be and what its contribution is. However, as will become clear when you know the solutions, the information is crucial to solving the challenge. This is also visual material that needs to be combined with the information that A has, but this may seem more difficult to convey, being a complex shape, although actually it is only the dimensions that are relevant.

C. Senior investigating officer

We need to know, was this murder or suicide?

Note for debriefing. This individual has very little to go on initially. The title may lead that person to think she has to take over all the decision making, but in fact it is bringing all the information together that is crucial. If C decides to go it alone with only limited information, thinking, for instance that he needs to make all sorts of inferences, then he will come very unstuck.

D. Profiler

A suicide would be out of public view.

Note for debriefing. This is deliberately ambiguous, apparently context-free information. It could easily be dismissed by the rest of the team. C for instance could assume this is nonsense and just fed into the mix to add confusion. But like the information that every member of the team has it is crucial for finding the solution.

E. Pathologist

- The body is that of a normal young man.
- It was found stretched out, not touching any bushes.

Note for debriefing. This information is totally verbal but needs to be brought together with the other information available in visual form in order to be made sense of. On its own it could be a very misleading basis for making all sorts of speculations of what a body would look like if it were murder or suicide.

Solutions

As is apparent from the details above, there are actually two different solutions to the question of whether the death was murder or suicide (see Figures 10.5 and 10.6).

Solution 1. A suicide would be out of view and therefore hidden from the road by bushes.

Bushes near the road

Figure 10.5 Solution 1. A suicide would be out of view and therefore hidden from the road by bushes

Solution 2. Because a suicide would not be in view of the road, this combination implies a murder.

Bushes near two walls

Figure 10.6 Solution 2. A murder would be in view and with bushes at the back

The teams and their networks

This information is not made available until after the game is concluded. It does, however, influence the way the message cards are written, indicating who can contact whom, and the network chart for recording the communication contacts.

The *Holmes* network shown in Figure 10.7 is a typical authoritarian one, with a central figure with whom everyone connects, but they cannot contact each other. Note also that the individual designated as the senior investigating officer, C, is not at the centre of this network. So how do they deal with that? Nor is the crucial role of the person who must give the news of their solution to the CPS in a central role. So although some aspects of this network can be quite efficient, it potentially has many problems. Not least the pressure that comes on B and the alienation that the other can feel if they are not involved in the decision process.

The communication contacts recording matrixes for each team are shown in Tables 10.1, 10.3, 10.5, 10.7, and 10.9. The recording matrix enshrines the available contacts in the network. This illustrates, for example, that B can contact A, C, D, and E but each of the others can only contact B. The idea is that the coders put a '/' into each box every time a message comes through from one of the members of the team to another. These can then be added at the end of the game and totals prepared. These then provide a fascinating insight into how the game unfolded. The frequency of contacts between team members and the total number of contacts each role received and sent links directly to the experiences people had of the game. Significantly it influences how much they enjoyed it and how significant they thought their role was.

It is also of value if the coder(s) number each message sequentially for each team. This adds as a check that that message has been recorded. It also provides a record if a particular message is sought later.

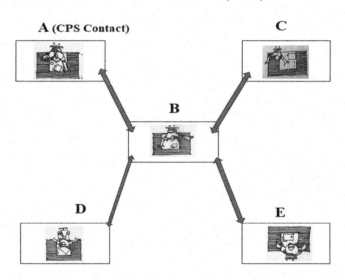

Team HOLMES (Star)

A (CPS Contact)   C

B

D   E

Classical authoritarian leadership pattern

Figure 10.7 Star network

Table 10.1 Coding matrix for Holmes team

HOLMES

*CPS Contact

To From	A*	B	C	D	E	Total
A*						
B						
C						
D						
E						
Total						

Table 10.2 Message slips for Holmes team

Team	HOLMES			
FROM A	TO	B	CPS	
Message:				

Team	HOLMES					
FROM B	TO (circle one)		A	C	D	E
Message:						

Team	HOLMES		
FROM C	TO	B	
Message:			

Team	HOLMES		
FROM D	TO	B	
Message:			

Team	HOLMES		
FROM E	TO	B	
Message:			

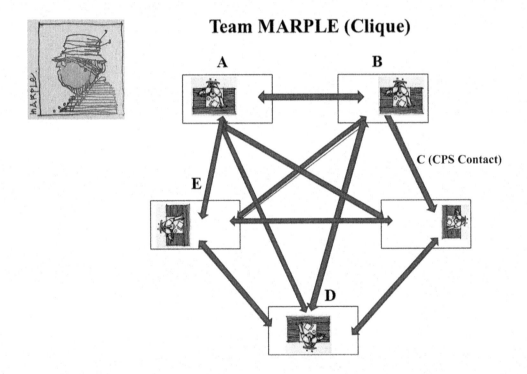

Team MARPLE (Clique)

Typical open, democratic team

Figure 10.8 Clique network

The *Marple* network shown in Figure 10.8 reflects an open, democratic process in which everybody can contact everyone else. This means ideas and information can be readily share shared. However, this is more difficult to manage and can give rise to conflicting individuals or subgroups trying to take control. Gossip can quickly fly around destabilising the work of the team.

The coding matrix for the contacts in team Marple, as in Table 10.3, is completely open.

Table 10.3 Coding matrix for Marple team

MARPLE
*CPS Contact

To / From	A	B	C*	D	E	Total
A						
B						
C*						
D						
E						
Total						

Table 10.4 Message slips for Marple team

Team	MARPLE					
FROM A	TO (circle one)	B	C	D	E	
Message:						

Team	MARPLE					
FROM B	TO (circle one)	A	C	D	E	
Message:						

Team	MARPLE					
	CPS					
FROM C	TO (circle one)	A	B	D	E	
Message:						

Team	MARPLE					
FROM D	TO (circle one)	A	B	C	E	
Message:						

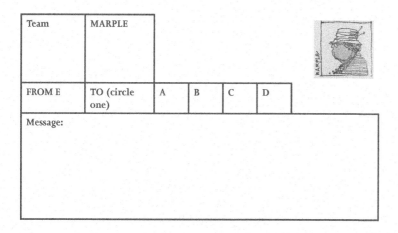

Team	MARPLE				
FROM E	TO (circle one)	A	B	C	D
Message:					

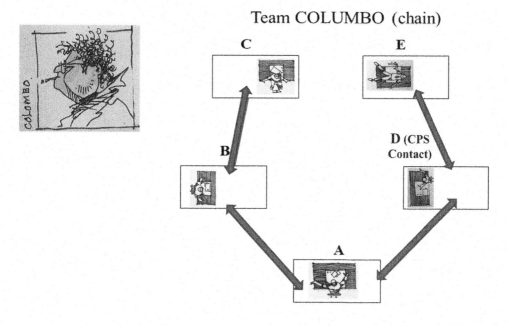

Hierarchical organisation

Figure 10.9 Chain network

The *Columbo* network, illustrated in Figure 10.9, is a stricter hierarchy than Holmes with C and E at the end of a communication chain, putting A in a significant position but, in effect, having B and D as lieutenants that have to be relied on to communicate with C and E. The room for confusing and messages going awry in this network are therefore considerable. Although A may not be under as much pressure as B, the counterpart in the Holmes star network, B still has the risk of alienating C and E who may not feel involved in the communications at all. In terms of destructive organisational psychology, because of their distance from the 'centre', it is C and E who offer the most potential for infiltrating the network or being turned into informers by the police.

Table 10.5 Coding matrix for Columbo team

COLUMBO
*CPS Contact

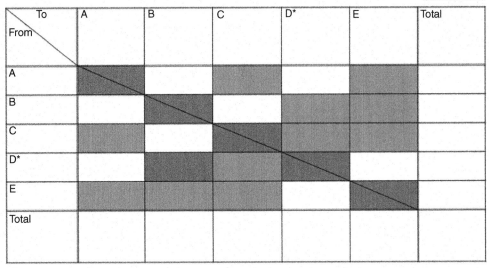

To / From	A	B	C	D*	E	Total
A						
B						
C						
D*						
E						
Total						

Table 10.6 Message slips for Columbo team

Team	COLUMBO			
FROM A	TO (circle one)	B	D	
Message:				

Team	COLUMBO			
FROM B	TO (circle one)	A	C	
Message:				

Team	COLUMBO		
FROM C	TO (circle one)	B	
Message:			

Team	COLUMBO	A	E		CPS
FROM D	TO (circle one)				
Message:					

Team	COLUMBO		
FROM E	TO (circle one)	D	
Message:			

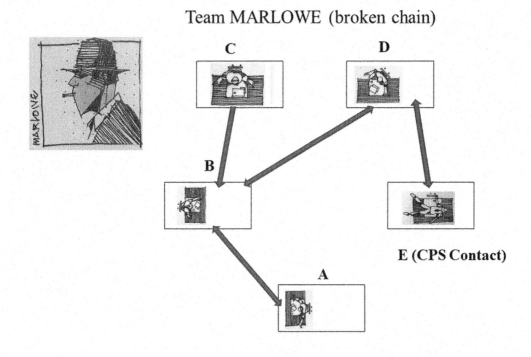

Figure 10.10 Broken chain network

The *Marlowe* network in Figure 10.10 is a complex hierarchy. B can contact three people but A, C, and E can only contact one. D is therefore potentially in a lieutenant role because of the link to E. This is potentially a very important role because E has the all-important CPS contact capability. Without knowing the structure of this network, it can become very confusing. It reminds me of the way that, in universities, assistants to professors can have very important roles, like D, because they can liaise with students and the professor, although their significance can be greatly underrated.

Network *Poirot* is a recipe for confusion, as shown in Figure 10.11. Messages can literally go round in circles. There is no obvious centre or hierarchy. Different subsets in contact with each other are likely to form subgroups that may try to control the network. Gossip and invention of possibilities beyond the immediate information available is very likely.

Table 10.7 Coding matrix for Marlowe team

MARLOWE
*CPS Contact

From \ To	A	B	C	D	E*	Total
A						
B						
C						
D						
E*						
Total						

Table 10.8 Message slips for Marlowe team

Team	MARLOWE				
FROM A	TO (circle one)	C	D	E	
Message:					

Team	MARLOWE	
FROM B	TO (circle one)	E
Message:		

Team	MARLOWE			
FROM C	TO (circle one)	A	D	E
Message:				

Team	MARLOWE		
FROM D	TO (circle one)	A	C
Message:			

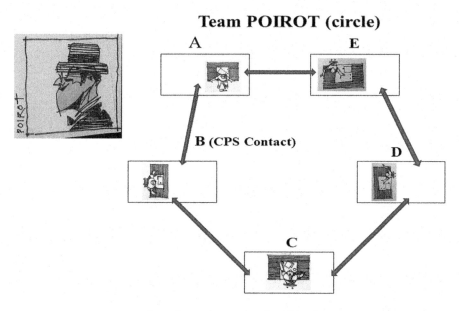

Figure 10.11 Circle network

Table 10.9 Coding matrix for Poirot team

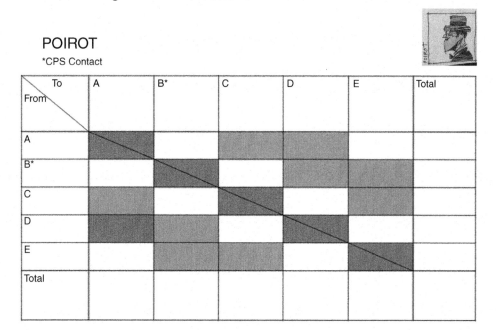

To From	A	B*	C	D	E	Total
A						
B*						
C						
D						
E						
Total						

Table 10.10 Message slips for Poirot team

Team	POIROT		
FROM A	TO (circle one)	B	E
Message:			

Team	POIROT	CPS	
FROM B	TO (circle one)	A	C
Message:			

Team	POIROT		
FROM C	TO (circle one)	B	D
Message:			

Team	POIROT		
FROM D	TO (circle one)	C	E
Message:			

Team	POIROT		
FROM E	TO (circle one)	A	D
Message:			

ANALYSIS

Who won?

Did any of the teams find a solution? Did anyone become aware that there were two different solutions? If they did not get the solution, where/what were the problems? In the debrief, do inform everyone of the solutions!

1. If there was a solution, which team came by it? What was it about their communication network that enabled them to bring all the facts together to work out the solution? Was there a particular leader who organised the team well?

2. One crucial aspect to be looked at is that teams need to go through some distinct phases:

   (a) They need to bring the five pieces of information together. This can be done by one person or happen with a number of people. It requires some sort of direction from one or more individuals. Someone needs to say, "Pass all the information to A", or at least, "We need to gather all the facts together". This can be seen as an authoritarian stage that benefits from clear 'central' direction. The star network *Holmes* should be best at this unless the person in role B does not take on that task and, for example, keeps on looking for "who is Watson?"

It helps if at least one member of the team has some idea of the network structure, but it is rare for people to seek that. Instead the first message is often "who are you?" or "what is your role?" These are actually irrelevant to solving the puzzle, but they show how significant people often believe their role designation is for their identity.

Often participants will try to guess what is going on. This can feed misleading information into the discussions between participants. Or an attempt will be made to come to a conclusion without all the facts (a common mistake in crime investigations).

(b) With all the information available there needs to be an interpretation of it and the solution it implies. This benefits from a number of people looking over the material. Such sharing is probably easiest with the *Marple* network, where everyone can communicate with everyone else.

3. There may have been a solution within the team but, not having taken notes, they did not remember that the solution had to be presented to the CPS. They did not know who in the group was able to contact the CPS. Or they found it difficult to communicate with that person to pass the message on. This is an illustration of how important it is:

(a) to keep the whole team involved; and

(b) to be aware that those who have contact with external agencies may be regarded as junior, but have a crucial role. Receptionists and messengers are an interesting example of this.[3]

This benefits from an understanding of the network structure and who has the CPS contact.

The interesting thing about these three phases is that they each require a different management style and benefit from different network structures. This is difficult for people to realise at the outset. This is where the placement of team members at different tables with their (letter) counterparts in different teams becomes an intriguing issue. You may have noticed that I did not say people in different teams may not talk to each other. Depending how competitive participants are and how strongly the competition aspect has been emphasised in the presentation of the rules, will influence whether people talk to each other around the tables. On the few occasions when the solution has been successfully found it has been because they talked to each other. This enables the strengths of the different communication networks to be harnessed. It also helps the participants to realise there are two different solutions.

Separate teams form an organisation

When participants talk together around the tables and compare notes, this turns the separate teams into one interacting organisation. The moral of course is that working together is better than ignorant competition. This coherence tends also to involve the messengers. They will often be cajoled into providing further information or sending illicit messages to roles that are not allowed. Such an organisation can turn on the organisers and the 'censors', believing they are being cheated in some way. From a social identity perspective, participants no longer identify with their team, but with all the other teams. This converts them all into the 'in-group' and the organisers who wished this on them become the 'out-group'.

Frequencies of contacts

Further detailed analysis reveals how the different teams worked and the consequences of their structure, communication, and management styles. This has direct influence on how team members felt about the game and their part in it.

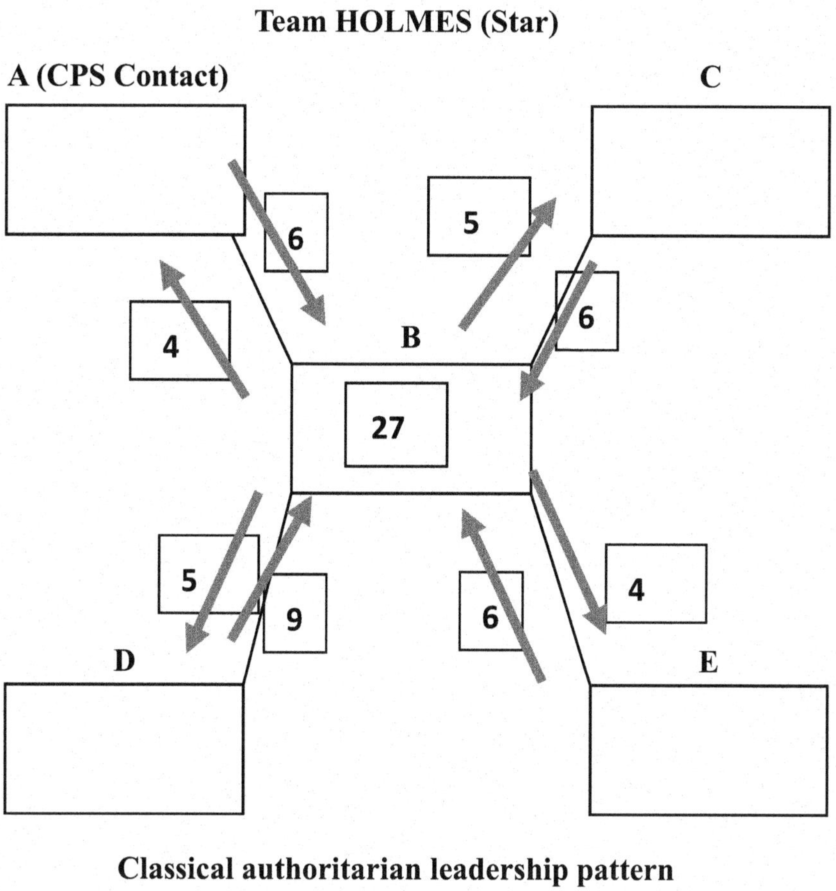

Team HOLMES (Star)

A (CPS Contact)   **C**

6

5

4

B

6

27

5

9

6

4

D   **E**

Classical authoritarian leadership pattern

Figure 10.12 Example message frequencies in star network

The first stage is to use the coding matrix to total the number of contacts

- from each person;

- to each person; as well as

- the *total* number of communications for each team.

If there is the possibility of writing these values on a projection of the networks this is very helpful for a debriefing process (as illustrated in Figure 10.12). This provides an indication of how the teams differed in terms of their overall activity, the extent to which they were generating messages and thus interacting with each other. The expectation is that the open network, *Marple* will produce the greatest number of messages in total. But any imbalance in these will indicate the formation of subgroups or cliques within the network. Discussion of who they are and why will be revealing. Did they have specific information or was it their role labels that caused them to think they should be working closely together?

Figure 10.12 provides an illustration of the number of messages to and from each person in the 'star' team *Holmes*. When considering the pattern of frequencies, Figure 10.12 illustrates what is typical of the very hierarchical star configuration. What is very clear is that B at the centre of the network is inundated with messages; in this example receiving 27. Often it is difficult for the person in that position to manage the load. Amusingly, other Bs at the same table, who are not getting very many messages because of their position in their network, may offer to help and become sort of secretaries to the Holmes B. This co-operation can open up the whole game and may even lead to it being solved.

The downside of the imbalance of the pressure under which B is put is that, unless B is an extremely thoughtful manager, the other members of the team may become alienated. They all send more messages than they receive. The frequencies in Figure 10.12 indicate, for example, that D may be quite frustrated, even angry, sending nine messages but only receiving five. The crucial CPS contact person at A may actually give up (I've had people go on strike, or even just go home). This can mean that when A is needed to send the result to the CPS they are no longer participating.

Various aspects of these communication patterns emerge for each team. In the debriefing some of the issues to look towards mentioning are:

• Who was under great pressure with a high frequency of messages?

• Who was likely to feel disenfranchised because they either got few messages and/or got no responses to their messages?

• Where did high-contact subgroups, 'cliques', of two or three people emerge? What was it about their circumstances that led to that?

• What did the messengers think about the process? What pressure where they under and why?

• What were the routes of any confusions? How did they arise?

• Did role labels (if you used them) make any difference?

What the simulation illustrates and participants learn

Key issues that emerge from the experience of taking part in this exercise:

• *Self-generated, but non-existent rules.* People tend to rely on stereotypical situations that they have experience of. In this exercise sitting people from different teams around a table usually carries the assumption that they should not talk to each other, as would be the case in an examination situation, or many competitive games. But that was never a rule of the game.

In police investigations it is often assumed that people act in ways that are considered usual. An instance of this is when police search for sexual contact between people as a way of deciding how significant their relationship is. But people can be extremely loyal to each other, or jealous of each other, without there being any sexual contact.

• *How misleading beliefs emerge.* Ambiguities in the process, especially due to being at the end of communication channels, may give rise to all sorts of assumptions about what is actually the case. For example, people not receiving responses to their messages sometimes generate beliefs about the situation. They have not got replies possibly because the person they are sending them to is too busy to respond or does not think they are significant. Yet they may start thinking the messengers, or the game organisers, are deliberately not delivering the messages.

The significance of this for destructive organisational psychology is to indicate that in organisations based on coercion and trust, any interference in the communication system can lead to a breakdown in the organisation.

• *The importance of physical closeness.* When people are able to talk to each other directly a variety of forms of expression are possible that are not available, or inevitably very crude, with distant – written – communication. In the game the messengers are free to talk to the team players. This makes the nature of their interactions with them rather different from the interactions between team members by writing. Similarly, those across a table from each other may open up discussions beyond those simply structured by the contents of the game itself.

When thinking about criminal activity, it surprising how little consideration is typically given by the police to whether offenders may be near each other, living in the same family, or have much more distant associations. Those who can spend a lot of time with each other are more likely to share objectives and values than those who meet from time to time or only have contact over the Internet.

- *Maintaining rigidly similar communication structures for all types of interaction.* The game shows the need to harness different forms of communication for different types of information. It would be extremely difficult to plan how to rob a bank without being able to look together at plans of the building and to discuss possible escape routes using maps. The Internet does allow much more of these sorts of visual contact, with the sharing of videos and maps, but these are also more open to surveillance. They are also open to faking. Paedophiles have been caught because they thought they were in contact with a child, when it was actually a police officer.

- *Different group structures are effective for different stages and types of problem solving and activity.* In a comparison of drug networks with burglary groups and hooligan gangs I was able to show that they tended to have different organisational structures (Canter, 2004). Understanding this assists in being more aware how to incapacitate them.

There is the related issue that different structures are necessary for different stages in any actions. When a plan is being hatched, ideas and information needs to be brought together. When it is being acted on clear instructions are necessary, with each person knowing what they are to do and when.

- *Ignoring the emotional significance of communications.* Involving people by communicating with them has powerful influence over their view of themselves. In this exercise I have repeatedly found that this carries emotional significance. You may think somebody is happy getting on with a task you have set them, but without contact they can feel they are not being taken seriously.

- *Undervaluing people who have contact with people outside the organisation.* It is often the most junior people in an organisation who have contact with those outside it. But that contact is usually crucial to the survival of the organisation.

OTHER STUDIES THAT COULD USE THIS RESEARCH DESIGN

As I've been at pains to emphasise, one of the crucial aspects of this study is the emotions it stirs up in the participants. Their reactions relate directly to their role in the game, which in turn is greatly influenced in the network they are part of and where they are in that network. This can be explored directly by asking people to complete a simple questionnaire at the end of the game.

What was your role in the game?	Team: Position:	
With 1 being not at all and 10 being very much indeed, how much did you enjoy your participation in the game?		
With 1 being not at all and 10 being very much indeed, how significant do you think your role was?		

These scores can then be put on the diagram of each of the networks with revealing results.

Mnay other challenges can be created using the same overall way of organising the game. The one mentioned in my book *Psychology for Architects* (Canter, 1975) was to design a Zen rock garden. Other simpler tasks can be put together, such as solving anagrams or even crossword puzzles.

Some participants have suggested to me that it would be interesting to rerun the game again with the same people to see if they would solve it much more effectively. I've never had the opportunity to do that, but it would be a good indicator of how much had been learned from participating the first time round.

NOTES

2 In the United Kingdom the Crown Prosecution Service (CPS) decides whether the evidence provided by the police is sufficient to take the case to court and then lead the prosecution. In other countries rather different people are involved.
3 You may forgive the following 'joke' as an illustration of this. Question: "How many professors does it take to change a lightbulb?" Answer: "I don't know but his assistant will be here soon and she'll be able to tell you."

REFERENCES

Canter, D. (1975). *Psychology for architects*. London: Applied Science Publishers. [See esp. chap. 9 'Organisations', pp. 124–145.]

Canter, D. (2000). Destructive organisational psychology. In D. Canter & L. Alison (Eds.), *The social psychology of crime* (pp. 321–334). Aldershot, UK: Ashgate.

Canter, D. (2004). A partial order scalogram analysis of criminal network structures. Behaviormetrika, 31(2), 131–152.

Dupuy, K., & Siri Neset, S. (2018). The cognitive psychology of corruption: Micro-level explanations for unethical behaviour. UR, 2. Retrieved from www.u4.no/publications/the-cognitive-psychology-of-corruption.

Glenny, M. (2009) *McMafia: Seriously organised crime*. London: Vintage Books.

Fellman, P.V., & Wright, R. (2014). Modeling terrorist networks: Complex systems at the mid-range. *Intelligencer: Journal of U.S. Intelligence Studies*, 14(1), arXiv:1405.6989 [physics.soc-ph]. Retrieved from https://arxiv.org/abs/1405.6989.

Haslam, S.A., Postmes, T., & Ellemers, N. (2003). More than a metaphor: Organizational identity makes organizational life possible. *British Journal of Management*, 14(4), 357–369. https://doi.org/10.1111/j.1467-8551.2003.00384.x.

Hesterman, J.L. (2013). *The terrorist–criminal nexus: An alliance of international drug cartels, organized crime and terror groups*. London: CRC Press.

Postmes, T., Baray, G., Haslam, S.A., Morton, T.A., & Swaab, R.I. (2006). Social identity formation. In J. Jetten & T. Postmes (Eds.), *Individuality and the group: Advances in social identity* (p. 215). London: Sage.

Reicher, S., Spears, R., & Haslam, S.A. (2010). The social identity approach in social psychology. In M.S. Wetherell & C.T. Mahanty (Eds.), *Sage identities handbook* (pp. 45–62). London: Sage.

Steffens, N.K.S., Haslam, S.D., Reicher, S., Platow, M.J., Fransen, K., Yang, J., … Filip Boen, F. (2014). Leadership as social identity management: Introducing The identity leadership inventory (ILI) to assess and validate a four-dimensional model. *Leadership Quarterly*, 25(5), 1001–1024.

Tajfel, H. (Ed.) (1978). *Differentiation between social groups: Studies in the social psychology of intergroup relations*. London: Academic Press.

APPENDIX A
Guidelines for ethics in psychological research

ONLINE GUIDANCE

There are many templates of the forms that should be used to obtain consent from participants in your research. A particularly wide range of such templates is available from the World Health Organisation at www.who.int/rpc/research_ethics/informed_consent/en.

Every professional body and university have online guidance relevant to psychological research. As for example, the following websites:

- American Psychological Association (APA), *Five Principles for Research Ethics*, at www.apa.org/monitor/jan03/principles.

- British Psychology Society (BPS), *Code of Human Research Ethics*, at www.bps.org.uk/sites/bps.org.uk/files/Policy/Policy%20-%20Files/BPS%20Code%20of%20Human%20Research%20Ethics.pdf.

- City University of London has very detailed *Guidance and Resources for Ethics Applications*, at www.city.ac.uk/research/ethics/help-and-guidance.

- City University of New York has an online Collaborative Institutional Training Initiative (CITI) research compliance training course. You can register as an independent learner to take one or more of these course at www.citiprogram.org/Default.asp.

INFORMATION FOR PARTICIPANTS

The following headings cover the main information that should be made available to participants.

Invitation to participate
Nature of the study

Why have I been asked to participate?

[Description of how participants have been selected here]

What is the aim of the study?

Who is organising the study?

What will I be asked to do?

What if I want to know more before I decide to participate?

[Details here of who to contact/website for more details about the study]

How do I take part in the study?

Further information about the study

What will I be asked to do?

What will happen to the information collected?

The information that we collect from you is confidential. That is, your name will not appear on any of the information you give. Instead, you will be allocated a research number. No one outside the research team will be able to identify the information you give. All identifiable information, such as names of people, will be replaced with allocated research numbers.

What are the possible benefits of taking part?

Thank you for your time.

INFORMED CONSENT FORM

A typical form of relevance to the sorts of studies described in this book is as follows:

Title of research project here

Please tick box

❑ I have read and understand the information sheet.

❑ I have had the opportunity to ask questions.

❑ All of my questions have been answered to my satisfaction.

❑ I understand that my participation is voluntary and I am free to withdraw from the study at any time, without my medical or legal rights being affected.

❑ I give my permission for the interview to be audio-recorded [if appropriate].

❑ I am over 18 years and I agree to take part in the [title of project here].

❑ I have received a list of free counselling services [if appropriate].

❑ I understand that if I have any further comments or questions I can contact [insert appropriate contact details here].

Please print your name	*Signature*	*Date*
Researcher	*Signature*	*Date*

EXAMPLE ETHICAL COMMITTEE APPROVAL FORM

(Ethical approval form for undergraduate, taught master's programme, and other postgraduate students)

PART 1 DECLARATION TO THE ETHICS COMMITTEE

Name:

Brief summary of proposed research:

I confirm that I have read the BPS Code of Practice concerning ethical principles for research (available from school web pages and student year handbooks).

Signed (proposer of the research):

Date:

PART 2 ETHICS CHECKLIST

Who are the participants in the study?

Do any special ethical conditions apply to this group? YES/NO (delete as appropriate) If YES, give brief details below and outline steps to deal with special conditions.

How will participants be selected?

Do any special ethical considerations apply? YES/NO (delete as appropriate) If YES, give brief details below and outline steps to deal with special conditions.

What will be required of participants?

Do any special ethical requirements apply? YES/NO (delete as appropriate) If YES, give brief details below and outline steps to deal with special conditions.

Are there any particular hazards associated with this research? YES/NO

If YES, give brief details below and outline steps to deal with special conditions they consider necessary.

Have matters of confidentiality been addressed? YES/NO Further details [e.g. confidentiality will be protected by anonymising the data immediately after collection and storing it in a stand-alone laptop computer, the data will not be shared with anyone outside the research team]

Have data protection issues been addressed?

YES/NO Further details

Are there any other ethics matters that need attention (e.g. deception)?

YES/NO Further details [e.g. the purpose and method of the research will be explained to the participants]

Will informed consent (or equivalent) be obtained?

YES/NO Attach copy of participant consent sheet

Will participants be provided with an information sheet?

YES/NO Attach copy of participant information sheet

Where will the research take place? Include full details.

Has permission, where necessary been obtained from the relevant external organisation(s)? Attach copies of relevant correspondence.

Does this work require formal ethics approval from an external organisation?

YES/NO Further details

Please provide letter of approval.

PART 3 SUPERVISOR'S RECOMMENDATION

After consideration of the proposal and the student's ethics checklist my recommendation with respect to ethics approval is as follows [please select most appropriate alternative]:

Refer to school ethics committee

Refer to external ethics committee

Proposal approved by the supervisor

Any additional comments:

If in your view an external ethics committee recommendation is appropriate please confirm that such a submission has been made, indicating which committee and providing contact name and address.

Signed supervisor of the project

APPENDIX B

A very brief introduction to smallest space analysis (SSA)

There are two aspects of SSA that should be noted.

MULTIDIMENSIONAL SCALING

SSA is part of a large number of statistical procedures that represent relationships as distances in a notional space. These procedures are generically termed *multidimensional scaling* (MDS) procedures.

The Wikipedia account of MDS is reasonable but rather technical. A detailed account with examples is given at https://ncss-wpengine.netdna-ssl.com/wp-content/themes/ncss/pdf/Procedures/NCSS/Multidimensional_Scaling.pdf.

All of these accounts distinguish between metric and non-metric MDS. SSA is a form of non-metric SSA, as explained in what follows. A full examination of how it operates is given by Borg and Lingoes (1987). James Lingoes did develop the software with Guttman. The original software packages were consequently called the G-L Package. When Borg and Lingoes published their account, they chose to say that SSA stood for *similarity structure analysis*. This was to reflect directly the role of SSA within facet theory.

FACET THEORY

SSA was developed within the context of *facet theory*, an approach to research developed by Louis Guttman (1959), elaborated by Gratch (1973). His long-time collaborator, Shlomit Levy (2014), summarised facet theory as follows:

> A systematic approach to coordinating theory and research. It integrates the constituents of scientific endeavor: the formal definition of the research problem in the form of facets (a facet is a set for classifying research issues), and the construction of hypotheses which link the definitional framework with aspects of the structure of the empirical observations defined by the facets. Thus, facet theory allows for promotion of the systematic development of scientific generalizations in cumulative fashion.

The crucial relationship of SSA to facet theory is that the SSA statistical procedure is regarded as representing the facets of a theoretical framework, such that the regions of the SSA indicate aspects of the structure in the empirical observations. This structure is taken to consist of a set related facets, which form the definitional system that specifies the research problem.

It is helpful to appreciate that when this approach is used in an ongoing research setting, the definitional system can be the starting set of hypotheses that define the domain being studied, which is then tested in the SSA to establish if the regions reflect those hypotheses. This is illustrated in Study 6 where Figure 6.3 is a test of the hypotheses summarised in Table 6.2.

Mapping Sentence

Guttman provided a process for specifying the definitional system, built on ideas from set theory, which he called a **mapping sentence**, described in detail by Borg and Shye (1995).

A mapping sentence representation of Table 6.1

Potency intimacy	High	Low
High	Revenger (quest)	Victim (irony)
Low	Professional (adventure)	Hero (tragedy)

is as follows:

The extent to which person p describes their experience during a crime as

Intimate		Potent		
				[Not at all]
[High]		[High]		[Just a little]
	and		⟶	[Some]
[Low]		[Low]		[A lot]
				[Very much]

Where p is drawn from a population P of people who remember a crime they have committed.

This gives the four combinations of both intimacy elements with both potency elements. In the actual questionnaire, three questions were created for each of these four combinations. This framework for a questionnaire owes a lot to the factorial design of experiments (Fisher, 1935)

		1	2	3	4	5	6	7	8	9	10	11	12
Professional	1												
Was right	2	−18											
Interesting	3	3	−11										
Routine	4	36	−3	−30									
Job	5	23	−17	−37	71								
Own back	6	31	61	−34	34	19							
Mission	7	49	3	6	24	41	29						
Helpless	8	29	54	−19	37	3	87	25					
Victim	9	−10	62	−50	3	12	72	15	63				
Get it over	10	43	7	−50	64	60	56	44	57	47			
Revenge	11	−5	44	−33	−8	−3	58	−1	42	60	14		
Hero	12	41	27	29	37	15	33	49	28	2	7	6	

Figure 11.1 The correlation matrix for the 12 questions used in Study 6

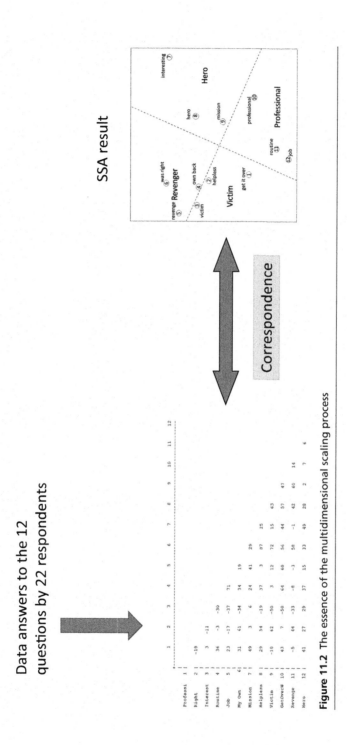

Figure 11.2 The essence of the multidimensional scaling process

The essence of an SSA calculation

1. An association matrix is created of the relationships between all the variables. With a questionnaire this is the correlation matrix of how every question correlates with every other. For the example of the 12 questions for Study 6 the correlation matrix is shown in Figure 11.1

2. These correlations are arranged in rank order (this is what makes the procedure 'non-metric'.

3. This is the clever bit, a way of representing these correlations as distances in a notional multidimensional space is generated by placing a point for each variable in that space. The rank orders of the distances between those points is then compared with the ranks of the correlations and the points are adjusted until the best match can be achieved. This is known as the 'fit' between the ranks of the distances and the ranks of the correlations. The size of this fit can be measured by a 'stress' measure or the *coefficient of alienation*. This varies between 0 and 1.00.

This process is illustrated in Figure 11.2.

Software availability

In Study 9 a very crude method of creating relationships using a form of simple linkage analysis is presented. To carry out SSA there is a well-established package – the Hebrew University Data Analysis Package (HUDAP), available at www.europhd.net/sites/default/files/international_labs/3rdinternationallab/hudap_manual.pdf.

Shye (2014) has also developed a version that he calls faceted SSA. There are also versions available within standard statistical packages such as SPSS.

Further Reading

Samuel Shye has an excellent video on YouTube describing facet theory, available at: www.youtube.com/watch?v=taEUU9rJneY.

Other useful sources of information on SSA are available from the following:

Canter, D. (1984). Putting situations in their place. In A. Furnham (Ed.), *Social behaviour in context* (pp. 208–239). New York, NY: Allyn & Bacon.

Canter, D. (Ed.). (1985). *Facet theory: Approaches to social research.* New York, NY: Springer Verlag.

Cohen, E.H. (2000). A facet theory approach to examining overall and life satisfaction relationships. *Social Indicators Research, 51,* 223–237.

Elizur, D. (1984). Facets of work values: A structural analysis of work outcomes. *Journal of Applied Psychology, 69*(3), 379–389.

Guttman, L. (1954). A new approach to factor analysis: The radex. In P.F. Lazarsfeld (Ed.), *Mathematical thinking in the social sciences* (pp. 258–348). Glencoe, IL: Free Press.

Guttman, L. (1968). A general non-metric technique for finding the smallest coordinate space for a configuration of points. *Psychometrika, 33,* 469–506.

Guttman, L. (1982). What is not what in theory construction. In R.M. Hauser, D. Mechanic, & A. Haller (Eds.), *Social structure and behavior* (pp. 331–348). New York, NY: Academic Press.

Guttman, L. (1991). The language of science. In L. Guttman, *In memoriam: Chapters from an unfinished textbook on facet theory* (pp. 38–69). Jerusalem: Israel Academy of Sciences and Humanities and the Hebrew University of Jerusalem.

Levy, S. (1976). Use of mapping sentence for coordinating theory and research: A cross-cultural example. *Quantity and Quality, 10,* 117–125.

Levy, S. (1985). Lawful roles of facets in social theories. In D. Canter (Ed.), *Facet theory: Approaches to social research* (pp. 59–96). New York, NY: Springer Verlag.

Levy, S. (1990). The mapping sentence in cumulative theory construction: Wellbeing as an example. In J.J. Hox & J. de Jong-Gierveld (Eds.), *Operationalization and research strategy* (pp. 155–177). Amsterdam, the Netherlands: Swets & Zeitlinger.

Levy, S. (Ed.) (1994). *Louis Guttman on theory and methodology: Selected writings*. Aldershot, UK: Dartmouth Publishing.

Levy, S., & Guttman, L. (1975). On the multivariate structure of well-being. *Social Indicators Research, 2*, 361–388.

Levy, S., & Guttman, L. (1989). The conical structure of adjustive behavior. *Social Indicators Research, 21*, 455–479.

Levy, S., & Guttman, L. (2005). *Encyclopedia of social measurement* (vol. 2). Amsterdam, the Netherlands: Elsevier.

Lingoes, J.C. (1968). The multivariate analysis of qualitative data. *Multivariate Behavioral Research, 3*, 61–94.

REFERENCES

Borg, I., & Lingoes, J.C. (1987). *Multidimensional similarity structure analysis*. New York, NY: Springer.

Borg, I., & Shye, S. (1995). *Facet theory: Form and content*. Thousand Oaks, CA: Sage.

Fisher, R.A. (1935). *The design of experiments*. Edinburgh: Oliver & Boyd.

Gratch, H. (Ed.) (1973). *Twenty-five years of social research in Israel*. Jerusalem, Israel: Jerusalem Academic Press.

Guttman, L. (1959). *Introduction to facet design and analysis: Proceedings of the Fifteenth International Congress of Psychology*. Brussels, Belgium: North-Holland.

Levy, S. (2014). Facet theory. In A.C. Michalos (Ed.), *Encyclopedia of quality of life and well-being research*. Dordrecht, the Netherlands: Springer. https://doi.org/10.1007/978-94-007-0753-5_978.

Shye, S. (2014). Faceted smallest space analysis (faceted SSA; FSSA). In A.C. Michalos (Ed.), *Encyclopedia of quality of life and well-being research*. Dordrecht, the Netherlands: Springer. https://doi.org/10.1007/978-94-007-0753-5_978.

Index

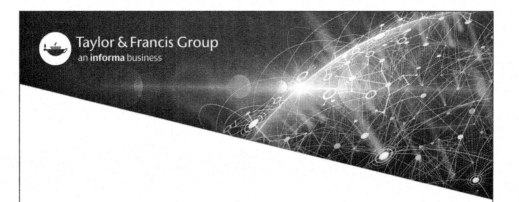